NEW FRONTIERS IN MARINE TOURISM: DIVING EXPERIENCES, SUSTAINABILITY, MANAGEMENT

ADVANCES IN TOURISM RESEARCH

Series Editor: **Professor Stephen J. Page**
University of Stirling, UK
s.j.page@stir.ac.uk

Advances in Tourism Research series publishes monographs and edited volumes that comprise state-of-the-art research findings, written and edited by leading researchers working in the wider field of tourism studies. The series has been designed to provide a cutting edge focus for researchers interested in tourism, particularly the management issues now facing decision-makers, policy analysts and the public sector. The audience is much wider than just academics and each book seeks to make a significant contribution to the literature in the field of study by not only reviewing the state of knowledge relating to each topic but also questioning some of the prevailing assumptions and research paradigms which currently exist in tourism research. The series also aims to provide a platform for further studies in each area by highlighting key research agendas, which will stimulate further debate and interest in the expanding area of tourism research. The series is always willing to consider new ideas for innovative and scholarly books, inquiries should be made directly to the Series Editor.

Published:

Benchmarking National Tourism Organisations and Agencies
LENNON, SMITH, COCKEREL & TREW

Extreme Tourism: Lessons from the World's Cold Water Islands
BALDACCHINO

Tourism Local Systems and Networking
LAZZERETTI & PETRILLO

Progress in Tourism Marketing
KOZAK & ANDREU

Destination Marketing Organisations
PIKE

Indigenous Tourism
RYAN AND AICKEN

An International Handbook of Tourism Education
AIREY & TRIBE

Tourism in Turbulent Times
WILKS, PENDERGAST & LEGGAT

Taking Tourism to the Limits
RYAN, PAGE & AICKEN

Tourism and Social Identities
BURNS & NOVELLI

Micro-clusters & Networks – The Growth of Tourism
MICHAEL

Tourism and Politics
BURNS & NOVELLI

Tourism and Small Businesses in the New Europe
THOMAS

Hospitality: A Social Lens
LASHLEY, LYNCH & MORRISON

The Critical Turn in Tourism Studies
ATELJEVIC, MORGAN & PRITCHARD

Travel Medicine
WILDER-SMITH et al

Tourism Research
TRIBE & AIREY

Battlefield Tourism
RYAN

For other titles in the series visit: www.elsevier.com/locate/series/aitr

Related Elsevier Journals — sample copies available on request
Annals of Tourism Research
International Journal of Hospitality Management
Tourism Management

NEW FRONTIERS IN MARINE TOURISM: DIVING EXPERIENCES, SUSTAINABILITY, MANAGEMENT

EDITED BY

BRIAN GARROD

University of Wales
Aberstwyth, UK

STEFAN GÖSSLING

Lund University
Helsingborg, Sweden

ELSEVIER

Amsterdam • Boston • Heidelberg • London • New York • Oxford
Paris • San Diego • San Francisco • Singapore • Sydney • Tokyo

Elsevier
Linacre House, Jordan Hill, Oxford OX2 8DP, UK
Radarweg 29, PO Box 211, 1000 AE Amsterdam, The Netherlands

First edition 2008

Notice
No responsibility is assumed by the publisher for any injury and/or damage to persons
or property as a matter of products liability, negligence or otherwise, or from any use
or operation of any methods, products, instructions or ideas contained in the material
herein, Because of rapid advances in the medical sciences, in particular, independent
verification of diagnoses and drug dosages should be made

British Library Cataloguing in Publication Data
A catalogue record for this book is available from the British Library

Library of Congress Cataloging-in-Publication Data
A catalog record for this book is available from the Library of Congress

ISBN: 978-0-08-045357-6

For information on all Elsevier publications
visit our website at books.elsevier.com

Printed and bound in The Netherlands

07 08 09 10 11 10 9 8 7 6 5 4 3 2 1

Contents

List of Figures

List of Tables

List of Photographs

List of Boxes

Contributors

Dr. Nola Barker is currently Policy Officer with the Marine Stewardship Council in London, UK, a non-profit organisation dedicated to reversing the decline in fish stocks worldwide through its certification programme. She specialises in natural resource management and ecotourism, and has worked for government and non-government organisations in the UK, Africa and the Caribbean.

Dr. Carl Cater is a Lecturer in Tourism at Griffith University, Queensland, Australia. His research centres on the experiential turn in tourism and the subsequent growth of special-interest sectors. He is a fellow of the Royal Geographical Society, a qualified pilot, diver, mountain and tropical forest leader, and maintains an interest in both the practice and pursuit of sustainable outdoor tourism activity. He is co-author (with Dr. Erlet Cater) of *Marine Ecotourism: Between the Devil and the Deep Blue Sea* (CABI, 2007).

Christopher Coxon is currently employed as the Principal Advisor (Diving) for Workplace Health and Safety Queensland. In this role, he combines regulatory functions, including incident investigation and prosecution, with proactive advisory and educational work. He has been the leading player in the development and implementation of the regulatory regime for diving work in Queensland. His background in diving commenced with his undergraduate dissertation whilst at Cambridge University and has continued mainly in the recreational dive industry in the Caribbean, Mediterranean and on the Great Barrier Reef. The opinions expressed by this author do not necessarily represent those of the Department of Employment and Industrial Relations or the state of Queensland.

Susanna Curtin is a Senior Lecturer in Tourism Management at Bournemouth University. She has published a number of articles on marine ecotourism particularly regarding the tourist experience and the management of swimming with marine mammals. Her PhD is on the psychological and experiential benefits of nature-based/wildlife tourism.

Kay Dimmock is completing PhD studies at Southern Cross University, Lismore, Australia. In-water comfort with scuba divers is the central theme of that research. Her research interests include tourism and hospitality education and dive tourism. She has published in areas including risk management in outdoor adventure, managing dive tourism operations and international tourism education.

Dr. Michael Eisinger is a marine ecologist with focus on coral reef ecology reef rehabilitation. He was born in 1969 in Ludwigshafen am Rhein, Germany, and studied biology at the University of Heidelberg and marine biology at the Northeastern University, Boston, USA. In 2005, he completed his PhD on ecological and economical aspects of coral reef rehabilitation. Since 1996 he is research assistant at the University of Duisburg-Essen in Germany and participated in numerous projects in the Mediterranean, the Red Sea and the Golf of Aden, including consultancies for UNDP and the Global Environmental Facility (GEF).

Dr. Brian Garrod is Senior Lecturer and Head of Tourism at the Institute of Rural Sciences of the University of Wales Aberystwyth. His research interests span all aspects of tourism and recreation, but focus particularly on sustainable tourism, ecotourism and heritage tourism. He is Book Review Editor of the Journal of Heritage Tourism, Associate Editor of the Journal of Ecotourism, and an editorial board member of Tourism in Marine Environments and the International Journal of Sustainable Development. He has published three books, and written over thirty journal papers and book chapters.

Dr. Stefan Gössling is an Associated Professor working at the Department of Service Management, Lund University, and research coordinator at the Centre for Sustainable- and Geotourism, Western Norway Research Institute. He has worked extensively in the various islands of the Western Indian Ocean, focusing on eco- and sustainable tourism development. His recent edited books include *Tourism and Development in Tropical Islands: Political Ecology Perspectives* (Edward Elgar, 2003) and *Tourism and Global Environmental Change* (Routledge, 2005, with Michael C. Hall).

Jeanette Liljenberg, **Jayne Helmersson** and **Serwa Qwarm** are former students of the Service Management programme, Lund University. In 2004, they participated in a project 'Students do Research' in Mauritius, an initiative to collect data in tropical destinations, with the ultimate goal to improve the working knowledge of quantitative methods.

Dr. Olof Lindén is professor of coastal environmental management at the World Maritime University in Malmö, Sweden, and holds an adjunct professorship at the University of Kalmar in Sweden. His research focuses on climate change and its impacts on coastal ecosystems. He is the project leader for the Indian Ocean-wide CORDIO project to assess the impacts of global change on coral reefs of the region. He has also carried out research on issues related to the impacts of maritime activities on coastal and marine ecosystems. His latest book is *Places of Refuge for Ships: Emerging Environmental Concerns of a Maritime Custom* (2006) (Publications in Ocean Development, Vol. 51). Leiden, The Netherlands; Boston, MA: Martinus Nijhoff (co-authored/edited with Dr. Aldo Chircop).

Anna Lindgren, **Jessica Palmlund** and **Ida Wate** recently completed the Masters programme in Service Management at Lund University, focusing on management issues in the dive industry. They now hold various positions in the service industry, but still have an interest in marine environments, sustainable tourism, and corporate social responsibility.

Dr. Callum Roberts is Professor of Marine Conservation at the University of York in England. His research focuses on threats to marine ecosystems and species, and on finding the means to protect them. His work includes studies of the profound historical and recent alteration of marine ecosystems by fishing, on the extinction risk of marine species and on global conservation priorities for coral reefs. His best-known work is on the performance and design of marine reserves, areas that are protected from all fishing. His latest book, *The Unnatural History of the Sea*, charts the effects of 1000 years of exploitation on ocean life. Callum is a Pew Fellow in Marine Conservation.

Claudia Townsend's interest in the sustainable marine tourism developed while working as a scuba instructor in the British Virgin Islands. Her personal and professional interest in the marine environment has continued over the past 6 years through her work on sustainable tourism in the UK, Caribbean and Africa.

Dr. Peter van Treeck was born in 1963 and from 1991 worked as research assistant and responsible coordinator for marine projects of the department of Hydrobiology at the University of Essen (Germany). His research has focused on reef restoration and rehabilitation technologies applying electrochemical accretion technologies and coral transplantation. In 2005, he completed his PhD on colonisation patterns of artificial reef substrates in the Red Sea near Aqaba (Jordan). In various projects he worked on integrated concepts of reef protection and innovative approaches for reef protection and sustainable tourism mainly in the Red Sea area. Additional work was as marine ecological consultant in the Emirates, Egypt and Iran and as project leader for a multinational EU project on natural marine resources and aquaculture in the Mediterranean (NOMATEC) completed his scientific features. Since 2005, he has been a high school teacher and ecological consultant.

Dr. Jeff Wilks is Director of Strategic Development with Surf Life Saving Australia and a Director of JTA Tourism, a company providing health and safety advisory services to the tourism industry. A qualified psychologist and lawyer, Jeff acts as a consultant to the United Nations World Tourism Organization and holds the position of Visiting Professor of Law at Northumbria University, UK.

Preface

Colourful fishes in coral reef environments, clear blue waters, white sands: a growing number of tourism destinations have made such images central to their advertising strategies. Accordingly, diving tourism has become an important market segment for destination countries to target and exploit. Marine environments are also the focus of countless documentaries and many movies, which has created and sustained an interest in dive experiences that is now being expressed in more and more countries. In its 2020 tourism forecast, the World Tourism Organization (WTO, 2001, p. 38) stated that "scuba diving is one of the fastest growing sectors of the tourism trade" and this claim is validated by the certification statistics of dive organisations. The Professional Association of Diving Instructors (PADI, 2007), for example, estimates that some 600,000 new divers are certified every year, representing a growth rate of about 6%. As their diving careers develop, many of these newly certified divers will want to combine their interest in diving with their holidaymaking.

While it is difficult to be precise about the overall size of the diving tourism market, observers generally agree that it has been subject to significant growth in recent years. PADI (2007) estimate that the total number of active certified divers now exceeds 10 million, while the WTO (2001) argues that one in three of these will take a diving-based holiday in any one year. Moreover, many diving resorts offer people the option of taking their diving certification while they are on holiday. It might be argued on this basis that diving has moved from a niche, special-interest form of tourism towards being a mass tourism activity. Indeed, as the WTO (2001) notes:

> Whilst scuba diving is a sport, which is well known and practised worldwide, it is a market segment that is forecast to show strong growth over the next five to ten years. As the world becomes increasingly explored, and fewer destinations are left for tourists to discover, there is a trend to travel to unusual 'territories'. Travel underwater is therefore gaining appeal in the marketplace (WTO 2001, p. 88).

The WTO goes on to note that 'underwater sports', also including submarine excursions, underwater walks and other such activities, are widely believed to hold the potential to grow as large as the ski tourism sector (WTO, 2001). According to the WTO, there were approximately 25 million downhill skiers worldwide in 2001, with a further 10 million snowboarders, cross-country skiers and participants in fringe winter sports such as sledding and snow-biking. This suggests that the diving tourism market is expected to expand very quickly in the specified time frame.

Given the significance of diving in terms of absolute diver numbers, and projections for further growth, it is perhaps surprising that the subject of diving tourism seems to be of so little interest to the scientific community. Indeed, reviewing the scant scientific literature on diving tourism reveals just a modest number of studies that have appeared in journals, with the occasional chapter on diving being included in an edited book. Most of the scientific material on diving tourism is therefore to be found in a range of reports, which are diverse in terms of their focus, precision, depth and public availability. Furthermore, the current literature seems to focus largely on environmental impacts, with only a very limited reference being made to management issues. In view of these observations, the authors decided that an edited volume on diving tourism, integrating aspects such as the sustainability, safety, education, experiences and management of diving tourism would be in order.

Many people have supported this book, although we regret to report that none of the large dive organisations such as PADI, CMAS or NAUI was willing to cooperate with us in carrying out a survey that would have substantially improved our understanding of divers and the diving tourism market. We are thus particularly thankful to all those who have directly or indirectly support this book with comments, ideas, material or practical help. More specifically, the editors would like to thank Stephen Page for including this volume in his series, staff at Elsevier, in particular Joanna Scott and Helen Collins. We would also like to thank Tobias Klose (Dive Island) for providing us with information on diving at Thingvellir in Iceland and Malmö Dyktjänst for participating in a small survey on cold water diving. Carol Scarpaci, Carl Cater, Roger Horrocks, and André Maslennikov for providing many of the photographs included in this book. Stefan would also like to thank Robert Bockermann, Meike and Linnea Rinsche, Mathias Gößling for discussions and support, Johan Hultman, Szilvia Gyimothy, Erika Andersson-Cederholm, Mikael Bergmasth, Christer Eldh, Ola Thufvesson and Richard Ek for the fun-working environment on Level 4, Service Management — *här är roligare än på tredje våningen*. Brian would like to thank Alison, Lydia, Drew and Nick Garrod for their love and support.

Clearly, this book would not have been possible without the chapter contributors who have so graciously given their time and energies to writing up their chapters and responding to our editorial comments, and have been so forbearing to our various requests for additional information and material. We extend our warmest thanks to them. Meanwhile, we gladly accept any remaining errors or omissions as our own responsibility.

Finally, we would like to thank you for picking up this book. We hope that it meets your needs and expectations. Your feedback would be most welcome.

Brian Garrod and Stefan Gössling
Editors

References

PADI (2007). Statistics. http://www.padi.com/english/common/padi/statistics/3.asp (Accessed 7 February 2007).

WTO. (2001). *Tourism 2020 vision*. Vol. 7. Global forecasts and profiles of market segments. Madrid: WTO.

SECTION I:

INTRODUCTION

Chapter 1

Introduction

Brian Garrod and Stefan Gössling

Diving has been a recreational activity for at least 75 years. Sport divers in the Mediterranean, for example, hunted fish by holding their breath as long ago as in the 1930s (Cherry, 1976, quoted in Dimmock, 2007). Basic forms of diving, such as free diving (or 'breath-hold' diving) and snorkelling, require a minimum of equipment, usually including only a mask, snorkel, fins, and some weight. The difference between free diving and snorkelling is that snorkellers remain primarily on the surface of the water, while free divers descend, holding their breath for one or two minutes. In contrast, scuba diving involves portable air supplies to remain underwater for longer periods of time and attain greater depths. Technically speaking, 'scuba' is an acronym (SCUBA), standing for 'self-contained underwater breathing apparatus', although the term is now so well known that it has been received into many languages as a simple noun (hence 'scuba diving', 'scuba equipment', and so on). The earliest prototype scuba-diving equipment, known as the aqua-lung, was developed by Jacques-Yves Cousteau and Emile Gagnan in the early 1940s. This apparatus, consisting of a diving cylinder containing high-pressure air and a regulator supplying the diver with it at ambient (i.e. reduced) pressure, is still the most commonly used in recreational scuba diving.

There are also a number of new technologies which enable underwater swimming, including rebreathers, which are technically different to scuba equipment in that they enable the user to rebreathe their exhaled air, either in a closed or semi-closed system, rather than for the air they exhale simply to be released into the surrounding water as bubbles (Orams, 1999). There is also 'snuba', a cross between scuba and snorkelling where the participant breathes air from tanks that are attached to a raft on the surface of the water, rather than being strapped to the participant's back. This form of diving is particularly attractive in that it enables the diver to stay underwater for a longer period of time and to descend deeper than a free diver or snorkeller would be able to, yet does not require the formal certification that a scuba diver would normally require (Garrod & Wilson, 2003). Other new technologies include the DPV (diver propulsion vehicle), or 'scooter', and the

New Frontiers in Marine Tourism: Diving Experiences, Sustainability, Management
Copyright © 2008 by Elsevier Ltd.
ISBN: 978-0-08-045357-6

Photo 1.1: Diving means immersing oneself in an alien environment.

'sled', which is pulled along the surface of the water by a boat. Divers hang on to such devices, enabling them to travel faster and thus further underwater.

Many divers dive simply for the fun of it, to enjoy the freedom of being underwater, to view the splendour of the underwater environment, to socialise with other participants and to tell their tales afterwards. This type of diver can conveniently be termed 'recreational divers' (Photo 1.1). However, there are also a number of distinct diving specialisms. These include various forms of technical diving (diving in challenging environments such as cave diving, wall diving, wreck diving, altitude diving, ice diving, night diving and drift diving); underwater photography and videography; diving with marine mammals such as whales, dolphins, seals and sea lions; undertaking underwater biological, geological or archaeological surveys; underwater rescue and many others. Some writers consider technical diving to represent a subset of recreational diving, while others separate the two because of the greater demands in terms of the knowledge, skills, equipment and physical exertion required of technical divers. Any of these diving specialisms may involve one or more of the diving formats noted above. Thus, for example, while swimming with marine mammals is something that is often restricted by law to free divers and snorkellers, in some countries scuba divers are also permitted to swim with marine mammals.

Defining Diving Tourism

Defining diving tourism is not entirely a straightforward task. The World Tourism Organization (WTO) defines scuba-diving tourism as comprising "persons travelling to destinations with the main purpose of their trip being to partake in scuba diving. The attraction of the destination is almost exclusively related to its dive quality rather than any other factor, such as the quality of accommodation or land-based attractions" (WTO, 2001, p. 85). However, it might well be argued that this definition raises more issues than it clarifies. Theobald (2005) argues that definitions of tourism usually seek to serve one or both of two rather different purposes. The first is to serve as a conceptual definition, the function of this being to distinguish clearly between those individuals who may be described as tourists and those who may not. This is to enable meaningful theories to be developed and tested regarding such issues as tourists' motivations, preferences and chosen activities. The second type of tourism definition is a technical definition, the purpose of these being to distinguish efficiently between tourists and non-tourist so that data on tourists may be collected for statistical, legislative purposes. In the case of diving tourism, the task of either type of definition is rather more complex, since such definitions must distinguish between four groups of individuals: diving tourists, divers who are not tourists, tourists who are not divers, and those who are neither tourists nor divers. The principle is nevertheless the same: to be practically useful, any definition of diving tourism will need to be able to distinguish effectively between those individuals who can be said to count as diving tourists and those who cannot.

There are, moreover, a number of complications in defining diving tourism, and considering these can shed some light on the adequacy of the WTO definition given above. Firstly, the degree to which going diving forms part of an individual's travel motivation tends to vary considerably, with on one end of the scale the dedicated diving tourist who will make their choice of holiday timing and destination based very largely on the quality of the diving to be found at that time of the year in that particular diving location. On the other end of the scale will be the occasional diver, for whom the timing of their holiday and choice of tourism destination will have little to do with the availability of opportunities to dive, let alone the quality of diving to be found at the destination at that particular time of the year. Furthermore, while the former group of diving tourists may intend to dive every day (perhaps even twice daily), those in the latter group may intend to dive only when diving conditions are particularly favourable or when they have no other leisure activities planned for the day. This latter group has been termed 'sideliner divers' by the WTO (2001) and 'resort divers' by Davis and Tisdell (1995). However, it is clear from the WTO definition given above that such individuals would not strictly be considered to be diving tourists, since scuba diving is not their prime motivation for taking the holiday.

Secondly, diving is clearly not an activity that is undertaken exclusively by tourists. Certainly it is true that modern international tourism and the recreational sport of scuba diving both have their origins in the period immediately following the Second World War. It is also true that both activities witnessed a considerable and unabated growth in popularity over the second half of the twentieth century. Indisputably, the growth of international tourism has played an important role in increasing the popularity of diving, enabling enthusiasts to partake in their sport in a wider range of locations and times of the year than would be possible if they were restricted to diving in their home locality. Indeed, many divers reside in the northern hemisphere developed countries, over one-third being European (WTO, 2001). Many are also from the United States. Meanwhile the majority of 'world-class' diving locations are in the tropical regions, particularly where coral reefs are to be found. International travel is hence very much a part of the way in which divers tend to access their recreational opportunities. Yet, as the WTO (2001) acknowledges, only one

Photo 1.2: Free diver, in the background Zambezi sharks (*Carcharhinus leucas*) (Photograph: Roger Horrocks).

in three scuba divers regularly take an overseas diving holiday. The remainder dive either close to home, on the basis of a day trip, or else travel further within their own country to go diving, over a period of more than one day. The latter can confidently be described as diving tourists, since they are travelling away from their place of residence in order to undertake diving activities. The former group should not, however, be overlooked in any analysis of diving as a form of recreational leisure activity. Indeed, the volume and value of such activities worldwide is not well known in either case, owing to a severe paucity of data on diving activities in general, and dive tourism in particular. Information at the national, regional and local levels is at best only patchy. It may therefore be that these activities are substantially more significant than international diving tourism, about which the data are rather better (although still inadequate) and slightly more is known.

Thirdly, and perhaps most importantly, diving tourists are not just interested in scuba diving. As we have seen in the previous section, a number of other important diving formats exist, including free diving (Photo 1.2), snorkelling, snuba and the use of rebreathers. While there are many specialists, who like to participate in just one of these diving formats, there are also a good many generalists. An individual may thus go scuba diving on one day of their holidays and snorkelling on the following day, or scuba dive in the mornings but go free diving in the afternoons. The same may be observed in terms of the diving formats an individual chooses over their diving 'career'. Thus, for example, an individual diver may get into the sport at a young age through snorkelling, perhaps while they are on a family holiday, and then take up scuba diving once they have the personal finances needed to acquire the necessary certification and buy some diving equipment.

In view of the foregoing discussion, the following conceptual definition of diving tourism is offered:

Diving tourism involves individuals travelling from their usual place of residence, spending at least one night away, and actively participating in one or more diving activities, such as scuba diving, snorkelling, snuba or the use of rebreathing apparatus.

Unlike the WTO definition given above, the definition offered here does not require diving to be the main motivation for their trip; nor does it require them to participate specifically in scuba diving. On the other hand, the definition offered here does require travellers to spend at least one night away from home, thus ensuring that they are genuinely tourists rather than 'day visitors'. It should be noted, however, that this does not imply that they should undertake international travel. Indeed, domestic diving tourism is entirely possible under this definition.

The Development of Diving Tourism

Orams (1999) suggests that scuba diving and snorkelling are by far the most popular diving activities worldwide. Unfortunately, reliable data on either of these activities is scarce, particularly at the global level but also at the national, regional and local levels. As such it is not possible to determine the relative significance of these two diving formats. Snorkelling is rather more accessible as a recreational activity because of the lower demands of equipment and training, which ensures that it has a wider appeal and higher participation rate than scuba diving. On the other hand, snorkelling often generates the interest in marine environments that leads to a dive certification (see Lindgren et al., Chapter 6, this volume). Meanwhile, scuba diving has become an important recreational activity in its own right. PADI, the Professional Association of Diving Instructors, certified more than half a million new divers in 2000, with cumulative dive certifications in 2000 totalling more than 10 million since 1967, the year in which the organisation was founded (PADI, 2007). Figure 1.1 illustrates the growth of diver certification with PADI, which may be taken as indicative of the numerical growth of divers worldwide. PADI, which claims to certify 60% of all divers worldwide, estimates that there are now more than 10 million active divers worldwide (PADI, 2007).

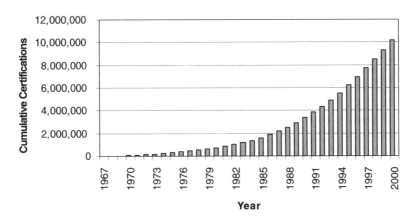

Figure 1.1: PADI certifications worldwide
(*Source*: PADI, 2007).

A similar estimate for the year 2000, i.e. 7 million, has been presented by the World Tourism Organization (WTO, 2001), along with a forecast of 10 million active divers by 2005. Cater and Cater (2001), meanwhile, quote a higher figure of 14 million active divers (taken from Viders, 1997) which, assuming a rate of growth similar to that predicted by the WTO, would imply that there are at least 28 million active divers in the world today. The WTO (2001) estimate that one in three divers will take an international holiday every year. Accordingly they estimate the international diving tourism market to be worth between US$4–6 billion (€4.7–7.1 billion; all Euro values are in the following provided for the respective year; values before 1999 are calculated as ECU equivalent) in 2000. The WTO report also indicates that divers are becoming more adventurous, with one in four active scuba-diving tourists constantly seeking new dive locations. More and more locations around the world are consequently trying to tap the diving tourism market and establish themselves as international diving destinations. This recent strong growth in the dive market might be explained by an increasing societal interest in marine tourism in general (e.g. Garrod & Wilson, 2003), the search for new, adventurous leisure activities (Swarbrooke, Beard, Leckie, & Pomfret, 2003), and cheaper and more easily accessible tourism destinations offering diving opportunities, particularly in tropical islands such as the Maldives or Seychelles (Photo 1.3).

Historically, the interest in marine environments has also been shaped by television and movies. Jacques-Yves Cousteau deserves to be mentioned here as one of the first marine explorers making underwater environments accessible to a mass audience. His first film was made as early as 1936, and during his life, Cousteau presented over a 100 films, including

Photo 1.3: Glass-bottom boats allow everyone to see marine life (Photograph: Stefan Gössling).

the Oscar-winning documentaries Silent World (1956), The Golden Fish (1959) and The World Without Sun (1965) (Cousteau Society, 2007). Even movies such as the James Bond films Thunderball (1965) and Octopussy (1983), The Big Blue (1989), Disney's The Little Mermaid (1989), Finding Nemo (2003), and recent documentaries such as Deep Blue (2004) and Sharkwater (2007) have heightened the interest in marine environments and experiences. These films have simultaneously raised interest in warm, tropical destinations. Indeed, movies like Thunderball might have been among the first to deliver images of the 'tropical paradise' to a broad audience, presenting coastal zones and marine environments as playgrounds for the wealthy jet set of that time. Other movies, such as Steven Spielberg's Jaws (1975), are not likely to have shaped perceptions of marine environments favourably, but the movie is nevertheless important, as it has created particular understandings of the open sea as a dangerous place, inhabited and dominated by dangerous creatures. Jaws might have influenced the perception of an entire generation, turning sharks into dangerous, aggressive predators. Such images of the sea are important, as they simultaneously create an understanding of diving as an adventurous activity. Indeed, divers are often portrayed as tough, and diving certainly contains an element of machismo and sexuality. This image can be reinforced by movies, such as the more recent Into the Blue (2005), a narcissist adventure of a group of young divers. However, the image can also be encountered in dive destinations, where tight neoprene suits underline masculinity as well as femaleness, while powerful boat engines (Photo 1.4) and the often military-like arrangement of dive excursions emphasise an element of seriousness and toughness. This might indicate that diving is not just a recreational activity containing elements of play, freedom, spontaneity and fun, as for instance pointed out by Dimmock (2007), but may also be seen as serious leisure. An apparent paradox is that the very same dive experience might contain both elements of fun and seriousness, with an individual, diver-dependent gradient existing between the two extremes.

Photo 1.4: Powerful boats and engines are part of the diving experience (Photograph: Stefan Gössling).

Table 1.1: 100 Top dive sites.

1. Yongala, Australia
2. Thistlegorm, Egyptian Red Sea
3. Blue Corner Wall, Palau, Micronesia
4. Barracuda Point, Sipadan Island
5. Shark and Yolanda Reef, Egyptian Red Sea
6. Manta Ray Night Dive, Kailua Kona, Hawaii
7. Navy Pier, Australia
8. Big Brother, Egyptian Red Sea
9. Great Blue Hole, Belize
10. Liberty, Bali, Indonesia
11. Elphinstone Reef, Egyptian Red Sea
12. Sodwana Bay, South Africa
13. Ras Mohammed, Egyptian Red Sea
14. President Coolidge, Vanuatu
15. Sha'ab Rumi South, Sudan
16. Bloody Bay Wall, Little Cayman
17. Straits of Tiran, Egyptian Red Sea
18. Great White Wall, Tavieuni Fiji
19. Tubbataha, Palawan, Philippines
20. Richelieu Rock, Thailand
21. Grand Central Station, Gizo, Solomon Islands
22. Darwin Island, Galapagos
23. Similans, Thailand
24. Osprey Reef, Coral Sea, Australia
25. Poor Knights, New Zealand
26. Blue Hole, Dahab, Egyptian Red Sea
27. Cod Hole, Northern Great Barrier Reef
28. The Zenobia, Cyprus
29. Darwin Arch, Galapagos
30. Jackson Reef, Egypt
31. Barra Reef, Mozambique
32. Stingray City, Grand Cayman
33. Pedras Secas, Noronha, Brazil
34. Holmes Reef, Coral Sea, Australia
35. Puerto Galera, Philippines
36. Shark Alley, Grand Cayman
37. Half Moon Wall, Belize
38. Protea Banks, South Africa
39. Wolf Island, Galapogos
40. Peleliu Express, Palau
41. Dos Ojos (Los Cenotes), Playa Del Carmen, Mexico
42. The Canyons, Utila, Hondura
43. Canibal Rock, Komodo, Indonesia
44. Mnemba Island, Tanzania
45. Cozumel, Mexico
46. Gili Air, Indonesia
47. The Point, Layang Layang
48. Dirty Rock, Cocos Island, Costa Rica
49. Rainbow Warrier, New Zealand
50. The Express, Kuredu, Maldives
51. Daedelus, Egyptian Red Sea
52. Garuae Pass, Fakarava Island, French Polynesia
53. Hilma Hooker, Bonaire
54. Hanging Garden, Sipadan
55. Booroo, Isle of Man
56. Sound Drift, Isle of Man
57. Chickens Rock, Isle of Man
58. Toucari Caves, Dominica
59. Wreck of the Bahama Mama, New Providence, Bahamas
60. Blue Hole, Malta
61. Joel's, PNG
62. Tiputa Pass, Rangiroa, Polynesia
63. Seal Rocks, NSW, Australia
64. Diamond Rocks, Kilkee, Ireland
65. Fujikawa Maru, Truk Lagoon (Chuuk Lagoon)
66. Sugar Wreck, Grand Bahama Island
67. Umbria, Sudan
68. Fish Rock, off South West Rocks in NSW, Australia
69. Office, Mozambique
70. South Point, Sipadan
71. Chios Island, Greece
72. Pixie Pinnacle and Pixie Wall, GBR, Australia
73. Palancanar Bricks, Cozumel, Mexico
74. Bay of Pigs, Cuba
75. Tiputa Pass, Rangiroa, New Zealand
76. St Johns, Egypt

Table 1.1: (*Continued*)

77. Turtle Tavern, Sipadan	90. Santa Rosa Wall, Cozumel, Mexico
78. Hin Muang, Thailand	
79. Great Basses Reef, Sri Lanka	91. New Dropoff, Palau
80. Port Royal, Roatan, Honduras	92. Kunkungan, Lambeh Strait, N. Sulawesi, Indonesia
81. Eye of the Needle, Saba	
82. Steel Forest, Nassau Bahamas	93. Cenotes, Playa Del Carmen, Mexico
83. Alcyone, Cocos Island, Costa Rica	
84. Tormentous, Cozumel, Mexico	94. Fernando de Noronha, Brasil
85. Eel Garden, Dahab, Egyptian Red Sea	95. Port Jackson, Sydney, Australia
	96. Punta Sur, Cozumel, Mexico
86. Boulari Pass, New-Caledonia	97. Lake Malawi, East Africa
87. Am Chesonet, St Lucia WI	98. Japanese Gardens, Koh Tao, Thailand
88. Aliwal Shoal, South Africa	
89. RMS Wreck of the Rhone, British Virgin Islands	99. James Barrie, Scapa Flow
	100. Los Testigos Islands, Venezuela

Source: Scuba Travel (2007).

The most popular dive destinations are primarily in warm waters. Dimmock (2007), for instance, lists the costal areas of the United States, Australia and Japan, the Wider Caribbean, the Pacific coast of Central America, the Pacific Islands, Papua New Guinea, Thailand and Malaysia, as well as the Red Sea, the Indian Ocean and the Philippines as important dive destinations. A similar list is provided by WTO (2001). A more specific distribution of popular dive sites can be derived from the list of 100 favourite dive locations provided by Scuba Travel (2007), a UK-based travel website providing the opportunity for divers to rank their favoured dive sites (see Table 1.1 and Figure 1.2). While there might be other rankings offering somewhat different insights, the Scuba Travel list highlights dive hotspots in the Wider Caribbean (22 sites) and the Red Sea (11 sites), the latter probably representing the highest spatial concentration of dive sites. Countries that are especially popular for diving include Egypt, Australia, South Africa, and Thailand. The ranking is likely to also provide an indication of the overall number of diving participants, as it might be reasonable to assume that more-frequently dived sites might be chosen more often as top dive sites. The list also reveals that the distribution of dive spots is skewed between tropical, temperate and cold waters. Tropical waters account for the great majority of dive sites, while only few temperate (e.g. Cyprus and Malta) or what might be considered cold-water dives sites (such as the Galapagos, the Isle of Man and Orkney) are represented in the list. It is also interesting to note that 99 dive spots are in the sea, while there is only one lake (i.e. Lake Malawi).

Indeed, temperate and cold-water destinations and lakes have become increasingly significant in recent years, even though in terms of absolute growth, tropical destinations remain far more important. For many destinations, temperate and cold-water diving opportunities have opened up new business opportunities, also addressing new tourist markets and contributing to a growing interest in marine protected sites (e.g. at the location of wrecks). Temperate and cold-water diving sites might generally offer another kind of

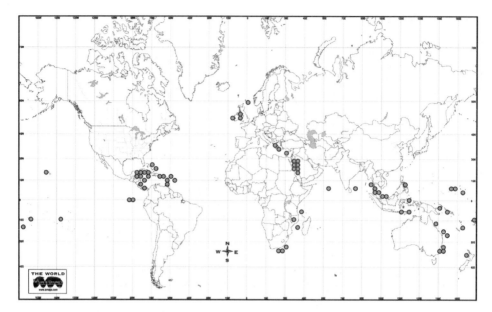

Figure 1.2: Geographical distribution of top dive locations
(*Source*: http://www.mapstoprint.com (2006) and http://www.scubatravel.co.uk/topdiveslong.html (2007)).

experience, as attractions may, in the absence of colourful marine life, more often include wrecks or geological formations. These attractions become available with the expansion of dive markets in temperate and cold waters, but sinking ships and other structures may also increasingly create wreck-dive attractions. Malta and Gozo, islands in the Mediterranean, are examples of destinations that have started to do this systematically, with the goal to expand dive tourism. One goal of Malta's Tourism Plan, published in 2006, is to "continue support-ing the scuttling of wrecks aiming at providing a fair distribution of this product offer around the various diving areas of the islands" (Ministry for Tourism and Culture, 2006, p. 44), indi-cating that dive tourism is increasingly considered in national tourism development plans.

Visibility might be another important attraction factor that can help to develop a dive destination. Dive sites such as Thingvellir in Iceland, said to be the clearest freshwater body in the world, boasts visibilities exceeding 100 m. There are several dive sites at Thingvellir, the most popular being Silfra, a tectonic rift between the Euroasian and American plates. The lake in which Silfra is located, Þingvallavatn, is filled primarily with water from a nearby glacier. Low nutrient levels, water temperatures of 1–3 °C, the national park status of the area, and low human pressure contribute to the unique visibil-ity found in this water body. The geological feature of the rift, with depths of 40–60 m adds to the attractiveness of the dive site:

> Diving is permitted in two submerged rifts in the National Park, Silfra and Davíðsgjá. Silfra is one of the best spots for diving in Iceland and many peo-ple find the rift unique on an international scale. The reason for its fame is the astounding visibility in the clear, cold ground water and the magnificent

surroundings. Davíðsgjá is in the north-eastern part of Lake Þingvallavatn. The rift is in the lake itself and to reach it you have to swim some distance. It is quite shallow nearest to the bank, but deepens and widens further out.

Divers have to fulfil all regulations and conditions regarding qualification and equipment for diving. They must abide by all rules concerning diving and agree to respect the National Park regulations. It is prohibited to dive alone, to enter caves while diving and to dive to a greater depth than 30 metres. Diving is entirely at the divers' own responsibility and risk. (Thingvellir, 2006, p. 1)

Thingvellir is thus providing an example of an emerging dive site that simultaneously appears to be well managed. Environmental problems associated with diving seem to primarily come into existence in emerging dive destinations seeing rapid growth in diver numbers (e.g. Barker & Roberts 2004; Hawkins et al., 1999; Tratalos & Austin 2001; Zakai & Chadwick-Furman, 2002), and in areas where coastlines are still poorly managed.

Environmental, Economic and Social Aspects of Diving

Diving has become a global activity, involving most water bodies, and occurring in the tropical, temperate and even arctic latitudes. As pointed out earlier in this chapter, diving is most popular in warm waters, with a concentration of diving activities in certain regions, notably the Red Sea. Particularly in these regions, and specially at popular dive sites within them, diving has sometimes put significant pressure on marine ecosystems, with environmental impacts including the breakage or abrasion of corals, the raising of sediments, behavioural change and altered feeding habits of marine fauna, and disturbances caused by diving with marine mammals (for a detailed overview of these impacts see chapters by Lindgren et al., Chapter 6; van Treeck & Eisinger, Chapter 8; Curtin & Garrod, Chapter 5, all in this volume). However, while these impacts of diving can potentially be addressed through soft and hard management strategies (see Lindgren et al., Chapter 6; Barker & Roberts, Chapter 9; van Treeck & Eisiniger, Chapter 8, all in this volume), one of the most problematic and largely unrecognised impacts associated with diving tourism may be its contribution to climate change.

Diving is highly energy intense due to its tendency to involve long-haul flights, often to remote corners of the planet (see Figure 1.2), the use of energy-intensive accommodation and powerful, fuel-hungry boat engines. In fact, with the exception of cruise ship vacations (Klein, 2002), there might be no other form of tourism involving such high energy use on a per capita, per day basis.

However, diving is seldom the sole reason for local environmental change (e.g. Rouphael & Hanafy, 2007; Wilkinson, 2004), and some authors have pointed out the dive industry's potential to contribute to the preservation of ecosystems. Diving can for instance generate revenue for marine protected areas (MPAs), which have been established in many parts of the world to provide refuge and breeding habitat for overfished or otherwise threatened species (Roberts & Hawkins, 2000). MPAs can, after relatively short periods of time (i.e. several years), see increases in marine species abundance and diversity, and thus become of interest for divers. As Roberts and Hawkins (2000, p. 90) point out, "the mere act of designating a site as a reserve increases its attraction for divers, and the protection offered will pay further dividends over time as animal populations build up".

Numerous studies have addressed the economic value of diving for protected and other areas. For instance, Cesar and van Beukering (2004) calculated that more than 14.6 million snorkelling trips and 870,000 dives were sustained by coastal zones in Hawai'i, corresponding to a total economic value of US$264 million (€216.7million) for snorkelling and US$40 million (€32.8 million) for diving. White and Rosales (2003) report that virtually all local divers and close to 80% of foreign divers were willing to pay user fees for diving at Moaboal, Cebu, Philippines. Locals were willing to pay US$1.25 (€1.06) per person per trip, while the foreigners' bid was almost US$9 (€7.8) per person per trip. A similar survey in Siquijor, Philippines, revealed even higher willingness to pay. Here, 87% of locals and 83% of foreigners were positive to paying entrance fees, with average per trip bids of US$4.62 (€4) for locals and US$17 (€14.8) for foreigners (White & Rosales, 2003). However, both Roberts and Hawkins (2000) and White and Rosales (2003) report that it is of great importance for divers to know that such revenue is invested in conservation of marine areas rather than being collected by the government for other purposes.

The economic contribution of divers can also provide alternative income opportunities, easing the pressure on marine resources. For instance, Roberts and Hawkins (2000, p. 43) report:

> In southern Belize, some commercial fishers in the area of a coastal marine park are being retrained as fly-fishing guides, easing the pressure on the fishery and enabling them to improve their incomes. Others have been undertaking scuba diving courses, improving their appreciation of local coral reef resources and allowing them to get work as dive guides for tourists.

Such developments can be promising alternatives to exploitive fisheries and other activities degrading the marine resource base (for a review of the economic value of diving see also Barker & Roberts, Chapter 9, this volume). However, in a systems perspective, it is worth noting that tourism always increases resource demands, particularly through the tourists' preference of certain types of seafood, thus increasing pressure on marine resources – locally or elsewhere. As Roberts and Hawkins (2000, p. 35) report, a single bluefin tuna can yield prices of US$10,000 (€10,490) in Japan, with the consequence that this rare and endangered species is hunted intensely. In fact, the catch is so valuable that spotter planes are used to locate remaining shoals of the fish. Similar mechanisms might also be found in tourism. In many areas, the purchasing power and demand of the tourism industry increases prices for marine resources, making even the time-consuming fishing of already rare species profitable, and thereby aggravating problems of overfishing (e.g. Gössling, 2001; Gössling, Kunkel, Schumacher, & Zilger, 2004). Tourism is thus, in environmental terms, usually a double-edged sword, and it remains difficult to say whether the benefits it can bring will always outweigh the costs.

It is clear that environmental education and management could generally improve the situation in many areas, but is so far not comprehensively addressed by dive organisations and tour operators (see Lindgren et al., Chapter 6, this volume), even though there might be some progress recently (Barker & Roberts, Chapter 9, this volume). However, the majority of operators do not as yet seem to focus on environmental education, informing their customers of the kinds of environmental impact associated with diving and asking them to take appropriate action to avoid or minimise such impacts. One positive example might be the online tour operator Responsible Travel, which provides guidelines for appropriate diver behaviour (see Table 1.2).

Table 1.2: Responsible diving guidelines, Responsible Travel.

Make sure your dive does not destroy what you have come to see
It is a privilege to be able to enter and experience the magical underwater world. However, coral reefs around the world are under extreme threat, and if we want to ensure that our kids can enjoy the same wonderful experiences then we need to dive responsibly. My top tips for responsible diving:

1. Anchors cause serious damage to reefs. Ask your skipper if they will be using a mooring, and about how they ensure the reefs will not be damaged.
2. Make sure that your point of entry to the water is away from fragile corals, it is all too easy to damage them as you enter.
3. Practice your buoyancy over sand before moving towards corals and reefs. Even the sand kicked up by fin kicks close to corals and vulnerable organisms can damage them.
4. Look — do not touch. Even robust looking corals and polyps can be destroyed by the gentlest touch.
5. Resist the temptation to feed fish and discourage others from doing so. You might affect normal patterns of behaviour and/or encourage aggression.
6. Ask your tour operator for their responsible tourism and diving policy — if they have not got one they are probably not taking it seriously. Find responsible dive operators on www.responsibletravel.com.
7. Coral reefs are under immediate threat from global warming. If you have flown to your destination offset the carbon emissions of your flight via www.co2.org.
8. Poorly treated waste from hotels destroys water quality and corals. Ask your hotel how they manage grey water.
9. Do not buy and gifts or souvenirs that are made from corals, shells or hardwoods. If you witness trade in these items report it to www.earthdive.com via their science log.
10. Remember that local communities may have used the seas and reefs for their own purposes for generations. Make sure that they are compensated for allowing us to enjoy their heritage by ensuring local communities benefit financially from tourism — think local about hotels, restaurants and where you buy your crafts.

Finally, a word about diving with sharks. The state of Florida banned chumming to attract sharks in 2001 because it changes their natural behaviour (and in some cases may attract sharks to tourist areas with possible consequences for safety).

Of course diving with sharks is a huge thrill, valuable as a way to educate people about sharks, and a good way to earn local communities an income. However, if you choose to dive with sharks our view is that you should do so with a responsible operator that dives with small groups, causes minimal obtrusion to the environment and ideally does not use the enticement of chumming.
Justin Francis, Managing Director, Responsible Travel

Source: Responsible Travel (2007).

Who Are Divers and Who Are Diving Tourists?

What kinds of people go diving? What kinds of people go on diving holidays? The former question is probably easier to answer than the latter, although both a fraught with difficulties. There is the general paucity of data and, even when data are available, they tend to be only partial in their coverage. Most of the dive organisations collect some kind of statistical data on the people who take their qualifications with them, but this gives us only historical data on that snapshot of divers at the particular time they achieved their certification, making it extremely difficult to draw conclusions about the characteristics of divers who are still active in the sport. Furthermore, such data only cover scuba divers, thereby ignoring other important forms of diving such as snorkelling and particular practices such as 'try diving' (a diving format wherein participants are offered the chance to try out scuba diving without having to be qualified). Furthermore, data on divers are not necessarily representative of diving tourists. Indeed, if certain types of diver are more likely to go on a diving holiday — perhaps older people or those with higher incomes — then the data on divers generally will not be representative of diving tourists specifically.

Diving, and particularly scuba diving, has traditionally been a male-dominated sport. Commentators sometimes put this down to the tough and often macho image that has tended to accompany the sport (as noted above) or to the physical demands required to move about in heavy scuba equipment and to make an underwater descent. Surveys of divers have therefore tended to show a high proportion of male respondents. Tabata (1992), for example, quotes a readership survey conducted by the US magazine *Skin Diver* in 1989, which suggests that around 65% of all scuba divers are male. This finding is confirmed in a report by Tourism Queensland (2006), which claims that two-thirds of all divers certified by PADI are male. In certain contexts the male domination may be even higher. Todd (2004), for example, reports that 80% of divers living and diving in New York State are male and argues that this is due to the tough image and harsh rigours of cold-water diving. Ditton and Baker (1999), meanwhile, conducted a study of divers on an artificial reef in Texas, 81% of whom were Texas residents, and found that most were white males, aged between 21 and 39 years.

Perhaps not surprisingly, this male domination soon carried over into diving tourism. Certified divers gained experience and soon began to look for opportunities to take holidays to places where different and more challenging, adventurous or exotic dives are to be found. Thus, Mundet and Ribera (2001) report that 80.6% of respondents in a study of divers in the Medes Islands of Spain were male, while O'Neill, Williams, MacCarthy, & Groves (2000) found that 71% of divers on an artificial reef in Western Australia were male. Musa (2003) found that males made up nearly 65% of his sample of diving tourists in Sipadan in Malaysia. However, Musa, Kadir, & Lee (2006) argue that the male-dominated image of scuba diving is changing and this is reflected in a growing proportion of females participating in diving tourism. Their study found that females were better represented among diving tourists in Layang Layang, Malaysia, making up 46.9% of the total.

It would appear, therefore, that while diving is still very much a male-dominated sport, the gender balance of diving tourists is becoming more even. This finding has yet to be explained but could be associated with the additional opportunities to learn to dive and become qualified in a relatively short period of time at many of the dive resorts around the world (see Lindgren et al., Chapter 6, this volume).

Many surveys of divers suggest that it is a sport dominated by those in their 30s and 40s. Mundet and Ribera's (2001) study, for example, found that 56% of divers in the Medes Islands of Spain were aged 31–45. They link this result firstly to the requirement for purchasing power. The equipment and training required to engage in the sport of scuba diving implies that it can be an expensive hobby, which tends to limit its appeal to older participants who have built up sufficient wealth. Secondly, Mundet and Ribera argue that there is the issue of physical fitness, the physical demands of scuba diving sometimes (but by no means always) prevent older people from participating. Other studies of scuba divers, and indeed diving tourists, confirm this finding. Tabata (1992), for example, quotes a *Skin Diver* magazine readership survey from 1989 which suggests that the median age of US divers was 35.3 years. Interestingly, this is higher than the median age of respondents from the 1987 survey, which was 30.8 years. Arguably, these figures are not truly representative of divers, especially if older divers are more likely to read diving magazines. On the other hand, a number of studies do back this finding up. Musa (2003), for example, found that the average age of tourist divers in Sipadan, Malaysia, was 34.9 years, while Musa et al.'s (2006) study of tourist divers in Layang Layang, Malaysia, found the average age to be 38.5 years. Meanwhile, O'Neill et al.'s (2000) study of divers on an artificial reef in Western Australia reported that 53% of respondents were aged between 25 and 34 years old.

What is true of diving tourists is not necessarily true of divers in general. Tourism Queensland (2006), for example, state that 60% of all individuals certified through PADI are aged between 15 and 34 years. Of course, given the comments made earlier about the need for spending power in order to remain an active participant in the sport of diving, we might expect divers to begin their diving careers at an earlier age than they begin taking diving holidays. Moreover, the age range quoted in this report clearly relates to divers who are beginning their diving career, rather than those who have achieved certification and are progressing through their diving careers as active divers. Under such circumstances, the median age group of the former is clearly going to be less than that of the latter. Todd (2004), meanwhile, reports that the average age of divers both living and diving in New York State is 43 years.

Scuba diving as a sport also tends to attract participants who are more highly educated. Thus, for example, Tabata (1992) quotes a *Skin Diver* magazine readership survey from 1989 which suggested that 84.2% of US divers attended college or beyond. At this time only 35.6% of Americans had received a college education. This finding is confirmed in a more recent survey by Todd (2004), who reports that 75% of divers living and diving New York State had attended college. Thailing and Ditton's (2003) study of mainly US divers in Texas reported that divers had an average of 16 years schooling, which is the equivalent of a four-year degree. Cater and Cater (2001), meanwhile, quote a report by PADI which suggests that 80% of newly certified divers have a college education. The domination of the sport by highly educated individuals is often linked to the high cost of participating in the sport, only those with well-paid jobs being able to afford the substantial and ongoing equipment and certification costs.

There is evidence to suggest that this pattern is carried over into diving tourism. Musa (2003), for example, found that 71% of diving tourists in Sipadan. Malayasia, had at least some years of college education. Musa et al. (2006), meanwhile, found that 66.3% of diving tourists to Layang Layang, Malaysia, had a university degree or postgraduate qualification. Gössling et al. (Chapter 4, this volume) found that 58% of diving and snorkelling tourists in Mauritius held a college degree. These findings might, however, be influenced by the fact that Malaysia and, particularly, Mauritius tend to be high-cost tourism destinations. The market is thus naturally limited to those who have the incomes associated with higher educational qualifications.

Studies tend to confirm that divers typically have a higher-than-average income, reflecting the relatively high equipment and training costs typically associated with engaging in the activity. Thus Tabata (1992) notes that while the average annual household income of US residents in 1989 was $35,000 (€29,000), for respondents to a *Skin Diver* magazine readership survey in that year it was $64,300 (€53,650). Todd (2004), meanwhile, reports that half of those diving and living in New York State earned at least $60,000 (€47,700) a year. Ditton and Baker (1999) found that the median income of divers on an artificial reef in Texas (of whom 81% were Texan residents) was in the range $60,000–69,000 per annum (€57,500–66,150).

This finding can generally be carried over to diving tourists. The WTO (2001), for example, suggests that 78% of international diving tourists are in full-time employment, compared with 55% of other international tourists, while the average income of a US diving tourist is $80,000 per year (€94,000), which the report states to be considerably higher than the average income of other travellers. Similarly, Gössling et al. (Chapter 4, this volume) found that diving and snorkelling tourists in Mauritius had a relatively high median net income of $73,000–96,000 per year (€60,000–79,000).

Studies also suggest that diving tourists are relatively more experienced than certified divers in general. Mundet and Ribera (2001), for example, found that 57% of divers in the Medes Islands of Spain possessed advanced diving qualifications and 23.4% had intermediate qualifications. Furthermore, 60% had at least 6 years diving experience and approximately one-third had 10 years diving experience or more. Only around a quarter of divers were diving for the first time. In Musa et al.'s (2006) study of diving tourists in Lyang Lyang, Malaysia, 51% divers considered themselves to be experienced and 37.8% considered themselves intermediate. Only 8.2% of divers considered themselves to be novices. Gössling et al. (Chapter 4, this volume) found that the average diving experience of diving tourists in Mauritius was 8.8 years and for snorkellers it was 13.4 years. Finally, Cottrell and Meisel's (2004) survey of divers in Florida found that 25% were beginners (holding a basic, Open Water certificate), while 39% held intermediate certification. The remainder held higher diving qualifications. On average, divers had 4–6 years diving experience. On average, each diver had logged 11–25 dives in their diving career, while 19% had logged 100 or more.

Diving tourists also tend to be have well-developed tourism careers. As mentioned previously in this chapter, the WTO (2001) suggests that one in three divers regularly takes an overseas diving holiday. Tourism Queensland (2006) state that 80% of world's divers hold a valid passport. Mundet and Ribera (2001), meanwhile, found that two-thirds of diving tourists in the Medes Islands of Spain had visited the area two or more times previously. Furthermore, Thailing and Ditton's (2003) study of mainly US divers in Texas found that respondents were well-travelled, in the last 12 months having spent on average 5.1 days diving in Texas, 0.7 days diving in Florida, 2 days diving in Mexico, 3.3 days diving in Caribbean and 2.1 days elsewhere. Adding these figures up suggests that the average diver in the study had gone diving on 14.2 days in the previous year, of which at least 5.3 days involved international travel.

Care is required, however, in interpreting the findings above. While the evidence does seem to indicate a clearly defined socio-demographic profile for divers, with some relatively minor modifications required so that it can be transferred across to diving tourists, it would be entirely wrong to conclude that divers are all the same. As Cater suggests (Chapter 3, this volume), divers vary considerably in terms of their motivations — both to participate in diving and to go on a diving-based holiday — their particular interests and specialisms (particularly in terms of the proposed divide between recreational and technical diving, as noted above), the centrality of diving to their lifestyle, and so on. It is thus possible to imagine a number of scales or continuums along which different categories of diving tourists could potentially be distributed. Thus, for example, it is possible to distribute diving tourists along a scale according to their principal motivation for travelling. At one end would be 'mainliners', for whom the prime motivation would be diving, while at the other would be 'sideliners', who are primarily going on holiday for other reasons but if they have the opportunity to go diving they may choose to do so. Most diving tourists would probably be located somewhere between these polar extremes, their tourism motivations being based essentially on a mix of diving and non-diving factors. To understand the continuum of dive motivations, we furthermore suggest that it is possible to distinguish fanatics and dabblers, experienced divers and novices, highly qualified divers and 'try' divers, specialists and generalists, mariners and socialisers, independents and group divers, learners and enjoyers, as well as 'homies' and 'remotes'. For an explanation of these suggested continuums, see Table 1.3.

Outline of Section Themes

The book is organized in three sections covering the diving tourism experience (Section II), the environmental, economic and social impacts of diving tourism (Section III) and the management of diving tourism (Section IV). The following section, the diving tourism experience, consists of two chapters providing an analysis of diver characteristics, motivations and behaviour. An understanding of these aspects is paramount in that it helps to frame 'the experience' associated with diving. Divers constitute an important tourist segment that seems to have particular characteristics in terms of socio-demographics, motivations and expectations, while within this segment, various types of divers can be distinguished.

Diving tourists are not a homogenous group, nor indeed should diving tourists be confused with divers more generally. Indeed, the characteristics, motives and behaviours of the subset of divers who choose to take diving holidays (or, alternatively, go diving while on holiday) do not necessarily reflect those of divers in general. Understanding that diversity is an important step to the achieving the effective planning, management and

Table 1.3: Possible continuums of diving tourists.

Continuums of diving tourists
Mainliners–Sideliners, i.e. those for whom the travel motivation is primarily diving vs. those for whom tourism is the main motivation
Fanatics–Dabblers, i.e. those for whom diving is central to their lifestyle vs. those for whom it is peripheral
Experienced–Novices, i.e. those who have made many dives vs. those who are new to diving
Highly qualified–'Try' divers, i.e. those who are highly trained vs. those who are completely untrained
Specialists–Generalists, i.e. those who specialise in one diving activity, e.g. underwater photography vs. those who like to participate across the full range of diving specialities
Mariners–Socialisers, i.e. those primarily interested in marine encounters and experiences vs. those putting a high value on social contacts and interaction
Independents–Group divers, i.e. those diving by themselves or with a partner vs. those preferring to dive in organised groups
Learners–Enjoyers, i.e. those trying to expand their knowledge of marine environments vs. those who are primarily interested in the dive experience itself
Homies–Remoties, i.e. those regularly and mostly diving at home vs. those diving abroad, often in remote locations

marketing of diving tourism experiences, and in Chapter 2, Brian Garrod suggests four alternative approaches that can be potentially employed to achieve this. The first involves segmenting the market according to participants' socio-demographic characteristics, such as gender, age, income and so forth. Indeed, a review of some of the previous studies which provide an indication of the main socio-economic characteristics of the diving tourists is provided in this introductory chapter. As can be seen, segmentation on this basis is useful, but it does not provide a fully convincing analysis of the diving tourist market: one that will be especially useful for planning, managing and marketing the activity. To meet that purpose, alternative approaches are required, such as segmentation on the basis of involvement or specialisation. This approach works on the basis that the diving tourists market can be sub-divided into statistically distinct subgroups according to the depth of their involvement in the activity as demonstrated by their knowledge, equipment, activity-setting preferences and so on. Alternatively, market segmentation could be undertaken on the basis of diving tourists' 'travel careers'. This approach follows the work of Pearce and others, which argues that tourists typically pass through a travel career, over the course of which their demographic characteristics, motivations and behaviours may vary systematically. Another approach, meanwhile, is called benefit segmentation. This relies on the observation that different types of diving tourists will typically seek different benefits from different aspects of the diving tourism product. These approaches are often presented as competing with one another. The chapter concludes, however, by suggesting that these different approaches may in fact be best applied in combination with one another, and there is no theoretical or practical reason why they could not be. The chapter concludes by calling for a serious and robust market segmentation of the diving tourism market to be undertaken.

In Chapter 3, Carl Cater brings us closer to an understanding of what attracts people to marine environments. Diving implies immersing oneself in alien environments that human beings are not meant to inhabit. The mastery of these environments is a challenge requiring various skills, and the very process of successfully engaging in diving is thus both rewarding and satisfying. Cater distinguishes between four categories of diver motivations: stimulus-avoidance, social, competence-mastery and intellectual. Stimulus-avoidance is interpreted as escaping to an environment that is fundamentally different from those normally experienced. Social motives include interpersonal relationships that are necessarily part of the diving experience, for instance because of the need to 'buddy up' with a dive partner. Engaging in dive experiences also means to gain the esteem of others; for instance, discussing dive experiences and adventures after the dive can be a source of satisfaction, particularly for more experienced divers that have moved upwards on the diver career ladder. For divers with greater experience, competence-mastery will become a more important motivation. For instance, Cater describes cage diving with sharks as an experience most divers will engage in only once. Wreck diving, on the other hand, requires a greater level of skills, and might be seen as a form of diving in which divers engage in order to achieve, master, challenge or compete. Ultimately, cave diving would then require highest levels of competence-mastery within the leisure-diving continuum, and it is from here that divers might move on to technical diving. Finally, intellectual motives include 'entertainment, excitement and education', i.e. the desire to learn about marine life and marine environments, and to engage in the sustainable management of these.

Section III focuses on the environmental, economic and social impacts of diving tourism. With a growing number of divers and dive destinations coming into existence, the environmental, economic and social impacts of diving tourism gain increasing importance, particularly in dive 'hot spots', i.e. areas where large numbers of divers concentrate. Focusing particularly on environmental aspects, the three chapters contained in this section assess the contribution of diving tourism to environmental change as well as diving tourism's susceptibility to current/projected environmental change. Other topics included in this section are interactions of divers and snorkellers with marine mammals and the role of environmental education in diver certification.

In Chapter 4, Stefan Gössling and his co-authors investigate the interactions between diving and global environmental change. Marine environments, and coral reefs in particular, are coming under increasing stress from destructive fishing methods, various forms of pollution from agriculture, forestry and construction, as well as climate change leading to increasing surface temperatures, rising sea levels and more intense and frequent extreme weather events. All of these changes could potentially affect diving. As the findings of a survey of 289 divers and snorkellers in Mauritius show, however, such interrelationships are highly complex. For divers and snorkellers in Mauritius, few environmental parameters are particularly important, including physically intact reef structures, good visibility, abundance of marine life, and colourful or 'special' species such as turtles or sharks. Most divers and snorkellers believe that reefs are not in a 'good and healthy' state, with scientific studies indicating that marine ecosystems are indeed moderately affected by environmental change, but this does not seem to have a commensurate effect on the divers' and snorkellers' marine experiences. However, further deteriorating environmental conditions could very well influence diver and snorkeller perceptions, particularly if a theoretical threshold is reached beyond which experiences become negatively affected. As divers in Mauritius are to a large extent holiday divers, i.e. divers choosing the destination not primarily for the purpose of diving, the situation might also be fundamentally different in destinations attracting a higher share of experienced dive tourists. The authors thus conclude that for most destinations in the tropics, environmental change is not as yet a threat for local dive industries. However, this could change quickly in the future if El Niño phenomena or weather extremes cause large-scale damage to marine ecosystems. 'Must-dive' destinations are likely to be more vulnerable to such incidences than those serving holiday divers.

Tourists are increasingly seeking out close-up interactions with marine mammals, such as cetaceans (whales and dolphins) and pinnipeds (seals and sea lions) and this has led to an explosion of tours in many places around the world offering tourists the chance to swim with these 'charismatic megafauna'. This may involve scuba diving, although in many specific locations there are regulations restricting such interactions to swimmers (usually equipped with snorkelling gear) who may be required to remain stationary in the water, linked to a vessel by means of ropes (sometimes called 'mermaid lines'). In spite of such regulations, however, the negative impacts of such activities on the animals concerned are not well documented or well understood. In Chapter 5, Susanna Curtin and Brian Garrod review the scientific literature on the nature and magnitude of negative impacts arising from the close interaction of humans with marine mammals in the water, either as scuba divers or as snorkellers, and assess the adequacy of the management response to date. The major conclusions is that the adoption of a 'precautionary' approach to regulating the activity requires that the targeted animals are afforded an opportunity to withdraw from contact with humans if they so wish, and a network of marine-animal refuges will be needed to achieve this. MPAs offer a potential way forward in this respect. There is also a need for tour providers to uphold a more respectful standard of behaviour in order to avoid stressing the animals they seek out for close-up tourist-wildlife encounters.

In Chapter 6, Anna Lindgren and her co-authors evaluate environmental management and education in the dive industry. Divers are in an increasing number of studies depicted as a source of environmental damage, particularly in areas where large diver numbers are concentrated. Impacts include, for instance, direct damage to corals through physical contact, raising of sediments through fins, behavioural change and altered feeding habits of marine fauna, as well as disturbances caused by diving with marine mammals. Higher levels of environmental awareness, knowledge and behaviour as well as improved practical skills of divers could thus help to reduce environmental impacts. In their analysis of teaching materials provided by the PADI, the largest dive organization in the world, Lindgren et al. find that environmental issues are addressed only to a limited degree, while focus of the educational process clearly is on safety. Even of the 'speciality courses' offered to divers having completed the basic Open Water diver certificate, only few focus on environmental management. Regarding practical skills, which are of importance to control diver behaviour, there are demands on required skills, but these might not always be achieved given the rather short period of the training. This does not seem to affect certification, though. The authors thus conclude that the current educational process can, at best, raise awareness of environmental management to a level where newly certified divers incorporate the principle of 'do not touch'. These findings are confirmed by interviews with dive instructors, indicating that smaller group sizes and an extended training could improve divers' awareness and practical skills. Clearly, this also depends on individual dive schools and their dive instructors, as there might be substantial differences in between these in terms of commitment to environmental management.

The final section of the book is focused on the management of diving tourism. The section contains five chapters, indicating the growing importance of integrating management issues in diving tourism. Chapters focus on corporate social responsibility (CSR), options to create artificial reefs that can also be used for training purposes, diver attitudes towards regulation, the role of education in conservation and the increasingly important topic of safety management.

In Chapter 7, Claudia Townsend tackles the critical issue of CSR among the diving tourism providers. Indeed, if diving tourism is to make a positive and effective contribution to the sustainable development of the increasing number of places around the world where it is being developed, then ways and means need to be found of managing the use by the diving industry of the often fragile marine environment, as well as ensuring that the diving tourism industry contributes to the economy concerned and maintains full accountability to the local community in which it operates. This will necessarily involve the dive industry organisations and require them to adopt a completely transformed corporate agenda, as well as fundamentally different tools for implementing it. While noting a number of barriers to the development of CSR in the dive industry, including the diverse nature of the dive tourism sector, the financial cost of the investment required, and educational as well as language barriers, this chapter also notes that there is a growing interest in pro-poor, fair-trade and sustainable tourism among consumers, i.e. diving tourists. This interest needs to be harnessed by the many different organisations working in the sector, which will need to work together and share resources in order to achieve this. A long-term perspective will also need to be adopted. While this may seem a tall order, the chapter provides a wide range of examples showing what can be done by various different types of organisation working in the sector, including private businesses, donors and non-governmental organisations, and the dive-certification organisations. It is also argued that whatever the context of diving, whether in a remote location or a mass-tourism destination, there are benefits to be gained by allowing local people to participate in making decisions about diving tourism and how it effects them.

As coral reefs are coming under increasing pressure from diving, Peter van Treeck and Michael Eisinger investigate in Chapter 8 whether artificial reefs can meet the experience demands of divers. Such installations can not only serve as dive sites, but as well facilitate other uses, such as diver education and training, reef rehabilitation, or as spawning grounds for larvae that can contribute to the recovery of degraded reef areas. In presenting the Save Coral Reefs (SCORE) project, designed to divert diver pressure from natural reefs, to enhance reef recovery and to present training opportunities, the authors discuss Electrochemical Reef Construction technology, a method based on electrolysis, forming magnesium and calcium minerals on metal structures. These structures, having similar characteristics as reef limestone, are suitable to be colonised by reef organisms. Set up in a way to protect natural reefs in need of recovery, SCORE could help to provide alternatives for diving that can be of interest for divers because of the unusual character of the structures and their observable development over time towards more fully developed coral colonies. Van Treeck and Eisniger suggest that such structures should be more often used in the future to combine the development of the diving industry with the conservation of reefs.

Divers are used to regulation, being subject to a range of rules and requirements from the time they begin their diving careers by training with the various certification organisations. Surely, then, formal regulation will hold considerable potential for the prevention of diver impacts on the often fragile marine environments in which they undertake their activities. In Chapter 9, Nola Barker and Callum Roberts examine the evidence on divers' attitudes to and preferences for particular regulations, based on studies that have been conducted in various diving tourism destinations around the world but especially in the Soufrière Marine Management Area of St. Lucia in the Caribbean. The chapter considers four particular regulatory approaches: the education and supervision of divers; the establishment of quotas on the number of divers allowed to use the site at any one time; regulation by zoning specific areas for diving; and the use of diving fees as incentives to encourage or discourage diving at particular sites or at particular times. The chapter argues that diver education through briefings alone is not sufficient to ensure that divers do not have negative impacts on the underwater environment; these need to be reinforced by close in-water supervision, whatever the level of ability or experience of the divers concerned. With regard to limiting access, the chapter notes that divers often seek out MPAs as diving tourism destinations, as these are able to offer a better quality of environment and more abundant marine life. However, divers will typically want to see visible evidence that the area is indeed being actively protected through the use of rigorous and effective management and regulatory measures. Research has meanwhile shown that imposing user fees does not tend to put divers off diving at such sites; indeed many are willing to pay a good deal more to dive than they currently do. If this potential revenue could be effectively captured, then the authorities concerned could implement more and better management systems. These approaches are not necessarily mutually exclusive; nor are they exclusive with non-regulatory measures such as site management through the use of pontoons, walkways and so on. The chapter concludes by recommending that managers need to identify the best mix of regulatory measures according to the particular characteristics and requirements of their site, as well as the attitudes and preferences of their diving clientele towards these different measures.

Claudia Townsend returns in Chapter 10 to discuss the role of education as a conservation tool. Education and interpretation are important both to inform divers of relevant regulations and rules, but they can also serve as means to improve the divers' experience, for instance by providing information about dive sites, particular features of the marine environment, or necessary dive skills. Townsend outlines the character of messages that are more effective in achieving these goals — and those that are not. Warning divers not to damage the reef without providing practical advice of how to achieve this may for instance induce guilt rather than prevent damage. Messages thus need to be designed in such a way as to reinforce the diver's wish to engage in pro-environmental action, which ideally is based on a more holistic consideration of the dive experience. Small group sizes, for instance, can help to increase diver satisfaction, which in turn increases willingness to engage in conservation through payments, donations or spending time as a volunteer for activities such as surveys or beach cleanups. Educational messages, on the other hand, need to appeal intellectually and emotionally. If divers feel they are doing good through their diving behaviour, they are not only more likely to act in responsible manners, but will even open up in other contexts, such as of how to behave in more culturally sensitive ways. However, messages may not always be easy to deliver: there may be certain diver groups that are particularly difficult to reach (such as novice divers), while providing too detailed information might result in disinterest of other groups. Townsend thus concludes that environmental education and interpretation can, if messages are properly delivered, help to manage diver impacts on sites and to increase support for conservation. The challenge is to deliver this information in ways that enhance diver satisfaction and interest in these issues.

The final chapter of this volume, by Christopher Coxon, Kay Dimmock and Jeff Wilks, presents a safety-management approach to managing risk in the context of tourism diving. Most diving activities by their very nature have a high degree of risk attached to them, there being a high potential for accidents and injuries to occur, and this requires the adoption of an approach to risk management that is both proactive and robust. To this end, the chapter sets out a safety-first approach that combines a number of elements, including risk assessment, the adoption of a safety-management system and embracing a safety culture at the organisational level. First, the risk-assessment process is set out. The chapter argues that dive tourism operators can ultimately take one of four main stances in relation to risk assessment, each being illustrated by a particular marine species. Among 'grunions', both the assessment and management of risk is poor, and organisations of this kind tend to operate on the basis of little understanding of the risks implications they confront on a day-to-day basis. Like the grunion they are likely to end up washed up on the beach. 'Stellar's sea cows', on the other hand, are good at assessing the risks they confront but do little to address these risks effectively. Like the Stellar's sea cow they soon become extinct. 'Salmon', meanwhile, take an active approach to managing risk. Their attitude to risk is, however, poor, with procedural requirements developed to cover all conceivable risks. Like the salmon, these organisations will achieve their safety goal but will 'die on the return trip' as diving customers are put off by the seemingly draconian risk regimes they operate. 'Dolphins', finally have a positive approach both to risk assessment and risk management, and like their animal they constantly explore their environment, learn from what they discover and seek challenges in new directions. Overall, these will be the most successful dive operators. The risk-management process, meanwhile, is divided into five stages: commitment and policy formulation; planning; implementation; measurement and evaluation; and review and improvement. These stages form a circular system through which the organisation can identify and adapt to changes on an on-going basis. Lastly, the chapter considers the development of a positive safety culture critical to the success of risk management in the dive tourism industry. This is needed to ensure that the risk-assessment and risk-management systems outlined in the chapter have a real impact on the ground. Only then will the promised benefits in terms of reduced incident occurrences, customer approval and worker satisfaction be fully captured by the organisation concerned, thus making a maximum positive contribution to its bottom line.

Several conclusions can be drawn from the chapters contained in this book. First, dive tourism is an emerging form of mass tourism, with the potential to help developing new destinations. In fact, there is evidence that dive tourism could be developed far more systematically than has been done so far, with examples contained in this book including sinking old ships to attract wreck divers in Gozo and Malta, or cold-water, high-visibility diving in Iceland. Second, diving increasingly contributes to the generation of economic benefits, which can be of particular importance for peripheral, mono-structured economies. However, there is also evidence that environmental impacts from dive tourism are increasing, calling for a broader integration of innovative management approaches in diving. Particularly the growing contribution of diving to global emissions of greenhouse gases deserves attention, given the commitment of industrialized countries to reduce emissions. Finally, it seems clear that there is a huge potential to improve the management of diving, with many initiatives such as artificial reef generation being little explored so far. The dive industry is thus encouraged to address more seriously and broadly the issues of social corporate responsibility, environmental management, education and safety which play such an important role in their operations. This will help to ensure the positive development of this emerging tourism sector.

References

Barker, N. H. L., & Roberts, C. M. (2004). Scuba diver behaviour and the management of diving impacts on coral reefs. *Biological Conservation, 120*, 481–489.

Cater, C., & Cater, E. (2001). Marine environments. In: D. B. Weaver (Ed.), *The encyclopedia of ecotourism* (pp. 265–282). Wallingford: CABI.

Cesar, H. S. J., & van Beukering, P. J. H. (2004). Economic valuation of the coral reefs of Hawai'i. *Pacific Science, 58*, 231–242.

Cherry, G. (1976). *Skin diving and snorkeling*. London: Adam and Charles Black.

Cottrell, S. P., & Meisel, C. (2004). Predictors of personal responsibility to protect the marine environment among divers. In: J. Murdy (Ed.), *Proceedings of the 2003 northeastern recreation research symposium* (pp. 252–261). Newtown Square: USDA Forest Service.

Cousteau Society. (2007). http://cousteau.org (Accessed 20 May 2007).

Davis, D., & Tisdell, C. (1995). Recreational scuba-diving and carrying capacity in MPAs. *Ocean and Coastal Management, 26*, 19–40.

Dimmock, K. (2007). Scuba diving, snorkeling, and free diving. In: G. Jennings (Ed.), *Water-based tourism, sport, leisure, and recreation experiences* (pp. 128–147). Amsterdam: Elsevier.

Ditton, R. B., & Baker, T. L. (1999). Demographics, attitudes, management preferences, and economics impacts of sport divers using artificial reefs in offshore Texas waters. Report to the Texas Parks and Wildlife Department.

Garrod, B., & Wilson, J. C. (2003). *Marine ecotourism: Issues and experiences*. Clevedon: Channel View.

Gössling, S. (2001). Tourism, environmental degradation and economic transition: Interacting processes in a Tanzanian coastal community. *Tourism Geographies, 3*, 230–254.

Gössling, S., Kunkel, T., Schumacher, K., & Zilger, M. (2004). Use of molluscs, fish and other marine taxa by tourism in Zanzibar, Tanzania. *Biodiversity and Conservation, 13*, 2623–2639.

Hawkins, J. P., Roberts, C. M., van't Hof, T., De Meyer, K., Tratalos, J., & Aldam, C. (1999). Effects of recreational scuba diving on Caribbean coral and fish communities. *Conservation Biology, 13*, 888–897.

Klein, R. (2002). *Cruise ship blues: The underside of the cruise industry.* Gabriola Island, British Columbia: New Society Publishers.

Ministry for Tourism and Culture. (2006). Malta's national tourism plan. Draft. Discussion document for external consultation. http://www.tourism.gov.mt/filebank/pdfs/ TourismPLAN.pdf (Accessed 22 February 2007).

Mundet, L., & Ribera, L. (2001). Characteristics of divers at a Spanish resort. *Tourism Management, 22*, 501–510.

Musa, G. (2003). Sipadan: An over-exploited scuba-diving paradise? An analysis of tourism impact, diver satisfaction and management priorities. In: B. Garrod & J. C. Wilson (Eds), *Marine ecotourism: Issues and experiences* (pp. 122–137). Clevedon: Channel View.

Musa, G., Kadir, S. L. S. A., & Lee, L. (2006). Layang Layang: An empirical study on scuba divers' satisfaction. *Tourism in Marine Environments, 2*, 89–102.

O'Neill, M. A., Williams, P., MacCarthy, M., & Groves, R. (2000). Diving into service quality: The dive tour operator perspective. *Managing Service Quality, 10*, 131–140.

Orams, M. (1999). *Marine tourism: Development, impacts and management.* London: Routledge.

PADI. (2007). *Statistics.* http://www.padi.com/english/common/padi/statistics/ (Accessed 7 February 2007).

Responsible Travel. (2007). *Leave only bubbles.* http://www.responsibletravel.com/Copy/ Copy100784.htm (Accessed 7 February 2007).

Roberts, C. M., & Hawkins, J. P. (2000). Fully-protected marine reserves: A guide. WWF. Endangered Seas Campaign, Washington DC and Environment Department, University of York.

Rouphael, A. B., & Hanafy, M. (2007). An alternative management framework to limit the impact of SCUBA divers on coral assemblages. *Journal of Sustainable Tourism, 15*, 91–103.

Scuba Travel. (2007). 100 Top dive sites of the world. http://www.scubatravel.co.uk/topdiveslong.html (Accessed 7 February 2007).

Swarbrooke, J., Beard, C., Leckie, S., & Pomfret, G. (2003). *Adventure tourism. The new frontier.* Amsterdam: Butterworth Heinemann.

Tabata, R. S. (1992). Scuba diving holidays. In: B. Weiler & C. M. Hall (Eds), *Special interest tourism* (pp. 171–184). London: Belhaven.

Thailing, C. E., & Ditton, R. B. (2003). Demographics, motivations and participation patterns of sport divers in the Flower Garden Banks National Marine Sanctuary. In: *Proceedings of the Gulf and Caribbean Fisheries Institute No 54* (pp. 338–348). Gulf and Caribbean Fisheries Institute.

Theobald, W. F. (2005). The meaning, scope and measurement of travel and tourism. In: W. F. Theobald (Ed.), *Global tourism.* 3rd ed., (pp. 5–24). Burlington, MA: Elsevier.

Thingvellir. (2006). *Diving.* http://www.thingvellir.is/english/national-park/ diving/ (Accessed 1 July 2006).

Todd, S. (2004). Only 'real divers' use New York's Great Lakes? In: J. Murdy (Ed), *Proceedings of the 2003 northeastern recreation research symposium* (pp. 211–218). Newtown Square: USDA Forest Service.

Tourism Queensland. (2006). *Dive tourism.* http://www.tq.com.au/tq_com/dms/2F0335B4B50 A7B818A527A1CE5C4E434.pdf (Accessed 19 June 2006).

Tratalos, J. A., & Austin, T. J. (2001). Impacts of recreational SCUBA diving on coral communities of the Caribbean island of Grand Cayman. *Biological Conservation, 102*, 67–75.

Viders, H. (1997). *Marine conservation in the 21st century.* Flagstaff: AZ Publishing.

White, A., & Rosales, R. (2003). Community-oriented marine tourism in the Philippines: Role in economic development and conservation. In: S. Gössling (Ed.), *Tourism and development in tropical islands: Political ecology perspectives* (pp. 237–262). Cheltenham: Edward Elgar Publishing.

Wilkinson, C. (Ed.) (2004). *Status of coral reefs of the world: 2004.* Townsville: Australian Institute of Marine Science.

World Tourism Organization. (2001). *Tourism 2020 vision. Vol. 7. Global forecasts and profiles of market segments.* Madrid: WTO.

Zakai, D., & Chadwick-Furman, N. E. (2002). Impacts of intensive recreational diving on reef corals at Eilat, Northern Red Sea. *Biological Conservation, 105,* 179–187.

SECTION II:

THE DIVING TOURISM EXPERIENCE

Chapter 2

Market Segments and Tourist Typologies for Diving Tourism

Brian Garrod

Introduction

Divers are often diving tourists. The World Tourism Organization (2001) suggests that one in three scuba divers regularly take an overseas holiday, often with the aim of diving the world-class sites, such as Sharm El Sheikh on the Red Sea, the Caymans in the Caribbean, the Seychelles and the Maldives in the Indian Ocean or the Australian Great Barrier Reef. At such dives sites, the water is always warm and the underwater visibility good; the underwater landscapes are breathtaking and the seas teeming with marine wildlife. One does not have to look very far, so it would seem, to uncover the travel motivations of the scuba diver. Yet academics and practitioners have long recognised that diving tourism markets are extremely diverse (Tabata, 1992). Diving tourists vary widely according to their demographic backgrounds and socio-economic status, their previous experience of diving and aspirations for the diving holiday, their needs and expectations, the ways in which they approach the diving tourism product, and in many other respects. Even so, it appears that relatively little effort has been put into trying to understand the extent and nature of such diversity. The analytical techniques needed to achieve such insights are nevertheless available and prominent among these is market segmentation. The purpose of this chapter is firstly to set out the rationale for market segmentation and to explain how the technique works. Various approaches to market segmentation will then be explored that have been successfully used in other closely-related tourism markets, such as adventure tourism, sports tourism and ecotourism. The chapter will conclude by making recommendations for how a tourist typology based on an actual segmentation of the diving tourism market might be developed in practice.

New Frontiers in Marine Tourism: Diving Experiences, Sustainability, Management
Copyright © 2008 by Elsevier Ltd.
All rights of reproduction in any form reserved.
ISBN: 978-0-08-045357-6

Market Segmentation

Palacio and McCool (1997, p. 236) define market segmentation as "a process by which a large, potentially heterogeneous market is divided into smaller, more homogeneous components or segments". The segmentation can be based on the demographic, socio-economic, psychographic or behavioural characteristics of the tourists comprising the market. Most often, a combination of variables drawn from two or more of these groupings is found to produce the most incisive and serviceable market segmentation. The technique works by identifying both similarities and differences between tourists in the market. Each market segment is thus defined on the basis that the individuals comprising it have demonstrably similar characteristics, for example they may share a similar demographic background or seek the same kinds of benefit from the product. Each market segment is also defined on the basis of measurable differences between its tourists and those included in other market segments. Such differences could for example relate to tourists' socio-economic characteristics or the degree of specialisation they have in the activity concerned. The resulting spectrum of market segments is often presented as a tourist typology, and these can be invaluable tools in the strategic armoury of organisations, such as tour operators, tourism destinations and national park authorities. In particular, marketing and visitor-management strategies can be targeted at individual market segments, rather than at the market as a whole, thereby increasing their specificity, precision and effectiveness.

Market segmentation is extensively implemented in the tourism industry (Sarigöllü & Huang, 2005) and diving tourism is widely acknowledged to be one of the tourism industry's fastest growing markets (Cater & Cater, 2001; Musa, Kadir, & Lee, 2006; Tabata, 1992). While Orams (1999) points out that this claim could be made of almost any new sport, he goes on to suggest that scuba diving has become an immensely popular activity and this has undoubtedly fuelled the demand for diving tourism. Indeed, the World Tourism Organization (2001) suggests that scuba diving is now second only to winter sports as a form of active sports tourism, with an estimated annual turnover of €3.5–5.0 billion. Sung (2004), meanwhile, points out that tourism is becoming increasingly more specialist, with an ever-widening array of 'special-interest tourism' (SIT) market segments emerging and growing rapidly in their importance. Trauer (2006) argues that while tourism providers used to seek to cater for niche markets at the 'hard or specialised' or 'serious leisure' end of the spectrum, tourism providers have now diversified across into the 'soft' or 'novice' end of the SIT market. The main drivers of such growth are considered to be technological change, time squeeze, space contraction, affluence and the increased availability of leisure equipment.

Given the growing significance of diving tourism, it is perhaps surprising that no market segmentation study yet exists that focuses specifically on diving tourists. While a small number of segmentation studies exist that deal with sports tourists, adventure tourists and ecotourists — larger conceptual groupings to which diving tourists can be said to belong — the typologies that emerge do not seem to capture the either specifics of diving as a form of recreation or to provide much of an improved understanding of tourism as a means of participating in this activity.

The benefits of market segmentation are nevertheless widely appreciated, particularly in terms of the contribution that market segmentation can make to tourism marketing

(Fyall & Garrod, 2005). The value of market segmentation in planning and managing sustainable tourism has also been noted. Palacio and McCool (1997), for example, argue that sustainable tourism in natural areas requires that land managers, tourism providers and local hosts all appreciate the types of tourists they are dealing with, their particular characteristics, their motivations and behaviour, and the benefits they seek. This will enable tourism suppliers to design effective promotional campaigns by selecting appropriate messages, to provide facilities that are in keeping with the tourism setting but attractive to tourists, to determine an appropriate customer-base for a particular destination so that the tourism that takes place there remains in keeping with its physical and cultural capacities, and to appreciate more fully the economic and policy consequences of different tourism development strategies. Market segmentation thus provides the organisations involved in sustainable tourism with the information base they need to make their strategies effective. Hvenegaard (2002) echoes this view, arguing that tourism typologies based on market segmentation are vital ingredients in the effective planning and management of tourism. Tourist typologies are able to inform such issues as the nature and incidence of environmental and community impacts, how to involve tourists in conservation activities and the varying motivations of different types of tourists. The latter has particular implications for tourist satisfaction and the design of tourism products. Tourist typologies also enable managers to recognise and address the different motivations, experiences and impacts of various tourist types, as well as to understand which tourist types are more likely to be found at different stages in the lifecycle of tourism destination areas.

While the concept of market segmentation is well established, researchers do not always agree on the best variables to adopt in attempting to achieve a coherent and instructive segmentation. Swarbrooke and Horner (1999), for example, identify four groups of variables:

- *Geographical*: the market is segmented on the basis of the tourist's place of residence, distance travelled to the destination or, most frequently, nationality. For example, Hinch and Higham (2004) quote a World Tourism Organization study that found that French summer-sport tourists preferred diving and snorkelling, while Germans preferred walking and hiking.
- *Socio-economic*: the market segmentation is based on the occupation and/or income of tourists. It is often pointed out that scuba diving is a relatively expensive leisure activity because of the equipment and extensive training involved, and as such is more likely to be attractive participants with higher incomes (Cater & Cater, 2001).
- *Demographic*: market segmentation is done on the basis of tourists' gender, age or education. All of these variables are considered to be particularly relevant to scuba diving, the activity being largely male-oriented and restricted to younger people (World Tourism Organization, 2001). This is often put down to the physical demands involved in scuba diving, although Musa et al. (2006) argue that this seems to be changing, with a more even gender balance and a higher average age of participants emerging as the activity has become more well-known and popular. The educational status of scuba-diving participants also tends to be higher on average, although this is likely to be more to do with the close correlation between education and income than any intrinsic causal factor linked specifically to educational achievement.

- *Behaviouristic*: the market is segmented according to the behavioural relationships of tourists with the product. This behaviour might relate to the type of experience being sought (e.g. particular activities) or the tourists' motivations for participating in a particular activity. It is noted, for example, that for some tourists scuba diving will be their specific purpose for visiting the destination, while for others participating in the activity will be a secondary, even casual decision. Indeed, Davis and Tisdell (1995) remark on the growth of so-called 'resort diving' (also known as 'try diving'), where non-certified participants dive under close supervision. Cater and Cater (2001), meanwhile, note that increasing numbers of people who scuba dive whilst at a holiday destination are there actually on traditional 3S (sun, sand and sea) packages.

This system of classification is by no means generally accepted. Palacio and McCool (1997), for example, collapse the socio-economic and demographic categories together and include psychographics (based on tourists' attitudes and values) within the behavioural category. Sarigöllü and Huang (2005) also separate out psychographic and behavioural variables, while also including an additional category of benefits. The inclusion of the latter category recognises the increasing popularity of benefits segmentation as a basis for determining market segments (e.g. Frochot, 2005; Murphy & Norris, 2005; Palacio & McCool, 1997), although it could well be argued that benefits segmentation is essentially a variant of behaviouristic segmentation based on trip motivations. It should also be noted that market segmentation is often implemented on the basis of a number of variables drawn from two or more of the above groups. Indeed, if a more effective and instructive market segmentation is achieved by using a mixture of explanatory variables then it can surely be argued that this is exactly as it should be.

Each market segmentation strategy will clearly be specific to the market it is being applied to and its success or otherwise can only be judged on the outcomes it generates. However, there are some general preconditions that would appear to be relevant to any application of the market segmentation process. Indeed, according to Kotler (2001), individual market segments need to be:

- *Measurable*: the selected variables upon which a specific market segment is based can be measured empirically.
- *Actionable*: practical marketing programmes can be formulated for the various segments.
- *Differentiable*: the segments must be conceptually distinct and must respond differently to different combinations of the marketing mix.
- *Accessible*: each segment can be effectively reached and serviced.
- *Substantial*: each segment must be large enough to be profitable, given the added marketing costs involved in segmenting the market and the additional revenues likely to be received as a result.

It can also be added that the segments need to be *defendable* in the face of competition in the short, medium and long term (Fyall & Garrod, 2005). There may be little to be gained if rival companies are able to raid the segments by replicating the targeted marketing strategies that have been developed to address them. Bieger and Laesser (2002), meanwhile, indicate that the resulting market segments must also be *appropriate* insofar as they are compatible with the overall position of the service provider.

Segments of the Diving Tourism Market

Individuals clearly have a wide range of motivations for undertaking diving tourism experiences. While the literature has barely touched upon such motivations in the specific context of scuba-diving holidays, academics have long been interested in determining the basic motivational forces that underlie leisure behaviour more generally. Beard and Ragheb (1983), for example, construct and test an empirical model of leisure motivation. The work suggests that four components tend to dominate in leisure motivation:

- *Intellectual*: engaging in leisure activities that provide mental exercise, such as learning and teaching, exploring, discovering, creating and imagining.
- *Social*: engaging in leisure activities that involve inter-personal exchanges, thereby meeting the need for friendship and the need to earn the esteem of others.
- *Competence-mastery*: engaging in leisure activities in order to achieve, master, challenge and compete. Such activities are normally physical.
- *Stimulus avoidance*: engaging in leisure activities that allow the individual to escape from the everyday stresses of life, to avoid social contacts, to seek solitude and calmness, to relax and to unwind.

While Beard and Ragheb do not go on to use these motivational factors to segment any particular leisure market, there are certainly a number of very strong resonances between these general motivational factors and the specific reasons a person might have for taking a diving holiday. These will be further developed in the following chapter of this book.

With more specific reference to diving tourism, Tabata (1992) sets out two possible typologies that could be applied to participants in scuba diving. While neither was based on a practical market segmentation study or has been tested empirically, these typologies nevertheless provide an indication of the broad spectrum of individuals that participate in diving tourism. The first typology, following Rice (1987), divides scuba divers into three main groups: 'hard-core' divers, who choose a destination for its fauna and flora or its challenging dives; 'tourist divers', who include diving as part of their vacation; and 'novices', who have never dived before but are taking the opportunity to dive while on holiday. The second, proposed by Tabata himself, places divers along a spectrum, with 'adventure' motivations at one end and 'educational' motivations at the other. 'Adventure' divers seek excitement, such as wall dives and drift dives (where divers drift in currents and are to some degree at their mercy), while 'educational' divers want to see unique underwater marine life and/or geology. One possible criticism of this spectrum is that it is unclear where to fit in activities involving both high excitement and a strong desire to encounter marine wildlife, for example, the growing practice of diving with sharks. Indeed, it can be argued that both of these typologies are lacking both in precision and in a strong empirical basis.

Similar criticisms can be levelled at the World Tourism Organization (2001) typology, which divides diving tourists into four types: (i) cheap-and-cheerful dive tourists, comprising mainly younger tourists who are holidaying on organised, low-cost dive packages; (ii) dive fanatics at short-haul destinations, with the sole purpose of diving, usually with family and friends; (iii) dive fanatics to long-haul destinations, who are generally well off and wish to dive either as part of a beach holiday or are solely interested in diving; and

(iv) sideliner divers, who make one or several dives as part of a family beach-resort holiday. The latter group would seem to correspond to Davis and Tisdell's resort divers mentioned earlier in this chapter.

Keeling (2006), meanwhile, presents a market segmentation which he argues can be applied to any outdoor recreation activity, water sports being an example used for illustrative purposes. Four main market segments are suggested, based on the level of interest an individual has in the activity and the amount of leisure time he or she devotes to it. The four groups are:

- *Samplers*: these are undertaking the outdoor activity for the first time, or do so on a very occasional basis.
- *Learners*: those that are learning the skills involved in the outdoor activity, or wishing to improve.
- *Dabblers*: those who occasionally participate in the outdoor activity as part of the leisure time or holiday. They will have some knowledge and skill in the activity. Holidays present an opportunity for them to participate.
- *Enthusiasts*: those who regularly take part in the outdoor activity and will have expert skill and knowledge.

Keeling goes on to argue that this market segmentation can be applied to individuals or groups and that different outdoor activities will exhibit different mixes of sampler, learners, dabblers and enthusiasts. He also suggests that the segmentation can assist public-sector agencies in implementing tailored marketing strategies and in meeting the key product requirements of each market segment. Thus for water sports, in general, Keeling suggests that samplers will require accredited water sport centres, while learners will require accredited water sport centres and instructors. Dabblers, meanwhile, will require access to beaches and the sea, beach showers and changing facilities, equipment hire and accredited water sport centres. Enthusiasts, on the other hand, will require access to beaches and the sea, beach showers and changing facilities, and dive charter boats. The market segmentation is said to be developed "on the basis of the research and analysis undertaken for the Wales activity tourism strategies over the past 5 years" (Keeling, 2006, p. 5), although unfortunately no details of the specific type of research and analysis are given. The segmentation also appears to be anything but insightful, the key product needs for the four groups of water sports participants actually being strikingly similar to one another.

In view of the foregoing discussion, it can be argued that what is needed is a typology of diving tourists that is both highly instructive to those marketing, planning and managing this form of tourism, and based on a rigorous empirical segmentation of the market. The purpose of the remainder of this chapter is to identify some promising lines of inquiry and to sketch what a practical market segmentation of a dive tourism market might look like.

Segmentation on the Basis of Involvement or Specialisation

Several writers in the wider sports and adventure tourism literature have recommended segmenting these markets on the basis of participants' extent of 'involvement' or degree of 'specialisation' in the activity. Such concepts would appear to be highly relevant to scuba diving and, as such, might hold considerable promise as the basis for an actual segmentation of particular diving tourism markets.

The concept of recreational involvement, or specialisation, has been traced back to the pioneering work of Bryan (1977, 1979). In this work, Bryan postulated a spectrum of recreational behaviour, ranging from the general to the highly specialised, based on participants' ownership of equipment and their activity-setting preferences, knowledge about the activity, accumulated experience and skill level. Bryan initially applied this approach to developing a typology of trout fishermen (*sic*), although the approach has since been successfully applied to a diverse range of outdoor recreation activities including, *inter alia*, hunting, bird watching, canoeing and hiking. The approach has also been applied in the tourism context. Kerstetter, Confer, and Graefe (2001), for example, present a segmentation study of heritage tourists based on three dimensions of specialisation: previous experience, knowledge and investment. All three of these dimensions were found to be statistically significant in distinguishing between different types of heritage tourist, defined as those with low, medium and high levels of specialisation. The value of the approach is further confirmed in that several variables, such as income, age and gender were found not to be significant, even though they might have been considered to be important on *a priori* grounds.

Kim, Kim, and Ritchie (2006), meanwhile, incorporate the concept of specialisation in their segmentation study of Korean overseas golf tourists. Six variables related to the golf tourists' degree of involvement or specialisation were used: golfing stroke, number of overseas golfing trips since 2000, number of overseas golfing trips since 2003, number of golfing magazine subscriptions, age at which they started playing golf and expenditure on golfing equipment since 2003. Three distinct market segments were identified on this basis: beginner, intermediate and advanced. The advanced group tended to have a lower golfing stroke, higher expenditure on equipment and magazine subscriptions, and to have started playing golf at a younger age. They also made more overseas trips and took more golfing trips. Beginner, intermediate and advanced golf tourists also tended to vary significantly in terms of their demographic profile and motivations for taking an overseas golfing holiday. Kim et al. argue that this serves to make their segmentation even more insightful and useful as a practical tool for the management and marketing of overseas golf tourism. Thus, advanced golf tourists tended to be motivated by the quality of the overseas golf resort and the opportunity to make business contacts, have relatively high incomes, travel independently and use their own knowledge as a source of information about the destination. Beginners, meanwhile, were more likely to be motivated by the cultural and entertainment facilities, be attracted by the ease of access to the resort, be a company employee or housewife, be on relatively low incomes, use information from friends and family to choose their destination and prefer package tours. The intermediate group, meanwhile, fell somewhere between the advanced in beginner group in these respects. Motivations relating to the appreciation of natural resources and boasting/prestige did not vary significantly between the three groups.

While the above research is clearly based on the specific case of golf tourism, the available evidence would seem to suggest that there is a great deal of scope to apply this approach to diving tourism. Indeed, scuba diving is a particularly good example of a recreational activity where equipment is of paramount importance, human survival in the underwater environment being impossible without sophisticated and therefore relatively expensive equipment. While this equipment can often be hired at the diving destination, many divers prefer to use their own equipment because they will be more familiar with how it works and can also be more confident that it is in good working order and well maintained. As noted above, most studies of scuba divers suggest that they tend to some from older age groups and earn an income that is above average. Cater and Cater (2001) suggest that this may be related to the expense of purchasing more and better equipment as the individual become more experienced as a diver. A similar set of arguments might well be said to apply to the issue of skills. Indeed, a survey undertaken on behalf of Tourism Queensland (2006) found that around a quarter of diving tourists wanted to develop their scuba-diving and/or snorkelling skills. As divers gain experience they will typically wish to dive in more challenging activity settings, such as wrecks, underwater caverns and wall dives, and in more challenging ways, such as drift diving, cold-water diving, encountering sharks or underwater photography (Ellegard, 2005). Indeed, the progressive system of dive training provided by the world's diving organisations, such as that used by the Professional Association of Diving Instructors (PADI), is specifically designed to enable divers to undertake additional training as they become more involved and/or specialised in the activity.

There are also a number of studies which, while not specifically focused on diving tourism, suggest that the involvement/specialisation approach has a real potential in that context. A paper by Sung (2004), for example, classifies a sample of US adventure tourists into six distinct market segments, each varying according to their degree of ego involvement in adventure tourism. Six dimensions of ego involvement were identified and used in this model, those being activity, experience, environment, motivation, risk and performance. Thus 'general enthusiasts' (making up 27.2% of the market) and 'active soloists' (making up 14% of the market) showed the highest level of ego involvement and it was clear that issues such as a rugged activity-setting and the element of risk were of great importance to such tourists. These groups differed, however, in other respects, such as in their demographic characteristics and travel behaviour. For example, while the general enthusiasts preferred to travel in groups the active soloists preferred to travel alone. At the other end of the spectrum, meanwhile, soft moderates (making up 9.4% of the market) showed little ego involvement. Thus, for example, soft moderates prized familiarity and safety, with little or no risk involved in their tourism activities. This classification seems in some ways to echo the classic tourist typology suggested by Plog (1977), where tourists are placed along a spectrum with 'allocentrics' at one end, who crave exoticism and seek risk, and 'psychocentrics' at the other, who seek familiarity and shun risk.

The potential to apply market segmentation based on the involvement/specialisation approach is also evidenced in a paper by Trauer (2006) focusing on SIT. In this paper, Trauer presents a carefully argued theoretical segmentation of the SIT market based on two dimensions: the tourist's degree of involvement and the amount of complexity/challenge implicit in the activity being undertaken. This is shown in Figure 2.1. The four segments are characterised as:

- *Collector (low involvement, with high complexity/challenge)*: such tourists regularly undertake SIT but do not restrict themselves to one particular activity, such as windsurfing, canoeing or scuba diving. They effectively collect SIT experiences.

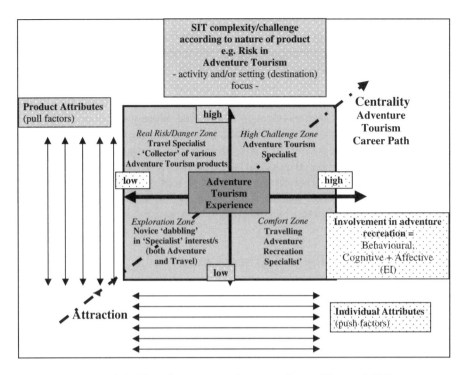

Figure 2.1: The adventure tourism experience (Trauer, 2006)

- *Expert/specialist tourist (high involvement, with high complexity/challenge)*: here the tourist is engaging in a special-interest activity that is fundamental to and central in their way of life and leisure.
- *Travelling expert/expert recreationists (high involvement, with low complexity/challenge)*: this group comprises individuals who are highly involved in the activity during their day-to-day leisure time but travel to undertake the activity only rarely or even as a one-off (and thus only 'dabbling' in tourism element of the SIT holiday).
- *Novice/dabbler (low involvement, with low complexity/challenge)*: this group is characterised by relative inexperience, lack of familiarity with the activity and limited exposure time to it. The 'novice' is thus defined as someone who is dabbling in *both* tourism and the activity.

While this model has clearly not been tested empirically, in terms of its conceptualisation it would appear to fit very well to the particular case of diving tourism. For example, the model is built on the notion that there is a spectrum of involvement on the part of divers, from 'hard-core' enthusiasts at one end, to casual 'resort divers' at the other. Indeed, this conforms well to our understanding of current trends in scuba-diving participation (Cater & Cater, 2001; Davis & Tisdell, 1995). The model also incorporates the notion of complexity and challenge, and these are considered to be increasingly important motivational factors as divers accumulate more and more diving experience. Orams (1999), for example, argues that diving is an activity that is well suited to the achievement of 'flow' on the part of participants. A state of flow (or 'peak experience') is said to be achieved when the individual's skill level is matched to the degree of challenge involved in the activity. This results in a feeling of empowerment and exhilaration. Often the individual loses perception of what is going on around him or her and may lose track of time. However, when the participant's skill level exceeds the level of challenge of the activity, the individual becomes bored. When the level of challenge of the activity exceeds the skill level of the participant, he or she becomes anxious and is in stress. Orams argues that diving represents an activity that allows a variety of skill levels (as the individual becomes more experienced as a diver) to be matched to a variety of levels of challenge (different diving locations and formats), and is thus an ideal vehicle for the achievement of flow. The notions of experience, skill level, challenge and flow link closely to the travel-career approach, which is the subject to which this chapter now turns.

Segmentation on the Basis of Travel Career

Pearce and Lee (2005) propose a travel-career approach to understanding tourists' motivations. This approach is itself a modification of the travel-career ladder proposed originally by Pearce (1988). The basis of the approach is that travel motivations tend to vary over the lifespan and travel experience of the tourist. Pearce argues that tourist motivations exist at a number of levels which relate broadly to Maslow's (1970) hierarchy of needs — those being relaxation, safety/security, relationship, self-esteem and self-actualisation — and an individual will seek progressively to meet these needs. While tourists are a very diverse group and will clearly not have just one set of needs, we might expect one of these needs to dominate in the decision making of an individual tourist at any given point in time. This suggests that tourism decision-making can be characterised as a 'ladder' up which the individual progresses as they develop their 'career' as a tourist. Less-experienced tourists will be expected to be motivated in significantly different ways to more-experienced tourists. Of course, the concept of a 'career' has a strong resonance with Bryan's notion of recreational involvement or specialisation (as discussed above). This is important in terms of the arguments being present in this chapter in that it implies that travel experience can potentially be used as a means of segmenting the market.

While the travel-career approach has not been tested in the context of diving tourism, it can be argued that it holds considerable promise as a robust conceptual basis for the empirical segmentation of such markets. Accumulated diving experience would certainly appear to be an important determinant of scuba divers' needs and motivations, with more experienced divers clearly seeking different experiences and requiring different types of product to meet those needs. Thus, as already noted, as scuba divers progress up their career ladder they tend to prefer more challenging diving environments. As Ellegard (2005, p. 65) notes, more experienced divers "want to experience a little more than brightly coloured fish and pretty coral … deeper waters, shark spotting and dive sites that challenge their skills tend to be the order of the day". Similarly, Meisel and Cottrell (2004) in their study of scuba divers in the Flora Keys suggest that for those with little previous diving experience the following motivations are the most important:

* To show myself I can do it
* Because its an impressive sort of thing to do
* To develop my diving skills and knowledge
* To have an experience I can look back on
* Because it's a challenge.

These motivations tend, however, to decline as the diver becomes more experienced, while the following motivations tend to take over:

* For relaxation
* To share my knowledge
* To use my equipment
* To see shipwrecks.

These findings are based on a self-assessment by survey respondents of their diving experience, rather than on a robust empirical segmentation of the market, and should therefore be viewed with some caution. They are nevertheless indicative of the strong possibility that diving tourists motivations vary consistently as the individual extends his or her scuba-diving 'career'.

Previous applications of this approach to other forms of tourism also suggest that it has some promise as a means of segmenting the market. The study by Pearce and Lee (2005), for example, successfully differentiates between less- and more-experienced general tourists in Australia, with the motivations of the former group focusing on stimulation, personal development, security, self-actualisation, nostalgia and romance, and those of the latter group focusing on host-site involvement (e.g. experiencing different cultures) and being close to nature. Travel motivations shared by both groups included the desire to escape, relationship enhancement and self development. While these findings are certainly not directly transferable to diving tourism, they do at least demonstrate the potential of the travel-career approach as a basis for market segmentation in this context.

Benefits Segmentation

Benefits segmentation is based on the fundamental premise that consumer decision-making is focused primarily on the benefits that a particular product has to offer. Different groups of consumers, with different backgrounds and preferences, will be motivated by different combinations of benefits. This pattern, if it can be isolated, enables the researcher to identify subgroups of consumers in a market who share these various combinations of benefit motivations. Murphy and Norris (2005) even go so far as to argue that the benefits people are seeking to consume by purchasing a product are the basic reason for the existence of distinct market segments. If this is so, then we might expect benefits segmentation to have an invaluable role to play in informing the effective planning, management and marketing of tourism; particularly so with forms such as diving tourism which take place in the natural environment and, very often, in protected areas of one kind or another. Indeed, as Palacio and McCool (1997, p. 235) note:

> The benefits that people expect to derive from recreational use of natural resources influence how those natural resources are protected, managed and exploited. Understanding these benefits is an important step in developing a sustainable tourism strategy because it involves identifying specific values that natural resources provide, and thereby indicates the larger-scale social benefits that need to be sustained. Effectively utilising the natural environment for tourism similarly requires that protected area managers, tourism providers, providers and local hosts understand their clients' expected benefits from participating in recreational engagements in natural settings.

Given the proposed advantages of benefits segmentation, it is surprising that there are so few published studies applying the approach to nature-based forms of tourism (Palacio & McCool, 1997) and none at all more specifically on diving tourism. Two studies focusing on subjects relevant to diving tourism do, however, suggest that the technique has a strong potential to be applied in that context. The first is a study by Palacio and McCool (1997), which presents the results of a benefits segmentation of the ecotourism market in Belize, ecotourism representing a broader grouping of tourism activities to which diving tourism is sometimes argued to belong (see for example Cater and Cater, 2001). The other study, by Murphy and Norris (2005), is of the market for 'activity tourism' on Australia's Great Barrier Reef (GBR). As such, the sample used in this study includes tourists using the setting for scuba-diving and snorkelling activities. While the findings are not specific to diving tourism they are nevertheless insightful given the multi-activity context in which diving tourism typically takes place.

In the study by Palacio and McCool (1997), a total of 206 tourists were interviewed in the departure lounge of the Belize International Airport over 35 randomly selected days. In order to segment the market, respondents were asked to indicate the importance of 18 specific benefits from their visit. Additional data were also collected on the respondents' socio-demographic trip characteristics. Principal components analysis was then used to identify four main benefit domains: the desire to escape the pressure of everyday life, the desire to learn about nature, the importance of keeping fit and doing healthy activities, and the importance of sharing experiences with friends and/or family. A non-hierarchical cluster analysis was then performed, with the following segments emerging:

- *Nature escapists (21.5%)*: this segment scored appreciably higher on the 'learning about nature' and 'escape' domains, and lower on the other two, suggesting a narrow set of expected benefits. They were most likely to be visiting Belize in a small group or alone.
- *Ecotourists (18%)*: this segment scored relatively highly across all four benefit domains, with the highest scores being for wanting to learn about nature and wanting to share the experience with others. Individuals in the group were relatively young and tended not to have visited Belize before.
- *Comfortable naturalists (33.3%)*: for this segment the scores for the 'learning about nature' and 'escape' domains were moderate: below those of both the nature escapists

and the ecotourists. Meanwhile, their scores for the other two domains were between those of the nature escapist and ecotourist segments. While this segment sought nature and escape, they wanted to do so in relative comfort. This group had the highest levels of previous experience of travel to Belize and the longest period of stay.

- *Passive players (26.9%)*: this segment had low scores in all four benefit domains. A simple index showed that individuals in the group were significantly less likely to participate in activities than those in the other groups.

Palacio and McCool go on to indicate the advantages of market segmentation on the basis of benefits. They argue that the segments identified in the study require different facilities, desire different rates of participation and seek involvement in a diverse range of activities. As such, promotional and product-management efforts would have to be different for each group. Market segmentation based simply on the activities undertaken by tourists would not have been as detailed and instructive. Indeed, the authors conclude by noting that the 'ecotourist' segment actually comprises only 18% of the market, even though they visited the same destinations and attractions as individuals in the other groups. This, they argue, emphasises the inherent dangers of basing tourism management and development decisions on 'the average visitor', who probably does not even exist. Segmentation is therefore vital if we are to understand the diversity of tourists' needs, and the attendant management and marketing implications, and benefits segmentation is argued to be an optimum way of achieving this.

Murphy and Norris (2005), meanwhile, conducted a benefits-based segmentation of tourists on the Australian GBR. A number of tourists undertaking diving and snorkelling activities on the reef were included in the sample but this study was not specifically of diving tourists. The authors note that a common pattern in previous studies of the GBR was that visitors tend to exhibit significantly different preferences and behaviours. This pattern appears to be a consistent: for some the purpose of a visit to the reef was to be active and/or to learn, while for others the visit merely represented a chance to relax and/or socialise in a pleasant natural setting. This, in turn, suggested that the application of benefits segmentation might be of value.

The study involved a written questionnaire administered among passengers on reef operations on the GBR. A total of 2215 passengers completed the survey with a response rate of 75%. Cluster analysis was then used to identify four market segments:

- *Dive learners (24%)*: this group was more likely to be female and younger than average, and their primary motivation for taking a trip onto the reef was to scuba dive. They were thus more likely to engage in 'wet' activities and hear the educational reef talk (hence the term 'dive learners' refers to their desire to dive and learn about the reef, rather than to learn how to dive). In choosing their reef tour operator, dive learners tended to emphasise the opportunity of seeing marine wildlife and to go snorkelling. They also placed more importance on the opportunity to dive, the tour price and the size of the tour boat. Meanwhile, dive learners were more likely to indicate that the diving and underwater scenery were their best experiences of the trip, and less likely to indicate going on the semi-submersible or relaxing.
- *Nature relaxers (19%)*: this group were also more likely to be interested in scuba diving; however, they were also motivated by the opportunity to relax. They tended to be international visitors and were often repeat visitors to the GBR.

- *Nature family visitors (23%)*: this group were more likely to be accompanied by children and tended to have a higher daily expenditure than those in the other groups. They tended to emphasise the tour schedule and price when choosing a reef tour operator. As with the nature relaxers group, those in the nature family visitors group emphasised relaxation above involvement in physical activities such as swimming or diving.
- *Nature learners (34%)*: like the dive learners group, this group comprised more females than average. Nature learners were more likely to visit the underwater observatory and to indicate that the semi-submersible was their best experience of being on the reef.

The authors go on to argue that the most important findings from a management point of view relate to the differences between segments with respect to desired level of involvement with the reef and desire for information and/or learning. Indeed they conclude that:

> The recognition that not every visitor on the reef is seeking the same experience has important implications for visitor management on reef tours and trips. The differences have direct implications for tour operators with respect to infrastructure provision, trip activity planning and the provision of interpretive materials and programs to visitors. (Murphy & Norris, 2005, p. 84)

As such it is clear that there may be distinct advantages in developing different itineraries, at different prices, for each of the four segments. A tailored marketing approach would also be expected to have benefits for the management of the GBR insofar as specific visitor facilities, management systems and educational provision can be targeted at the individual market segments, thereby increasing its ultimate effectiveness and achieving maximum protection of the GBR.

Concluding Remarks and Recommendations

Given the potential for market segmentation to assist in the effective planning, management and marketing of diving tourism, it seems surprising that no market segmentation of the diving tourism market has been published to date. This chapter has set out to investigate the potential for segmenting the diving tourism market and concludes that the diving market is in many ways highly suitable for segmentation. Indeed, there are a number of ways in which the motivations and behaviour of different groups of scuba divers differ, and the existence of these differences suggests that a segmentation study could be both robust and insightful. The principal recommendation of this chapter is therefore that a market segmentation study of a specific diving tourism market should be undertaken in order to confirm the practicality of the approach and to illustrate its potential value in formulating and implementing effective planning, management and marketing strategies for diving tourism.

Three approaches that might be considered in implementing a market segmentation study in this area have been identified as particular useful in the course of this chapter: segmentation on the basis of involvement/specialisation, the travel career approach and benefits segmentation. This is not to suggest that these approaches are mutually exclusive.

Indeed, most market segmentation studies use a variety of tourist characteristics — including geographical, demographic, socio-economic and behavioural variables — in order to achieve a robust segmentation of the market. A corollary of the first recommendation is therefore that while the three approaches detailed in this chapter might hold considerable promise for the segmentation of diving tourism markets, the approach that is actually adopted may need to be a composite one, taking elements of two or more of the approaches suggested in this chapter.

The involvement or specialisation approach to segmentation certainly seems to hold considerable promise for application to diving tourism markets. Indeed, the studies by Kim et al. (forthcoming), in the case of golf tourism, and Sung (2004), in the case of adventure tourism, illustrate how such studies might successfully be designed and carried out. While these studies do not relate specifically to diving tourism, there are arguably strong parallels between golf tourism and diving tourism, particular in terms of the concept of involvement or specialisation. This approach assumes that there is a scale of involvement or specialisation along which tourists can be placed — depending on their levels of knowledge, skills, investment in equipment, activity-setting preferences, and so on — and this is strongly resonant of what is known about diving tourists. There are also strong parallels between adventure tourism and diving tourism, the latter usually being considered to be a subset of the former.

The travel-career approach, meanwhile, has not widely been applied to the specific case of diving tourism. However, the study conducted by Pearce and Lee (2005) of general tourists does show how the approach might be applied to diving tourism markets and how instructive such an approach might prove to be. This is perhaps not surprising given the strong affinity between the activity of scuba diving and the concept of the travel career. Indeed, the available evidence would seem to suggest that more-experienced scuba divers do indeed hold significantly different motivations for taking a diving holiday than less-experienced divers. Market segmentation on the basis of travel-career experience may therefore be a useful means of distinguishing between different groups of diving tourists, who are at different stages in their travel career and thus have different motivations, expectations and exhibit different behaviour as a result.

The third approach reviewed in this chapter, benefits segmentation, also seems to be well suited to the diving tourism context. Indeed, studies by Palacio and McCool (1997), of ecotourists in Belize, and Murphy and Norris (2005), of visitors to the Australian GBR, suggest that segmentation based on tourists' expected benefits can be not only robust but also highly insightful. Again, while these studies are not directly transferable to diving tourism, they do suggest that the approach is a promising one. The latter study, in particular, demonstrates the value in market segmentation on the basis of benefits, rather than activities, with a much more detailed and insightful segmentation emerging as a result.

Finally, the practical value of conducting market segmentation studies cannot be overemphasised. Indeed, most of the studies examined in this chapter suggest one or more of the following benefits:

- Market segmentation enables tourism marketers to target their marketing strategies more effectively by dividing the market into specific sub-markets, each with a different set of basic needs and purchase motivations.

- A market segmentation also enables marketers to develop products that will more effectively meet the requirements of different groups of consumers within the market as a whole. For example, different tour itineraries can be developed for different market segments on the basis of the facilities and activities demanded by these different types of tourists.
- Knowledge of the needs and requirement of different market segments may also help destination managers to provide tourism facilities that are appropriate both to the specific context of the destination and to the particular market segments that visit it.
- Market segmentation may assist protected-area managers in the efficient zoning of natural areas by allocating different market segments to different zones on the basis of geographical features, available facilities and the kinds of tourism activities suitable to that area.
- Understanding the diverse motivations of different markets may assist in the provision of educational and/or interpretive materials by enabling such efforts to be targeted to the specific types of tourist visiting a particular destination or attraction.
- Having a detailed understanding of the benefits sought by tourists from different kinds of environmental settings and natural resources can be a vital step in understanding how to manage the relationship more effectively, thereby potentially opening the door to more cogent and effective sustainable tourism strategies.

However, while the need for tourist typologies based on robust empirical market segmentation studies is recognised in the literature on diving tourism, the potential for such studies to revolutionise the way in which such activities are planned, managed and marketed still remains to be tapped.

References

Beard, J., & Ragheb, M. (1983). Measuring leisure motivation. *Journal of Leisure Research, 15*, 219–228.

Bieger, T., & Laesser, C. (2002). Market segmentation by motivation: The case of Switzerland. *Journal of Travel Research, 41*, 68–76.

Bryan, H. (1977). Leisure value systems and recreational specialization: The case of trout fishermen. *Journal of Leisure Research, 9*, 174–187.

Bryan, H. (1979). *Conflict in the great outdoors: Toward understanding and management for diverse sportsmen's preferences*. Tuscaloosa: University of Alabama.

Cater, C., & Cater, E. (2001). Marine environments. In: D. B. Weaver, (Ed.), *The encyclopedia of ecotourism* (pp. 265–282). Wallingford: CABI.

Davis, D., & Tisdell, C. (1995). Recreational scuba-diving and carrying capacity in MPAs. *Ocean and Coastal Management, 26*, 19–40.

Ellegard, P. (2005). How to dive them wild. *Travel Trade Gazette, 6 May*, 65–66.

Frochot, I. (2005). A benefit segmentation of tourists in rural areas: A Scottish perspective. *Tourism Management, 26*, 335–346.

Fyall, A., & Garrod, B. (2005). *Tourism marketing: A collaborative approach*. Clevedon: Channel View.

Hinch, T. D., & Higham, J. (2004). *Sport tourism development*. Clevedon: Channel View.

Hvenegaard, G. T. (2002). Using tourist typologies for ecotourism research. *Journal of Ecotourism, 1*, 7–18.

Keeling, A. (2006). Understanding the outdoor activity tourism market. *Countryside Recreation, 14*, 3–9.

Kerstetter, D. L., Confer, J. J., & Graefe, A. R. (2001). An exploration of the specialization concept with the context of heritage tourism. *Journal of Travel Research, 39*, 267–274.

Kim, S. S., Kim, J., & Ritchie, B. W. (2006). Segmenting overseas golf tourists by the concept of specialization, Unpublished working paper, University of Canberra.

Kotler, P. (2001). *A framework for marketing management.* Englewood Cliffs: Prentice Hall.

Maslow, A. H. (1970). *Motivation and personality.* New York: Harper & Row.

Meisel, C., & Cottrell, S. (2004). Differences in motivations and expectations of divers in the Florida Keys. In: J. Murdy (Ed.), *Proceedings of the 2003 Northeastern Recreation Research Symposium* (pp. 393–401). Newtown Square: USDA Forest Service.

Murphy, L., & Norris, A. (2005). Understanding Great Barrier Reef visitors: Segmentation according to reef trip benefits. *Tourism in Marine Environments, 1*, 71–87.

Musa, G., Kadir, S. L. S. A., & Lee, L. (2006). Layang Layang: An empirical study on scuba divers' satisfaction. *Tourism in Marine Environments, 2*, 89–102.

Orams, M. (1999). *Marine tourism: Development, impacts and management.* London: Routledge.

Palacio, V., & McCool, S. F. (1997). Identifying ecotourists in Belize through benefit segmentation: A preliminary study. *Journal of Sustainable Tourism, 5*, 234–243.

Pearce, P. L. (1988). *The Ulysses factor: Evaluating visitors in tourist settings.* New York: Springer-Verlag.

Pearce, P. L., & Lee, U.-I. (2005). Developing the travel career approach to tourist motivation. *Journal of Travel Research, 43*, 226–237.

Plog, S. C. (1977). Why destinations rise and fall in popularity. In: E. M. Kelly (Ed.), *Domestic and international tourism* (pp. 26–29). Wellesly: Institute of Certified Travel Agents.

Rice, K. (1987). Special report: Scuba diving — dive market requires specialized skill and information. *Tour & Travel News, Feb 9*, 24–27.

Sarigöllü, E., & Huang, R. (2005). Benefits segmentation of visitors to Latin America. *Journal of Travel Research, 43*, 277–293.

Sung, H. H. (2004). Classification of adventure travellers: Behaviour, decision making and target markets. *Journal of Travel Research, 42*, 343–356.

Swarbrooke, J., & Horner, S. (1999). *Consumer behaviour in tourism.* Oxford: Butterworth-Heinemann.

Tabata, R. S. (1992). Scuba diving holidays. In: B. Weiler & C. M. Hall (Eds), *Special interest tourism* (pp. 171–184). London: Belhaven.

Tourism Queensland. (2006). Dive tourism. http://www.tq.com.au/tq_com/dms/2F0335B4B50A7 B818A527A1CE5C4E434.pdf. (Accessed 19 June 2006).

Trauer, B. (2006). Conceptualizing special interest tourism: Frameworks of analysis. *Tourism Management, 27*, 183–200.

World Tourism Organization. (2001). *Tourism 2020 vision. Vol. 7. Global forecasts and profiles of market segments.* Madrid: WTO.

Chapter 3

Perceptions of and Interactions with Marine Environments: Diving Attractions from Great Whites to Pygmy Seahorses

Carl Cater

Introduction

> To swim fishlike, horizontally, was the logical method in a medium eight
> hundred times denser than air. To halt and hang attached to nothing, no
> lines or air pipe to the surface was a dream. At night I had often had
> visions of flying by extending my arms as wings. Now I flew without
> wings (Cousteau, 1953, p. 16).

The primary attraction of the scuba-diving experience is immersion in a strange and alien environment. Perceptions and interactions with the marine environment are heightened by the minimal communication that can take place underwater, and the highly physical and sensory nature of that engagement. This chapter will discuss this engagement and this discussion relates strongly to some of the diver typologies introduced in the previous chapter. Indeed, one useful division of motivations for leisure pursuits is that suggested by Beard and Ragheb (1983), which can be easily applied to scuba diving activity. These authors identified four possible areas for leisure motivation: stimulus-avoidance, social, competence-mastery and intellectual. These broadly correspond to a requirement for escape, esteem, expertise and education in scuba diving. In addition, the experience is one that is profoundly embodied, often requiring a significant amount of discomfort to achieve the sensations and feelings that are sought by participants. Ryan's (1997, p. 25) tourism mantra of "similar motivations, diverse behaviours" is important in understanding both the typologies described in the previous chapter and the range of experiences and attractions favoured by dive tourists tackled in this chapter.

Partly as a result of physical and monetary expense, divers seek out experiences that are 'world class', creating a portfolio of dive 'must dos' around the globe. Indeed, it is clear, as Orams (1999, p. 35) suggests, that divers are after "more than just a good time". Undoubtedly significant status is attached to seeing rare or distinctive species, and this is no less prevalent in the marine environment than it is in the terrestrial environment. Ironically, this motivation is probably stronger in the basic-to-intermediate dive tourist than in the career diver. It is suggested that this has some similarity to Pearce's (1982) travel career ladder model, wherein an initial desire to see the 'big stuff' is gradually supplanted by a fascination with smaller, and arguably more unusual, underwater inhabitants. Of course this recognition must be tempered by the fact that a number of extra skills are required to achieve successful underwater experiences, particularly in overhead (wreck and cave) environments. This chapter will illustrate these behaviours by examining a number of world-class diving locations and experiences. Understanding these interactions is vital if we are to manage their impacts effectively. Many might argue that the size of the scuba-diving industry, discussed in Chapter 1, means that it cannot be considered as a true form of ecotourism. Indeed, diving is often an example of what might be considered 'mass ecotourism', since many of the participants are actually on a 3S-format (sea, sand and sun) holiday. However, if we are to treat ecotourism as a method of tourism practice rather than a product of scale, as Weaver (2001) suggests, scuba diving may be considered one of the original ecotourism practices. Schuster (1992, p. 45) contends that ecotourism is neither a new word nor a new concept in diving, since "from the beginning dive travel has been a form of ecotourism since diving involves observing nature". This contention, however, assumes responsible behaviour, which is by no means automatic in the scuba diving context.

Underwater Perceptions

Probably, the first thing that divers perceive about the underwater environment is that it is unfamiliar compared with the terrestrial environment we are used to (Cousteau, 1953; Rebikoff, 1955). It is not one we are designed to inhabit, although we do have some biological inheritances that enable us to function more effectively, for example the diving reflex (a lowering of heart rate and increased blood flow to vital organs when entering the water). Perceptions of this alien space, therefore, are based on both the internal and external environment. The internal environment, or that of the body, has been overlooked in tourism studies until relatively recently (Tribe, 2006), despite the calls of such authors as Swain (2004) and Veijola and Jokinen (1994). The reduced role for the active body in many workplace settings means that we frequently seek physical activity during leisure and tourism experiences. While in early capitalism there was a close connection between the body and work, this has been eroded in the contemporary era, with the reduction of bodily work leading to "an entirely different and corrosive emphasis on hedonism, desire and enjoyment" (Turner, 1996, p. 4) as the focus for bodily concerns. Dive tourism is a prime expression of this.

Photo 3.1: Diving can involve considerable discomfort (Photograph: Carl Cater).

The fact that communication is limited underwater means that, to some degree, our senses are heightened. Part of the attraction of getting to know our bodies lies in the fact that they have the ability to surprise us. We can never really know how our bodies will respond to the hostile environment in which they have been placed, although some knowledge comes with repeated participation. However, as Radley (1995, p. 5) contends, "by virtue of being elusory, the body is empowered to configure the realms of experience". The fact that we cannot 'know' our bodies in their entirety, despite obvious intimacy, means that they have the upper hand in the negotiation of experience. Indeed, quite often the experiences of diving are not actually pleasant ones. Anyone who has been on or in the ocean can vouch for the pain and discomfort that can come with the territory: we may get seasick, we may be cold, biting sea lice may irritate us, we may have pain in our sinuses as we descend beneath the surface, the salt gets in our eyes and barnacles may cut us (Photo 3.1). Even things that we would expect have control over on firm ground may elude us in the water. Scuba divers constantly have to adjust their buoyancy and it is deeply frustrating for novice individuals to find they have difficulty staying in one place. Interviews conducted by the author with divers point to the strange experience of being able to breathe underwater, especially at the start of their diving careers. The feeling of being weightless is also often felt to be important when explaining the experience to non-divers. In addition, most divers identify that they feel relaxed when they are underwater. There seems to be a paradox here in that the scuba experience is simultaneously relaxing and physically demanding. This may seem strange given the focus of tourism on relaxation. However, this emphasises the point made by Ryan (1997, p. 32) that "to rest and unwind" does not necessarily mean "to relax physically". This corresponds to Csikszentmihalyi's (1975) concept of *flow*, which he uses to explain the popularity of activities that are intellectually or physically demanding. He endeavours to show that when there is a balance between the skills required and the challenges inherent in an activity such as scuba diving, positive feedback occurs in terms of satisfaction.

Perceptions of the external environment hinge on a similar assessment of the unusual. One of the motivators identified by Beard and Ragheb (1983) is that of *stimulus avoidance*, but somewhat paradoxically this can be interpreted as escaping to an environment that is different to that normally experienced. The very fact that the sea is an environment in which we are not designed to live serves to stimulate curiosity. The function of the foreshore as the last frontier emphasises the liminality of this space, as Urry (1990, p. 38) notes, "beaches are complex spaces, anomalously located between land and sea, nature and culture". When we disappear beneath the waves we have crossed this boundary and entered a world that is largely foreign to us. We make sense of this liminal space through narratives that make sense to us and almost all divers who have been interviewed by the author emphasise the alien nature of this world. This is perhaps compounded by the high species diversity at popular dive sites. For example conservative estimates put the number of coral reef species at 100,000 but, as Spalding, Ravilious, and Green (2001) suggest, the actual number of coral-reef species may be between 0.5 million and 2 million. The desire to experience the weird and wonderful is clearly central to dive tourism.

Underwater Interactions

Exploring the underwater environment therefore becomes the principal mode through which divers can come to understand it. Interactions with marine life, other divers, dive operators and certifying agencies become an important part of the production of knowledge (see Townsend, Chapter 10, this volume). However, these interactions are part of the attraction of dive tourism in and of itself, especially the buddy system used by most divers and dive operators. Indeed, the *social* component identified by Beard and Ragheb (1983) highlights the extent to which individuals engage in activities for social reasons, and includes two basic needs. The first is the need for friendship and interpersonal relationships, while the second is the need for the esteem of others. The dual components of the social motivation are interesting to examine, as they are defined not only in terms of the importance of a period of bonding with old friends and making new ones but also in respect of gaining esteem in the eyes of others. The opportunity for social interactions is clearly an important part of ecotourism experiences more generally, especially the ability to bond with like-minded individuals during an activity. As Miller (1993, p. 181) suggests, marine ecotourism may be studied as "symbolic interaction fostering social solidarity".

Indeed, the social interaction of diving is a fundamental part of the attraction. At a fundamental logistical level, the 'buddy' format of scuba diving, where divers should always dive in pairs, is an integral part of the activity. The system is primarily intended to promote safety but it also influences diver behaviour in other ways. The advantages when observing a marine environment are clear, as two pairs of eyes working together will find a greater number of interesting things than one pair. In addition, the continual monitoring of another person does reduce the opportunity of damage to marine environments, as buddies may be able to warn each other of unintentional harm that an action might cause to that environment (see Lindgren et al., Chapter 6, this volume). Examples might include hitting the reef with a fin or oxygen tank, as it is often difficult to know how much further these extend outside the body space. Author observation also highlights both the buddy-to-buddy disapproval and the personal feeling of guilt that such incidents provoke within the diving fraternity, especially if this involves breaking a piece of coral that may have taken tens or even hundreds of years to grow. Thus, in order for a dive to be successful, high levels of trust between individuals need to be built up. In many tourist dive situations this may be strained, as partners may not have dived with their buddy before. Satisfaction with the dive tourism experience can thus depend on the success of this relationship. Diver education and regulation is also an important part of minimising impacts on a reef, as discussed in Lindgren et al, Chapter 6, and Townsend, Chapter 10, both this volume.

In common with many other sport and leisure pursuits, scuba-diving participation is also closely linked to social ties. A survey of artificial-reef scuba divers in Texas (Ditton, Osburn, Baker, & Thailing, 2002) indicated that 56% of participants pursued this activity with friends, and 21% with a combination of family and friends. Over 60% listed 'being with friends' as either a very important or extremely important reason behind their dive trip. Of interest is the manner in which some marine ecotourism activities may be family based, especially those taken on vacation. Scuba diving is probably less so due to the need for qualifications, which may be held by only one family member. On disaggregating the results, the Ditton et al. (2002) study indicated that only 13% of divers were diving with family members and nearly 30% felt that 'family recreation' was not at all important on their trip. However, respondents indicated that it was not just the underwater experience that was important, as the opportunity for bonding as a group through the activity, particularly through discussing the adventure afterwards, was also a source of satisfaction. This is probably heightened in the dive experience because, as previously noted in this chapter, there is little opportunity for direct communication while underwater.

Esteem also comes through the stories that divers are able to tell others and, more importantly, tell to themselves, thereby revealing who they really are. Narrative psychology recognises the important social capital that is garnered through such processes. This narrative capital is discussed by Schiebe (1986), who suggests that adventurous tales form the basis of life stories that in turn are foundations of individual identity. In the same way that Pearce (1982) suggested that there is a travel career, there is clear evidence of a dive career observed by the author in the dive fraternity (see also Cater & Cater, 2007). As well as the status that can be gained through moving up the hierarchy of certification (PADI has no fewer than 14 qualification levels and 25 specialities), there is clearly status to be gained through having 'ultimate' diving experiences. Research by Norton (1996) on visitors to the African Savannah identified dissatisfaction when they were unable to see the 'big five'. Undoubtedly, significant status is attached to seeing rare or distinctive species and this is no less prevalent in the marine environment than it is in the terrestrial environment. The desire to see big fish, especially sharks, is a significant motivator for marine tourists wishing to acquire travellers' tales.

Some writers have taken a rather cynical approach to this factor in ecotourism, with the label 'egotourist' being applied to those who seek such experiences merely for the status that comes with them (Wheeler, 1994). Indeed, scuba diving is an activity patronised by those who can afford it and most studies of participants are skewed towards higher income brackets. Statistics from Professional Association of Diving Instructors (PADI) show that 80% of newly qualified Open Water divers have a college education, supporting Orams' (1999) suggestion that diving is an expensive hobby. Orams contends that relative to land-based activities, marine activities are patronised by upper socio-economic groups because of the significant costs involved in such pursuits. As mentioned in the previous chapter, the purchase of specialised equipment involves a considerable outlay. Basic training costs approximately US$200 (€160) and individual dives in a tourism destination are likely to be around US$50 (€40). A study of scuba divers in the western Mediterranean found that over half were in the 31–45 age group because the activity "requires a certain level of purchasing power not always within reach of younger people and a physical fitness that is not always found among older persons" (Mundet & Ribera, 2001, p. 505). Those experiences that have more status are by default more expensive, for example diving with whale sharks in Australia costs around US$200 (€160) for one trip.

Nevertheless, increases in disposable incomes and the growth of a global community of divers has created a range of signature dive tourism experiences that form a 'must-do' list of attractions, reinforced by dive schools, magazines and tourism organisations. Table 3.1 lists the top 10 dive sites worldwide, as voted by users of the UK-based website Scuba Travel (2006). Clearly such a list is subjective. However it is influenced by external organisations, with many of the listed dives centred on particular species, famous wrecks and legendary tales of clear visibility. As highlighted above, sharks have a particular fascination and this is related to their traditional image as a threat to humans when we are in the water. Such a perception is visually represented in Copley's famous eighteenth century illustration *Watson and the Shark*, based on a real shark attack in Havana Harbour at that time (Photo 3.2).

Table 3.1: Top ten dive sites around the world (Scuba Travel 2006).

Dive site	Type of dive/attractions
1. Yongala, Australia	Wreck, sharks, large fish
2. Thistlegorm, Egyptian Red Sea	Wreck
3. Blue Corner Wall, Palau, Micronesia	Wall
4. Barracuda Point, Sipadan Island	Drop off, barracuda
5. Shark and Yolanda Reef, Egyptian Red Sea	Drift dive, high diversity
6. Navy Pier, Australia	Artificial reef, sharks
7. Manta Ray Night Dive, Kailua Kona, Hawaii	Night dive, manta rays
8. Big Brother, Egyptian Red Sea	Drift dives, wall, sharks
9. Liberty, Bali, Indonesia	Wreck, high species diversity
10. Elphinstone Reef, Egyptian Red Sea	Pinnacles, sharks

Photo 3.2: John Singleton Copley, 'Watson and the Shark', 1778 (National Gallery of Art).

Underwater Attractions

Shark Diving

The desire to see sharks on dives and the added cachet of having 'survived' has led to the growth in a sub-industry of the dive world that involves encouraging sharks with bait. The feeding of sharks to encourage sightings has generated a great deal of debate in recent years. Experiences are available with either significant protection (for example cages, see Photo 3.3, or chain mail suits) or no protection, where only guides wear protective equipment and safety is based on behavioural understanding. George Burgess, the curator of the International Shark Attack File, which catalogues worldwide shark attacks, is deeply sceptical of shark-feeding operations. "My reservations about feeding-type dives are based on four interrelated factors: the safety of the divers; the likelihood for negative publicity directed at sharks if a shark bites a diver during one of these dives; the possibility for ecological disruption; and potential negative impact on multi-user recreational use of the feeding area" (Burgess, 1998, p. 1).

   Growing evidence that the fears outlined by Burgess were being realised, including over a dozen injuries in the Bahamas, prompted Florida, Hawaii and the Cayman Islands to outlaw shark feeding in 2001–2002 (Carwardine & Watterson, 2002). Despite this, a self-styled shark 'expert', Erich Ritter, suffered a serious leg injury in the Bahamas in April 2002 (Cyber Diver News Network, 2002), where the activity is still available, as it is in western

Photo 3.3: Shark cage diving in Kaikoura, New Zealand (Photograph: Carl Cater).

Fiji at the infamous 'shark supermarket'. Although the latter makes much of its community involvement, with a $10FJ (about €5) levy paid to the local village by each diver and many tours led by a local chief who claims to understand the sharks, behavioural and safety concerns are still present. Not least are reports that this individual is in the habit of hugging the sharks as a display of his mastery over the animal. Divers not on the feeding tour report unusual shark behaviour whilst on normal dives, with the shy animals coming closer than usual (Blue Oceans, 2005).

Great white sharks, also known as white pointers, have captured public interest through their size and reputation, and a number of operations provide viewing of this species in the wild. Internationally, white sharks are listed as 'vulnerable' on the The World Conservation Union (IUCN) Red List of threatened species (World Conservation Union, 2003), as well as being protected in South Africa, Namibia, the Maldives, Florida and California (US) and Malta. Despite an awareness of population decline, accurate figures on the actual status of this particular species are very hard to come by. This is related to very poor knowledge about the shark's stock structure and migration patterns, as well as piecemeal records of fishing by-catch and beach-net trappings (Topelko & Dearden, 2005). There are some concerns that the practice of 'burleying' or 'chumming', where bait is thrown into the water by tourism operators in order to attract the sharks, may alter shark behaviour and also have impacts on their prey relationships.

The opportunity to view the notorious but elusive great white has spawned a significant industry in South Africa. This was initially started at Gansbaii on the Western Cape in 1990, spreading to Mossel Bay in 1993 and most recently to False Bay in 1996. There are an estimated 10 operators serving some 4000 divers annually, and estimates indicate that activities related to cage diving contribute about 5 million Rand (€700,000) to the local economy (Kroese, 1998). Concerns with the 'cowboy' nature of the industry, which were confirmed by the author's visit in 1999, led to the establishment of a permit system and a code of conduct. The code of conduct makes recommendations on the level of technical training operators need, equipment standards in terms of cages and safety gear. The specific chum types, quantities allowable per day (no more than 25 kg), bait presentation and shark handling are also outlined (South African Collaborative White Shark Research Programme, 2005). However, there is growing evidence that the practice is significantly altering the behaviour of the sharks. In late 2004, one of the operators was bitten on his foot and in March 2005 a British tourist narrowly escaped an aggressive shark that caused serious damage to the cage which was supposed to be protecting him. The welfare of the sharks, which are a protected species in South Africa, is clearly of limited concern as "the captain had a big metal pole and was hitting it on the head and trying to push it off, but it was just making it worse" (BBC News, 2005, p. 1). It is likely that following a fatal attack on a skin diver in June 2005 (Cyber Diver News Network, 2005) there will be renewed calls for the industry to be discontinued. Similar tours continue in Australia and New Zealand (Topelko & Dearden, 2005).

Topelko and Dearden (2005) question whether the increase in shark-based tourism across the globe is a sufficient economic incentive to encourage a reduction in fishing pressure on sharks. They conclude that while the shark-watching industry may generate sufficient income to act as an incentive to conserve some species in some locations, given that an estimated 100 million sharks are caught each year worldwide it will provide limited impetus to providing adequate protection. In the face of such a large resource use, shark tourism can only work alongside government regulation and consumer education to "arrest the dramatic decline of shark populations worldwide" (Topelko & Dearden, 2005, p. 123). However, tourism may offer some potential for finding out more about these animals, as "regular viewing trips when properly managed offer good opportunities for data collection" (Commonwealth of Australia, 2002, p. 41). Indeed, in South Australia the permitting authority, the Department of Environment and Heritage (DEHSA), has made it a permit condition that licensed shark-cage dive operators fill out a logbook that records sightings of sharks and that that is passed on to government marine resource research organisations. Data collection of this manner, leading to a greater awareness of the status of marine resources, has been very successfully used in whale shark population monitoring in north Western Australia. A controlled interaction procedure and cooperation between operators and conservation authorities has created a good example of sustainable marine ecotourism (Cater & Cater, 2007).

The elusive whale shark is the largest fish in the ocean, yet very little is known about these animals, which can grow up to 12 m in length (Colman, 1997). However, reasonable numbers of juvenile males regularly visit the reefs of north Western Australia between April and June each year, coinciding with the coral spawning that occurs at the same time, which provides a significant food source for these animals (Davis, Banks, Birtles, Valentine, & Cuthill, 1997). They come to the surface periodically, for up to 20 min, before diving to feed. Predictably, in recent years the opportunity to dive with these behemoths has been a significant factor in a booming tourist industry in the North West Cape, centred on the town of Exmouth and Ningaloo Reef. Dive charters have been offering the chance to encounter whale sharks in their natural environment since the early 1990s, although the first dedicated operator did not commence until 1993. During that season, 14 boats handled approximately 1000 visitors, increasing to over 2000 by 1995 (Davis et al., 1997). It is estimated that some 500 interactions with sharks take place each year (B. Fitzpatrick,

Exmouth, 2004, personal communication), although it is likely that many of these are with the same individuals. Activities surrounding these highly specialised dive tourism experiences are estimated to contribute AU$12 million (about €7.2 million) to the local economy (Conservation and Land Management, 2004).

Despite their large size, their remarkable camouflaging, combined with the fact that they do not need to broach the surface to breathe like whales, means that sighting the whale shark is far from easy. Consequently, spotter planes are used to assist with the location procedure. On sighting an animal, tourist boats are directed to intercept it. Typically these boats will hold up to 20 tourists with snorkel gear, who will be split into waves and enter the water with a guide from the company in the path of the shark. These groups then split to allow the shark to travel, whilst the snorkellers swim alongside for up to 5 min (actual diving with the sharks is prohibited as it was found to stress the animals and could cut off their escape route). In some cases, another wave of tourists will be dispatched from the boat to replace that already in place. Alternatively, another operator will arrive to deposit their charges. On individual trips to visit the whale sharks there is likely to be a large number of repeat visitors, as frequently the whale sharks are not sighted at all, particularly in the shoulder periods of the year. Most operators offer a free second trip in this case, meaning that on any one outing approximately half of all individuals were repeating.

It is important to set the whale shark operations within a booming tourism industry context in the North West Cape. The pristine nature of Ningaloo Reef itself, the only extensive system anywhere to fringe the west coast of a continent (Collinsa, Zhua, Wyrwollb, & Eisenhauerc, 2003), brings increasing numbers of tourists, not all of whom are ecologically minded. Controversy raged in the late 1990s under a proposed marina resort to be built at Mauds Landing at the southern end of the reef (Morton, 2003). Public resistance and astute political–capital garnering by the incumbent government eventually stopped the construction of the resort, which would have had disastrous consequences for the health of the reef. Nevertheless, the threat of such developments remains. Re-zoning of the marine park in 2004 (Conservation and Land Management, 2004) sought to tighten up the management of the Cape's recreational opportunities. A large number of diving and snorkelling opportunities exist in the marine park, including diving at Navy Pier, part of the support structure for a US military listening post. The fringing nature of the reef itself allows drift-snorkelling opportunities directly off the beach, unavailable in sites such as the Great Barrier Reef. While clearly being very popular, as they do not require the hiring of boats, management of increasing numbers of visitors becomes a problem. To date, marine tourism activities seem to have been managed sustainably at Ningaloo. However, the growing reputation of the region for world-class experiences, coupled with increased access opportunities to what is a very remote location, will surely put stresses on this fragile environment (Fountain, Clark, Pforr, & Macbeth, 2005).

Wreck Diving

Although interactions with 'charismatic megafauna' such as sharks are significant dive tourism attractions, certainly forming an important part of dive tales, it is suggested that their relevance to repeat dive tourism experiences is limited. They are an important motivator for travel to specific destinations. However, once they have been 'ticked off' the list they have less pertinence. A parallel track to dive motivations is that of becoming a better diver, so skills-based experiences tend to take over as dive tourism attractions as individuals move up the diving career ladder. The extent to which individuals engage in leisure activities in order to achieve, master, challenge and compete is assessed by the *Competence-Mastery* component in Beard and Ragheb's (1983) scale.

One example of a dive attraction that requires improved skills is that of wreck diving. Indeed, it is important to remember that dive tourism attractions are not solely natural and there are a variety of anthropological resources both above and below the waterline that may form significant attractions. The density of shipwreck remains in English waters may be the highest in the world, with over 40,000 recorded sites, while Northern Ireland has 3,000, South Africa 2,500, Australia 6,000 and Canada 9,000 (Department for Environment, Food and Rural Affairs, 2002). In 2002, the National Heritage Act in the UK extended English Heritage's remit to include archaeological sites of all types in or under the seabed to the 12-mile limit around England in recognition of the nation's rich maritime history (Roberts & Trow, 2002). Similarly, the Caribbean island of St Kitts is host to hundreds of historic shipwrecks as a result of its trade importance, battles between the English and French, and hurricanes (Spooner, 2003). Since 2001, the Anglo-Danish Maritime Archaeology Team (ADMAT) has been working to preserve these wrecks. There are a number of threats to these resources, particularly from cruise-ship propeller wash and treasure hunters. However, the ADMAT programme proposes to catalogue, excavate and preserve these wrecks for heritage purposes. These wrecks can then form tourist attractions both above the waves, with salvaged material placed in museums, and below the surface, with protected wrecks becoming important dive sites. Malaysia is also waking up to the potential of its underwater heritage, promoting the maritime importance of destinations such as Malacca (Mustapa, 2005).

An alternative resource that is seeing increasing intervention and development in order to reduce pressure on natural reefs is that of artificial reefs. The term 'artificial reef' is deliberately vague and takes into account a broad variety of man-made structures that have been purposefully placed in the aquatic realm. Wrecks, jetties, beach-erosion barriers, walls, groynes and a variety of other structures are testament to human endeavour in the marine environment. They soon become colonised by marine creatures, however, and form attractions in their own right. Artificial reefs begin to aggregate fish and other mobile marine organisms very quickly after deployment and, given time, also host fixed life forms like algae, barnacles, soft and hard corals, mussels and sponges. In fact, 'established' artificial reefs have the potential to sustain a greater density and/or variety of biota (particularly fish species) than nearby natural reefs (Stolk, Markwell, & Jenkins, 2005). In the last decade, four ex-navy destroyers have been deliberately sunk around the coastline in Australia to form scuba-diving attractions for tourists (Club Marine, 2005). An abandoned 1.8 km jetty in Busselton, Western Australia was restored in 2001 specifically for its recreational potential (Stolk et al., 2005), both for diving and other marine pursuits.

The economic 'value' of these artificial marine resources can be significant. Research undertaken in south-east Florida estimated that spending associated with artificial reefs as a recreational resource was approximately one third of all expenditure related to reefs in the region (Johns, Leeworthy, Bell, & Bonn, 2001). In a state so reliant on marine tourism resources, this slice of the pie is considerable. This same report estimated that southeast Floridian reefs were the reason behind $873 million (€692 million) of residents' annual expenditure. Fishing was a $499 million (€396 million) industry, snorkelling $167 million (€132 million) and scuba diving was worth $207 million (€164 million) annually. Furthermore, users would be willing to pay some $26.7 million (€21.2 million) annually to invest in and maintain new artificial reefs.

In 2005, the Her Majesty's Australian Ship (HMAS) Brisbane, a destroyer decommissioned from the Australian navy was deliberately sunk as a dive tourism site off the Sunshine Coast in Queensland (Photo 3.4). This followed an extensive period of preparation, wherein a site was carefully selected and the vessel converted for deliberate sinking. In particular, significant marine pollutants had to be removed, such as any heavy metals, batteries, fuels, oils grease and any loose items. A 35 ha conservation park was set up around the wreck, with strict controls on diving activity in the area. Three local dive operators were issued with licenses to run trips to the ship and guide dive tourists around the vessel. By 2006, significant numbers of aquatic species had already colonised the vessel. A code of conduct is in place to ensure that new divers to the wreck are properly guided and that a minimum number of dives must be logged before penetration of the vessel is allowed (Environmental Protection Agency, 2006).

However, the project very nearly failed to 'sink', as there was a long period of negotiation between various authorities following decommissioning of the vessel in 2001. In particular, there was the issue of the public-liability insurance for 'creating' such a dive tourism attraction. Eventually, the federal government paid the estimated US$1.7 million (€1.35 million) cost of sinking the ship and the Queensland state government agreed to cover the annual insurance costs of the dive attraction. However, by most accounts the project has been relatively successful. An estimated 10,000 divers (Environmental Protection Agency, 2006) have

Photo 3.4: Diving on the HMAS Brisbane (Photograph: Carl Cater).

experienced the site in its first year of operation and one operator is planning a 'James Bond'-style heli-dive experience, where divers are dropped at the site by helicopter. It seems likely that a number of other destinations will follow suit. Indeed it now seems, in Australia at least, that coastal locations are clamouring for these vessels to be sunk off their shores.

Cave Diving

Cave diving is a very specialised dive tourism activity, accessible only to those with significant skills, experience and equipment. Owing to the presence of an overhead environment and often long routes of escape, risks in this activity are much higher, leading to few viable commercial operations. It is suggested that the majority of cave divers are originally cavers, who get into the activity as a way to further explore the underground realm, rather than divers who do the reverse. Nevertheless, these sites may be used in tourism promotion to dive tourists, for example Tourism South Australia uses images of caves on the limestone coast to promote diving in the area (South Australia Tourism Commission, 2004). The majority of cave diving is located in limestone areas and may be a significant distance from the sea. Areas of Florida and Mexico have become popular cave-dive tourism sites, and a few have developed commercial activity, for example the Hidden Worlds Cenote Park, Yucatan (Hidden Worlds Cenote Park, 2006). A less risky form of diving is that of cavern diving, which is defined as areas which still have natural sunlight, and therefore requiring fewer technical skills. In some senses this is a progression from 'swim throughs' that are popular at many reef dive sites.

Been There; Done That

It seems clear that experienced divers become less involved in novelty seeking that may characterise 'early-career' divers. Fortunately, the underwater realm offers such a diversity of attractions that there is still much on offer. As we have seen, divers have the opportunity to develop their skills in a variety of ways so that they can engage in more technical diving activity. They may also develop a more *intellectual* approach to diving, which mirrors the last of Beard and Ragheb's (1983) motivators. Observation by the author confirms that an initial desire to sight charismatic megafauna is gradually supplanted by a fascination with smaller underwater inhabitants. The most experienced dive instructors are more often than not excited by the most colourful nudibranch (a small underwater slug) than by sharks or turtles. For example the most popular attraction at the Walindi Plantation Resort, Kimbe Bay and Papua New Guinea is an endemic Pygmy Seahorse, that divers from all over the world come to view (Photo 3.5).

It is clear that with the acceleration in the numbers of qualified divers worldwide there will be an ancillary growth in the number and diversity of diving attractions such as those detailed in this chapter. It is apparent that many of these will be developed by dive tourism operators along the lines of the three 'E' travel motivators of the 21st Century suggested by Newsome, Moore, and Dowling (2002, p. 8): 'entertainment, excitement and education'. The challenge is to ensure that these attractions are sustainably managed, of which there are many examples. Indeed, scuba divers are largely characterised by a desire to seek

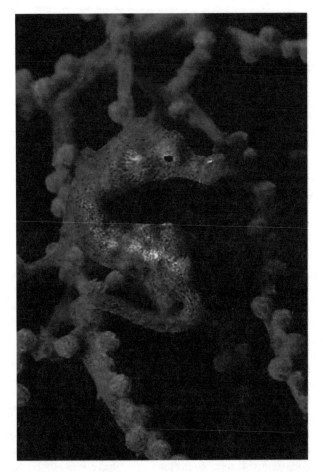

Photo 3.5: Kimbe Bay's pygmy seahorse (*Hippocampus bargibanti*) (Photograph: Cheyne Benjamin).

and protect the wonderful things that they know lie beneath the waves. Chapter 10 of this volume, by Townsend, details the ways in which divers learn about this underwater world and the efforts to direct this knowledge production in positive forms by various agencies. This is an important recognition, for divers feel that they are primary stewards of the resource that is their playground. To learn is central to this aim.

> The ordinary underwater excursion is perhaps the ultimate and the most magnificent adventure of modern times. Words cannot describe the sights that the depths of the sea can offer (Rebikoff, 1955, p. 154).

References

BBC News. (2005). Man relives shark attack escape. Saturday, 26 March, 2005. http://news.bbc.co.uk/1/hi/england/lancashire/4382621.stm (Accessed 3 May 2007).

Beard, J., & Ragheb, M. (1983). Measuring leisure motivation. *Journal of Leisure Research, 15*, 219–228.

Blue Oceans. (2005). http://www.blue-oceans.com/scuba/fiji/divereports.html (Accessed 3 May 2007).

Burgess, G. H. (1998). Diving with elasmobranchs: A call for restraint. *Shark News*, 12: July 1998. IUCN/SSC Shark Specialist Group.

Carwardine, M., & Watterson, K. (2002). *The shark watcher's handbook*. New Jersey: Princeton University Press.

Cater, C., & Cater, E. (2007). *Marine ecotourism: Between the devil and the deep blue sea*. Wallingford: CABI.

Club Marine. (2005). That sinking feeling. *Club Marine, 21*, 146–154.

Collinsa, L. B., Zhua, Z. R., Wyrwollb, K., & Eisenhauerc, A. (2003). Late quaternary structure and development of the northern Ningaloo reef, Australia. *Sedimentary Geology, 159*, 81–94.

Colman, J. G. (1997). A review of the biology and ecology of the whale shark. *Journal of Fish Biology, 51*, 1219–1234.

Commonwealth of Australia. (2002). *White shark (Carcharodon carcharias) recovery plan*. Canberra: Environment Australia, Commonwealth of Australia.

Conservation and Land Management. (2004). *Draft revised zoning scheme for the Ningaloo marine park and proposed additions to the marine reserve system*. Conservation and Land Management (CALM), Western Australian Government. Perth: Western Australia.

Cousteau, J. Y. (1953). *The silent world*. London: Hamish Hamilton.

Csikszentmihalyi, M. (1975). *Beyond boredom and anxiety*. San Francisco: Jossey-Bass.

Cyber Diver News Network. (2002). Shark feeding fanatic Erich Ritter in stable condition after shark attack at Walker's Cay Bahamas feeding site. *Cyber Diver News Network,* 25 Apr 2002.

Cyber Diver News Network. (2005). A scuba diver was swallowed by white shark says witness. *Cyber Diver News Network,* 5 June 2005.

Davis, D., Banks, S., Birtles, A., Valentine, P., & Cuthill, M. (1997). Whale sharks in Ningaloo marine park: Managing tourism in an Australian marine protected area. *Tourism Management, 18*, 259–271.

Department for Environment, Food and Rural Affairs. (2002). Taking to the water with English Heritage, *Wavelength* 7 (Autumn).

Ditton, R. B., Osburn, R. H., Baker, T. L., & Thailing, C. E. (2002). Demographics, attitudes, and reef management preferences of sport divers in offshore Texas waters. *Journal of Marine Science, 59*, 186–191.

Environmental Protection Agency. (2006). *The Brisbane wreck to reef one year on*. Australia: Environmental Protection Agency/Queensland Parks and Wildlife Service, Queensland Government.

Fountain, J., Clark, K., Pforr, C., & Macbeth, J. (2005). The reef and the resort: An investigation of visitors' knowledge and attitudes towards a large-scale development in a remote area of western Australia. *CAUTHE conference*, Alice Springs, February 2005.

Hidden Worlds Cenote Park. (2006). http://www.hiddenworlds.com.mx/ (Accessed 3 May 2007).

Johns, G. M., Leeworthy, V. R., Bell, F. W., & Bonn, M. A. (2001). *Socioeconomic study of reefs in southeast Florida final report 19*. Hollywood, FL: Hazen and Sawyer, P.C.

Kroese, I. (1998). Shark cage diving in South Africa–Sustainable recreational utilisation? *Shark News,* 12, July 1998. IUCN/SSC Shark Specialist Group.

Miller, M. L. (1993). The rise of coastal and marine tourism. *Ocean & Coastal Management, 20*, 181–199.

Morton, B. (2003). Editorial: Ningaloo. *Marine Pollution Bulletin, 46*, 1213–1214.

Mowforth, M. and Munt, I. (1998). *Tourism and sustainablity: New tourism in the Third World*. London: Routledge.

Mundet, L., & Ribera, L. (2001). Characteristics of divers at a Spanish resort. *Tourism Management, 22*, 501–510.

Mustapa, S. A. H. B. S. (2005). Showcasing maritime heritage artefacts for the benefit of the tourist industry in Malaysia. *International Journal of Nautical Archaeology, 34*, 211–215.

Newsome, D., Moore, S. A., & Dowling, R. K. (2002). *Natural area tourism: Ecology, impacts and management.* Clevedon: Channel View.

Norton, A. (1996). Experiencing nature: The reproduction of environmental discourse through safari tourism in Africa. *Geoforum, 27,* 355–373.

Orams, M. (1999). *Marine tourism: Development, impacts and management.* London: Routledge.

Pearce, P. L. (1982). *The social psychology of tourist behaviour.* Oxford: Pergamon Press.

Radley, A. (1995). The elusory body and social constructivist theory. *Body and Society, 1,* 3–23.

Rebikoff, D. (1955). *Free diving.* London: Sidgwick and Jackson.

Roberts, P., & Trow, S. (2002). *Taking to the water: English Heritage's initial policy for the management of maritime archaeology in England.* London: English Heritage.

Ryan, C. (Ed.) (1997). *The tourist experience.* London: Cassell.

Schiebe, K. (1986). Self narratives and adventure. In: T. Sarbin (Ed.), *Narrative psychology: The storied nature of human conduct* (pp. 129–151). New York: Praeger.

Schuster, B.K. (1992). What puts the eco in ecotourism? *The Undersea Journal, 1,* 45–46.

Scuba Travel. (2006). Top ten dive sites around the world. http://www.scubatravel.co.uk/topdives.html (Accessed 3 May 2007).

South African Collaborative White Shark Research Programme. (2005). http://www.sharkresearch.org/pages/index.html (Accessed 3 May 2007).

South Australia Tourism Commission. (2004). Dive South Australia. http://www.dive.southaustralia.com/ (Accessed 23 October 2006).

Spalding, M. D., Ravilious, C., & Green, E. P. (2001). *World atlas of coral reefs.* Berkeley: University of California Press.

Spooner, S. Q. (2003). How tourism benefits from the "ADMAT Model" for the preservation of underwater cultural heritage. Paper presented to 5th annual caribbean conference on sustainable tourism development, St. Kitts, September.

Stolk, P., Markwell, K., & Jenkins, J. (2005). Perceptions of artificial reefs as scuba diving resources: A study of Australian recreational scuba divers. *Annals of Leisure Research, 8,* 153–173.

Swain, M. (2004). (Dis)embodied experience and power dynamics in tourism research. In: L. Goodson, & J. Phillimore (Eds), *Qualitative research in tourism: Ontologies, epistemologies and methodologies* (pp. 102–188). London: Routledge.

Topelko, K. N., & Dearden, P. (2005). The shark watching industry and its potential contribution to shark conservation. *Journal of Ecotourism, 4,* 108–128.

Tribe, J. (2006). The truth about tourism. *Annals of Tourism Research, 33,* 360–381.

Turner, B. (1996). *The body and society* (2nd ed.). London: Sage.

Urry, J. (1990). *The tourist gaze.* London: Sage.

Veijola, S., & Jokinen, E. (1994). The body in tourism. *Theory, Culture and Society, 11,* 125–151.

Weaver, D. (2001). Ecotourism in the context of other tourism types. In: D. Weaver (Ed.), *The encyclopedia of ecotourism* (pp. 73–83). Wallingford: CABI.

Wheeler, B. (1994). Egotourism, sustainable tourism and the environment: A symbiotic, symbolic or shambolic relationship? In: A. V. Seaton, C. L. Jenkins, R.C. Wood, P. U. C. Dieke, M. M. Bennett, L.R. MacLellan, & R. Smith (Eds), *Tourism: The State of the Art* (pp. 647–654). Chichester: John Wiley.

World Conservation Union. (2003). 2003 IUCN Red List of threatened species. http://www.redlist.org/ (Accessed 3 May 2007).

SECTION III:

ENVIRONMENTAL, ECONOMIC AND SOCIAL IMPACTS OF DIVING TOURISM

Chapter 4

Diving and Global Environmental Change: A Mauritius Case Study

Stefan Gössling, Olof Lindén, Jayne Helmersson, Jeanette Liljenberg and Serwa Quarm

Introduction

Coral reefs are a major attraction to divers and snorkellers throughout the tropics, and are consequently of significant economic value (Cesar & van Beukering, 2004; White & Rosales, 2003). Coral reef ecosystems are characterised by high biodiversity and relatively high productivity. Coral reefs thrive in clear water with relatively high temperatures and closed nutrient cycles. However, over the past three decades a number of factors have caused increasing stress to coral reefs. These include destructive fishing methods on or near coral reefs, and various forms of pollution from land-based activities such as agriculture, forestry and construction (Wilkinson, 2004). Phenomena such as El Niño and global climate change, leading to increasing surface water temperatures, can cause additional stress to coral reefs. This has in many areas led to coral bleaching, a phenomenon occurring when symbiotic zooxanthelae residing within scleractinian corals are lost. As a consequence of these developments, coral reefs are now being damaged or destroyed at an increasing rate all around the world (Lindén, Souter, Wilhelmsson, & Obura, 2002; Lindén & Sporrong, 1999; Wilkinson et al., 1999).

The rapid degradation of coral reefs influences both current and future diving conditions. However, the literature on diver motivations and expectations has remained scarce, and little attention has been paid to the consequences of environmental change for the global diving industry. Clearly, physical destruction of coral through storms, the concomitant loss of species and other changes in dive conditions could negatively affect dive experiences. However, divers are not a homogeneous group with identical knowledge, motivations, experience and expectations, so perceptions of changing marine environments might be expected to vary. This, in turn, might have consequences for travel decisions, such as whether or not to visit a dive destination, or whether or not to recommend a particular dive destination to other divers. This chapter presents an overview of the state of coral reefs around the world, along with an outlook of how coral reefs are likely to be affected by global environmental change. Based on a case study in Mauritius, the chapter seeks to throw some light on diver perceptions of environmental change, with the ultimate goal of better understanding how dive destinations are likely to be affected by global environmental change. The case study, though not representative of dive tourism in general, identifies important elements of the diving experience and discusses how changes in the composition of these elements might affect diving tourism in the future. More specifically, it has the following four objectives: firstly, to provide an assessment of the importance of diving and snorkelling opportunities for the economy of Mauritius; secondly, to evaluate the state of the marine environment in Mauritius and its perception by divers and dive operators; thirdly, to understand which elements of marine environments are of greatest importance to divers; and fourthly, to analyse how future global environmental change might influence the attractiveness of the island for tourism.

Coral Reef Systems

Coral reefs are one of the oldest ecosystems on the planet. Reefs consisting of primitive corals and invertebrates were already in existence 600 million years ago. Today's highly diversified coral reefs are, however, of more recent origin. They are primarily found in shallow, clear waters in tropical regions in between 32 °N and 30 °S, with water temperatures ranging from 22 to 28 °C. Single reefs may contain up to 200 species of hard and soft corals, and even more species of fish. Particular locations can be even richer in biodiversity. For instance, around the tiny (about 6.5 ha) islet of Chumbe Island, Tanzania, almost 400 species of fish have been identified (CHICOP, 2007), representing some 10% of the 4000 species of reef fish existing in the vast Indo-Pacific Region stretching from the Red Sea to South Africa and the islands of Polynesia (Lieske & Myers, 1994). Reefs and single corals also exist in warm seas such as, for example, the West African coastline and islands and the east coast of South America. Corals are also found in deep cold-water areas such as the North Atlantic. In fact, one of the largest reef systems in the world is situated in 60–600 m depth along the coast of Norway and extending to areas north of the UK (Mortensen, Hovland, Brattegard, & Farestveit, 1995).

Coral reefs are for several reasons vulnerable to global environmental change, which can be explained by characteristics of reef ecology. The coral animal, a polyp, is the structuring organism on the reef. Without this organism there would not be an ecosystem for most other organisms that are found on a coral reef. What makes this coral organism so important is that it has the ability to build up a reef by fixing dissolved calcium carbonate from the water and build solid calcium carbonate as its skeleton. As the reef grows, new corals settle on the old ones and the old skeletons are gradually transformed into limestone rock, forming the foundation of the reef. Coral polyps of the tropical oceans live in symbiosis with a microscopic alga, also called zooxanthelae. This alga lives in the tissue of the corals and is thus protected by the coral from predation by other plankton. Zooxanthelae, like other algae, are primary producers, and their photosynthesis generates carbohydrates and oxygen, which benefit the coral animal. The alga requires carbon dioxide and mineral salts which are provided by the coral animal and are products of its respiration. Most coral animals living on the tropical reefs would not survive without this symbiotic relationship with the zooxanthelae, a relationship that has developed during millions of years of close co-habitation on reefs, where conditions have remained fairly stable. Another important characteristic of corals is that many of them are colonial: particularly those that build reefs. This means that, for example, staghorn corals or brain corals (*Acropora sp.*, *Lobophyllia sp.*) are in fact colonies consisting of a large number of individuals forming a layer of living organisms at the surface. A more general overview of the history of coral reefs, reef ecology and coral taxonomy is provided by, for instance, Veron (2000).

Coral reefs play an important role in coastline protection, recycling of nutrients, and the provision of food, breeding grounds, habitat and refuge to marine species. They are also important in the formation of sand, beaches and lagoons along the coast of most tropical countries. Relationships between corals and other species can be intricate. There are, for instance, fish species feeding directly on the coral polyp, while others graze on zooxanthelae algae. However, fish and other invertebrates also depend on the reef for shelter during parts of or the entire life cycle. The important role of coral reefs as breeding grounds and habitats also explains their high productivity. Net fish production of an intact tropical coral reef can be between 4 and 30 t of fish per km^2 per year (Talbot & Wilkinson, 2001).

The State of Tropical Reefs: An Outlook

Coral reefs are threatened by both local and global environmental change. By 1998, an estimated 11% of the world's reefs had been destroyed, and an additional 16% damaged in the 1997/1998 coral bleaching events, which were caused by high water temperatures (Wilkinson, 2002). Local environmental stress leading to the destruction of reefs can include overfishing, discharge of effluents, siltation, disease, disruption of food webs and tourism-related problems, including diving (e.g. abrasion of corals through contact with fins or gear; see Lindgren, Palmlund, Wate, and Gössling, Chapter 6, this volume). Global environmental change affecting reefs includes increasing ocean temperatures leading to more bleaching events, changes in ocean chemistry — increasing acidity and lowered concentrations of carbonate — as a result of higher concentrations of CO_2 in the atmosphere, and sedimentation as a result of shoreline erosion through sea level rise (Buddemeier, Kleypas, & Aronson, 2004; van Treeck & Schuhmacher, 1999; Wilkinson, 2002, 2004). Ahamada et al. (2004, p. 190) conclude for the coral reefs of the South West Indian Ocean Islands:

> If management does not improve and there are repeats of the recent climate-related stresses, it is predicted that most reefs in the region will have less than 20% live coral cover by 2014. Many species of corals and fish will be locally extinct due to losses from coral bleaching and over-exploitation of some fish and invertebrate species.

The interaction of local and global stressors is often complex. For instance, pressure on coastal zones has increased because of a growing number of humans living in coastal areas. An estimated 37% of the world's population now live in coastal zones within 100 km of the sea (Cohen, Small, Mellinger, Gallup, & Sachs, 1997), and total numbers are increasing. Consequently, formerly rural zones are turning into urbanised areas throughout much of East and South Asia, parts of Africa, Europe, the Americas and the Pacific region. Increasing human populations generally contribute to increasing stress on coastal ecosystems. Shallow waters are exposed to the release of various pollutants from land, particles from soil erosion, run-off, or river discharge including sediment loads and various pollutants from agriculture, forestry and industry. As corals are highly dependent on clear and clean water, even low nutrient or particle concentrations may upset the ecological balance of coral reefs. Ultimately, such reefs may be covered by algae and bacteria rather than living coral.

In addition to pollution from land, data from a number of regions (see e.g. Pauly, Christensen, Dalsgaard, Froese, & Torres, 1998) show that fishing activities have become an increasing problem. For coral reefs in tropical countries, fisheries are generally a persistent and growing threat because of the use of destructive fishing techniques on or near reefs. The use of bottom-set nets and the trawling and seining near or on reefs can break corals and transform a reef into rubble beds. When there are too many loose coral parts on a reef this may result in a cycle of self-destruction as wave action moves this loose material around, causing damage to other parts of the reef. Other very destructive fishing techniques include the use of explosives, although the magnitude of this problem is unknown. A stick of dynamite or a home-made bomb of fertilisers and kerosene can result in a 25 m^2 rubble bed on a reef. Finally, the use of poisons or bleach can affect reefs. In the process, a poison such as an insecticide is released into the water, and dead or dying fish are caught down current. The use of trawls and beach seines, bottom-set nets, explosives and poison is still common in tropical countries. Such methods are practiced extensively in Philippines, Indonesia, Vietnam, Sri Lanka, India, East Africa and large parts of the Caribbean (e.g. IUCN/UNEP, 1988).

Coral mining is another activity that can affect coral reefs. In some tropical countries, corals are collected from reefs and burnt in kilns to produce lime. While in some countries the activity is banned, it is still practised in parts of East Africa and South and Southeast Asia (see Photo 4.1). Often, the activity has the character of back-yard production at a relatively small scale. However, in some countries such as Tanzania, India and Sri Lanka, it is practised in an industrial or semi-industrial way, with significant impacts on the already-stressed coral reefs (Obura, 2005).

Tourism is now a common activity in coastlines all around the world, affecting the use of land, water, marine species and other coastal resources (for case studies in the Western Indian Ocean see Gössling, 2001a; Gössling, Kunkel, Schumacher, & Zilger, 2004). Tourism is also known to contribute to the transformation of local economies, which can either reduce or increase pressure on coastal ecosystems (Gössling, 2001b; Gössling, 2003). More generally, coastal tourism can have a wide range of consequences for coastal zones (e.g. Bramwell, 2004; Cater & Cater, 2007; Gales, 2003; Garrod & Wilson, 2003; Orams, 1999), and diving tourism in particular can affect reefs in various ways (see e.g. van Treeck & Eisinger, Chapter 8, and Lindgren et al., Chapter 6, both this volume).

Finally, global climate change is posing an increasing threat to coral reefs around the tropics. Corals have slightly different optimum temperatures but most of the tropical

Photo 4.1: Despite being banned in most countries, coral mining is still practised in many tropical developing countries (Photograph: Olof Lindén).

species thrive at temperatures between 26 and 29 °C, with 31 °C representing a lethal temperature for most species (Veron, 2000). Global warming will increase surface sea temperatures, and lead to more extreme events, such as the 1998 extreme El Niño event when water temperatures in many areas reached 30–34 °C. This affected weather patterns around the world and led to the death of many reefs (Photo 4.2), particularly in the Indian Ocean. Climate change is also expected to lead to more frequent and intense cyclones (Webster, Holland, Curry, & Chang, 2005), which can physically destroy reefs or affect them through the impacts of greater wave energy.

Considering these trends, it is not surprising that coral reef systems have been severely affected by local and global environmental change. The last report published by the Global Coral Reef Monitoring Network (Wilkinson, 2004) states that about 20% of the world's reefs are effectively dead. This appears to be a conservative estimate considering the situation in the Indian Ocean where, in some countries, 30–80% of coral reefs died in 1998, due to the extreme El Niño of 1997/1998 (Lindén et al., 2002; Obura, 2005). In addition, the report warns that there is an imminent risk of collapse of about 25% of the world reefs, while an additional 25% are under a long-term threat of collapse (Wilkinson, 2004). It is worth pointing out that these figures are averages; the situation in some countries may be considerably worse.

One can speculate if coral reefs would establish at higher latitudes with continued global warming. In principle this may be possible. However, there are very few sites in the world where the physical conditions exist that would make such colonisation possible. One can also speculate on whether coral species would adapt to warmer conditions and thereby

Photo 4.2: Coral bleaching caused by increasing water temperatures. (Photograph: André Maselennikov)

survive in significantly warmer temperatures. In the Persian Gulf, summer temperatures are significantly warmer than in the tropical Indian Ocean. Here a few species of corals exist but the diversity of corals is very low (Basson, Buchard, Hardy, & Price, 1977; Price, Sheppard, & Roberts, 1993). However, these corals can form reefs of similar character as the reefs of the tropical Indian Ocean.

Coral transplantation may be one way of re-establishing corals in areas where they have disappeared but where the conditions exist for coral growth. Techniques and procedures for this have been developed (e.g. Obura, 2005; van Treeck and Eisinger, Chapter 8, this volume). However, necessary prerequisites for such transplantations to be successful are, of course, that the stress factors that initially wiped out the corals have been sufficiently reduced or, preferably, eliminated.

The prospects of coral reef systems in the tropics are therefore rather dim. Growing human populations in coastal areas, few examples of successful coastal management, and global trends such as climate change going along with extreme weather events compound existing problems and indicate that the situation might worsen.

Case Study: Mauritius

An overview of the history, environment and economy of Mauritius, is provided in Box 4.1. Mauritius is a world-class diving destination, being surrounded by 150 km of fringing reefs, with two breaks in the South and West. The extent of the lagoon between the shore and the peripheral fringing reefs varies between 0.2 and 7 km, and the average depth of the lagoon between 1 and 6 m. Around Mauritius, a total of 159 species of Scleractinan corals have been identified (Pillay, Terashima, Venkatasami, & Uchida, 2002). There are also some 340 species of fish, many of them endemic (Terashima, Mosaheb, Chiranjiwa, & Vishwanitra, 2001). Lagoons and fringing reefs have in the past been damaged by fishing, tourism, siltation from development activities, discharge of nutrients and pesticides, coral bleaching events, as well as tropical storms passing the island (Ahmada et al., 2002).

Box 4.1: Mauritius: History, Environment and Economy.

Mauritius is located in the Indian Ocean at about 20 °S and 58 °E, roughly 800 km from the east coast of Madagascar. The island had a population of 1.24 million in 2006 and a terrestrial area of 2030 km² including the island of Rodriguez (Central Intelligence Agency, 2007). The island is of volcanic origin, with its highest peak, Mont Piton, being 828 m above sea-level (see Figure 4.1). Mauritius is surrounded by 330 km of coastline and has, according to the Ministry of Tourism and Leisure (2004), the third largest reef of the world. The climate is tropical and subtropical with a cyclonic season of about five months beginning in December. Water temperatures vary between 22 and 28 °C (Terashima et al., 2001).

Mauritius belongs to the group of small islands developing states (SIDS) (United Nations, 2005). SIDS are expected to be highly affected by medium- and long-term climate change, including sea-level rise and more frequent and intense storms (London, 2004; Nicholls, 2004). Mauritius has already seen major environmental change both locally, as expressed by large-scale sugarcane monocultures involving the use and subsequent seepage of fertilisers and pesticides, as well as globally in the form of incidences of tropical cyclones and El Niño Southern Oscillation phenomenon affecting the island's reefs. Economically, Mauritius is one of Africa's more wealthy countries with a per capita income of about €9,100 (PPP, 2003 estimate; UN, 2005). The island's economy is dependent principally on three sectors: sugar, textiles and tourism (Mauritius Tourism Promotion Authority and Ministry of Tourism and Leisure, 2004). However, world market prices for sugar have declined substantially in recent years, and the production of textiles has become economically unfeasible in the emergent economy of the island. Consequently, the focus is now on tourism. Tourist arrivals reached almost 720,000 in 2004, generating €630 million (Ministry of Tourism and Leisure, 2005). In terms of employment, tourism created 30,000 full time job equivalents in 2000 (Deloitte and Touche, 2002). Further growth is predicted. The consultancy Deloitte and Touche (2002) expects that tourism will generate a total of 63,000 full time job equivalents by 2020 with a concomitant growth in its contribution to the island's economy. In order to meet growth in tourist arrival numbers, the consultancy recommends extending the number of hotel rooms from 9623 in 2002 to 20,000 by 2020.

Diving conditions in Mauritius are best in summer, from December to March, even though there are occasional cyclones. During this period, it is usually hot, wet and humid, with an average air temperature of 30 °C. Mauritius also offers tourist-carrying submarine dives and an undersea walk, which are popular among tourists.

(Continued)

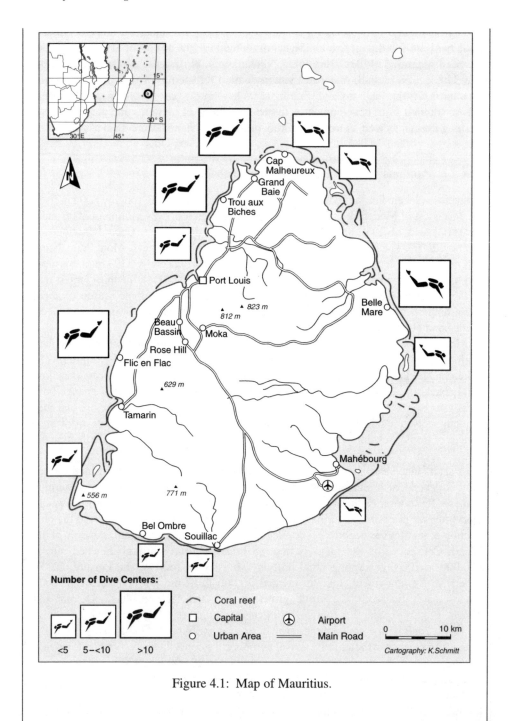

Figure 4.1: Map of Mauritius.

Coral Bleaching

During the major bleaching event in 1997/1998, relatively minor coral bleaching was observed in lagoons and on outer slopes of Mauritius. Quantitative monitoring at two sites at Trou aux Biches from March–May 1998 showed that about 6% of the corals were totally bleached and 27% were partially affected. Rapid surveys at 36 sites around Mauritius and inner islands showed that the reefs had suffered some bleaching in 1998, but most reefs were still healthy with the main signs of damage coming from boat and anchor damage and cyclones. The only large areas of dead standing coral were on the Barrier Reef off Mahebourg, even though mean bleaching was less than 10% at all sites. Around Rodriguez, there was a serious incident of coral mortality in March 2002. Rapid assessments recorded coral death at six of the 22 sites, with mortality concentrated in the north and west of the island (Ahmada et al., 2002). Coral colonies were still standing and being overgrown with turf algae. Mortality ranged from 10 to 75% (Ahmada et al., 2002). There was also a minor bleaching event in 2003 and 2004. Ahamada et al. (2004) report that in 2003, bleaching of corals occurred by mid-February, but by June, 95% of the bleached corals had recovered and another 2% were recovering. However, 3% had died. Trends in 2004 were similar to 2003, but coral mortality was slightly higher.

Sediments, Fertilisers and Eutrophication

It is clear that local development processes have had substantial effects on the reefs. Ahmada et al. (2002) report that in Trou aux Biches, run-off from agriculture continues to degrade the corals, both as a result of sediments and fertilisers increasing nutrient levels. Coral cover decreased slightly from 44% in 2000 to 39% in 2002. No changes in fish populations at Trou aux Biches were observed, but agricultural and tourist pressures were increasing, and the clarity of the water was deteriorating. At Bambou Virieux, the Grand River South discharges large sediment inputs, fertilisers and agricultural wastes. Live coral cover on the reef flat site near the coast decreased from 52% in 2000 to 38% in 2002, while algae had increased from 8% in 2000 to 23% in 2002 (Ahmada et al., 2002).

Cyclones

On average, one or two cyclones pass Mauritius annually, typically resulting in four days of intense winds and rain. However, few cyclones have actually hit the island. Since 1786, Mauritius was hit by cyclones in 1892, 1960 ('Carol', 297 km/h and 'Gervaise', 280 km/h), 1994 ('Hollanda', 216 km/h) and 2002 ('Dina', 278 km/h) (Mauritius Meteorological Services 2005). It seems that incidences of tropical cyclones have increased in frequency, and recent research suggests that cyclones in this area will increase in both frequency and intensity in the future as a result of higher water temperatures (cf. Webster et al., 2005, see also Emmanuel, 2005). Mauritius might thus see more cyclones passing or hitting the island in the future, which might affect diving conditions in various ways, including inaccessibility during storms (due to wave height), reduced visibility, or physical damage to coral reefs.

Overall, environmental change is thus likely to have a major effect on coral reefs in Mauritius. As diving seems of substantial economic importance for the island, this raises the question of the level of environmental damage that is tolerated by divers before their perception of a holiday destination becomes negative.

Method

In order to address the research objectives, a combined bottom-up (interviews with tourists) and top-down (interviews with dive instructors) approach was chosen. While it is clear that the understanding of tourist perceptions of the marine environment is central to the study, interviews with dive instructors served to provide additional information on divers, economics, and changes in the marine environment as seen from a dive-instructor perspective.

The study focused on leisure tourists, thus excluding an estimated share of 13% business tourists and tourists in transit (Ministry of Tourism and Leisure, 2003). The purpose of the study was always communicated in a general way ('a scientific survey on tourism'), and anonymity was assured. A structured questionnaire was used to interview tourists, addressing destination-choice motives, perception of the general environmental situation in Mauritius, the state of the marine environment, previous snorkelling/diving experience, the character of diving experiences, as well as socio-demographic information. Questions were either asked in open form, i.e. allowing tourists to answer freely, or in Likert form, i.e. asking tourists to rate their responses. In total, 289 tourists were interviewed, based on a judgement sampling technique. Tourists were approached in hotels, restaurants, on the street and on beaches in all major tourism zones in Mauritius, in an attempt to geographically embrace all places where tourists may go. The response rate was close to 100%, with very few tourists declining to participate in the study. All interviews were held in October 2004. Note that the number of valid answers is sometimes lower than the number of tourists interviewed, mostly because tourists had arrived only recently and could not as yet make statements on parts of the questions contained in the questionnaire.

Several aspects limit the representativeness of the study, including seasonality and sampling technique. Furthermore, interviews were held in English, German and French, but some communication problems could not be overcome, and tourists from France and La Reunion are underrepresented in the sample (see Table 4.1). Tourists from Seychelles, La Reunion and India are also underrepresented in the sample, because they were not as easily identified as a result of their physical similarity — from the perspective of the researchers — to the local population. It is not known neither whether tourists from Seychelles, La Reunion and India participate in similar holiday activities as their Western counterparts. For example, beach activities might not be as popular among these tourists as it is among European tourists and the chance of encountering these tourists on the beach might consequently have been lower. Another explanation is that travel motives of these visitors more frequently include visiting friends and relatives.

Table 4.1: Percentage of international tourist arrivals, Official Statistics and Sample, 2004.

	France	Reunion	UK	Germany	S. Africa	Italy	Other
Official arrivals	29.3	13.4	12.9	7.3	7.3	5.7	24.1
Case study	11		34	23	4	4	19

Source: Government of Mauritius (2007).

In addition to tourists, dive instructors, defined as the person in charge of a dive centre, were interviewed through semi-structured interviews to get an overview of diver numbers, dive-school economics, as well as dive instructors' perceptions of the quality of the reefs, and the importance of the quality of the reefs for tourist experiences. Dive instructors were contacted randomly at dive centres, and the scientific purpose of the study was outlined prior to each interview. Some dive instructors refused to answer questions, both as a result of time constraints and of suspicions that information might be used by competing companies or the government. Furthermore, out of the 72 dive centres identified in this study, some were difficult to reach (because of their remote location) or dive instructors were absent when the dive centre was visited. All interviews were held in English, lasted between 15 and 45 min, and were recorded by taking notes. The interviews were evaluated through comparative analysis. Overall, only ten dive instructors were interviewed. As the dive instructors willing to be interviewed owned or managed some of the rather large diving centres, diver numbers are not representative and figures difficult to extrapolate. However, with regard to the marine environment, the broad majority of the dive instructors interviewed had lived for many years in Mauritius, and were thus able to make statements on recent changes.

It is important to note that the study attempts to link the expectations and experiences of divers with environmental changes likely to occur in the future. Stated expectations, as well as negative perceptions, such as for instance poor visibility, are thus based on analogous experiences, i.e. dive conditions experienced elsewhere, or the imagination of such situations by the diver. As individual experiences are the basis for diver perceptions, they can only serve as a general indicator of the consequences of global environmental change for diving. Furthermore, Mauritius' reefs can be seen as only moderately degraded, and perceptions might be different in other, more badly-affected marine environments.

Results

Of the tourists interviewed ($n = 289$), 57% were men and 43% women. As men accounted for 52% of tourist arrivals in 2004 according to official statistics (Government of Mauritius, 2007), they are slightly overrepresented. More than one-third (34%) were of British origin, followed by Germans (23%) and French (from France and La Reunion, totalling 11%). Other countries of origin included Switzerland (5%), Italy (4%), South Africa (4%),

Netherlands (3%), Norway (3%), Austria (2%), Australia (2%) and 'other' (9%), including the USA, Ireland, Sweden, Belgium, Finland, Denmark, Spain, Zambia, Singapore and Greece. Regarding the level of education ($n = 287$), 58% of the respondents held a university degree, followed by college (24%) and secondary school (18%) qualifications. Annual net incomes ($n = 207$) of up to €19,000 were reported by 15% of the respondents, followed by €20,000–39,000 (31%), €40,000–59,000 (18%), €60,000–79,000 (15%), €80,000–99,000 (7%), €100,000–99,000 (8%) and more than €200,000 (6%).

The first question addressed respondents' reasons for choosing Mauritius as a holiday destination ($n = 289$). Responses on the open question indicate that 'weather' was the most important motive, as mentioned by 17% of the tourists, followed by 'recommendation by friends, family or colleagues' (9%), 'advertisement/travel-agency recommendation' (9%), 'honeymoon' (6%), 'beaches' (6%), 'friendly people and good service' (6%), 'dream vacation' (4%), 'anniversary or birthday' (4%), 'have family and friends here' (4%), 'relaxation' (3%), 'windsurfing, fishing and golf' (3%), 'nice hotels' (3%), 'the sea' (3%) and 'diving' (2%). Note that answers confuse proximate (e.g. 'honeymoon') and ultimate (e.g. 'weather') reasons for travelling to Mauritius. Respondents were then asked to rate the importance of snorkelling and/or diving to their vacation on a Likert scale from 1 (very important) to 5 (not important at all). Of the respondents ($n = 289$), one quarter reported that diving and/or snorkelling was very important or important, while another 20% reported that it was of some importance to them. Of the remaining respondents, 12% stated that diving and/or snorkelling was of minor importance, and for the majority (43%) it was of no importance at all. However, when asked about their participation in snorkelling and/or diving activities, 67% reported going diving and/or snorkelling at some point during their vacation. Out of these ($n = 194$), 93% went snorkelling and 26% diving, with 19% of the sub-sample participating in both diving and snorkelling activities. On average, divers reported going on at least one diving trip per day on 7.0 days of their vacation and snorkellers stated going for at least one snorkelling trip per day on 5.9 days of their vacation, with an average vacation length of 15 days.

The questionnaire also addressed the experience of snorkellers and divers ($n = 194$). Snorkellers were defined as anyone participating in snorkelling activities, but not going scuba diving. Divers, on the other hand, were defined as anyone participating in scuba diving activities (including snorkelling activities). As shown in Table 4.2, almost half of the divers and one-third of the snorkellers had only recent diving experience (1–5 years), and another 25% had between 6 and 10 years of experience. On average, divers had a diving experience of 8.8 years, and snorkellers 13.4 years.

Divers who had already undertaken several dives in Mauritius ($n = 38$) were asked whether they would recommend Mauritius as a good place for diving on a Likert scale from 1 (very good diving) to 5 (no good diving at all). About two-thirds ($n = 26$) stated that Mauritius was a good or even a very good place for diving, while it represented a moderately good place for diving for about a quarter of respondents ($n = 10$). Two respondents rated Mauritius as 'not so good for diving' or 'no good for diving at all'. Note that it is unclear whether divers considered the state of local dive sites when answering the question, or whether they compared Mauritius with other dive destinations they had visited. The answers thus need to be seen as representing a general perception of local dive sites.

Table 4.2: Length of experience of snorkellers and divers.

Years	Divers (%)	Snorkellers (%)
1–5	49	30
6–10	26	25
11–15	11	13
16–20	8	14
21–25	3	3
26–30	1	9
31–35	1	2
36–40	0	3
41–45	1	1
	100	100

Table 4.3: State of coral reefs in Mauritius: 'good and healthy'?

	Yes (%)	No (%)	Don't know (%)	Total
Divers	19 ($n = 8$)	49 ($n = 21$)	33 ($n = 14$)	$n = 43$
Snorkellers	23 ($n = 26$)	48 ($n = 53$)	29 ($n = 32$)	$n = 111$
Sample	22 ($n = 34$)	48 ($n = 74$)	30 ($n = 46$)	$n = 154$

The subsequent section of the questionnaire addressed the state of the marine environment in Mauritius. Divers and snorkellers ($n = 154$) were then asked whether coral reefs in Mauritius were in a good, healthy state (see Table 4.3).

Overall, one-fifth of divers and snorkellers (22%) believed that coral reefs were in a good and healthy state, while almost half (48%) did not think this is the case. About one-third of the respondents (30%) were undecided.

Respondents ($n = 284$) were asked whether global environmental change would have consequences for diving tourism. Answers were skewed, with 68% answering 'yes', and 13% 'no'. A further 19% were undecided. 'Yes' answers included a wide variety of ideas and perspectives, such as 'if the water gets very hot, certain species/corals will die', 'if temperatures get higher, the Northern countries will get better diving and maybe people will go diving closer to home', 'the diving sites will change and there will be fewer possibilities to go diving', 'the marine life will change', 'the fish will disappear' or 'islands like the Maldives will disappear in 100 years time because of seawater rise'. 'No' answers included 'not really, the corals get worse everywhere and the divers will go diving anyway', 'no, the sea level is rising, but this is not a problem, unless fish migrate elsewhere', and 'I don't believe in global climate change'.

Finally, divers ($n = 45$) and snorkellers ($n = 94$) were asked whether reduced visibility, broken corals, fewer species, algae growth or dead corals would influence their choice of

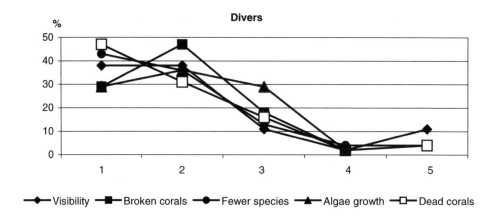

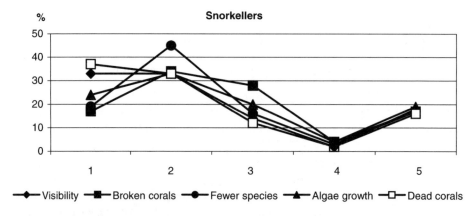

Figure 4.2: Parameters influencing diving experiences.

Mauritius as a destination on a Likert scale from 1 (great influence) to 5 (no influence at all). Figure 4.2 shows that for most parameters 'great influence' dominates, indicating that deteriorating environmental conditions influence the diving or snorkelling experience. For example, almost 80% of the divers stated that dead or broken corals would have an influence (1 or 2 on the Likert scale) on their choice of a destination. However, there was also a small (divers) to considerable (snorkellers) share of tourists stating that changing conditions of the marine environment would have no consequences for their choice of destination. While perceptions follow similar trend lines for all parameters, broken or dead corals seem of greatest relevance for divers, while visibility is, after dead corals, the most important aspect for snorkellers.

In order to understand which marine experiences are of importance to snorkellers ($n = 117$) and divers ($n = 54$), an open question addressed 'the best diving/snorkelling experience' (i.e. no choices were offered and multiple answers were accepted). Experiences where then coded into different groups, depending on whether they focused

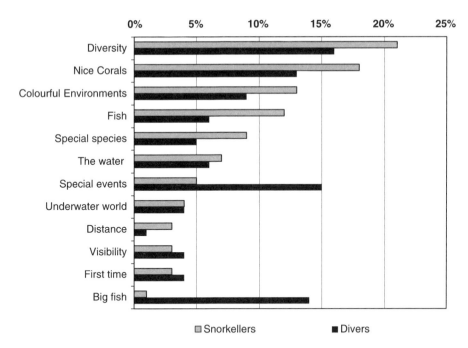

Figure 4.3: Factors influencing diving experiences.

on 'diversity', 'colourful environments', and so on. Answers reflecting 'diversity', such as different kinds of fish, were the most common in both groups, followed by 'nice corals', i.e. coral formations perceived as aesthetically appealing (see Figure 4.3). The third most often mentioned aspect was 'colourful environments', including marine flora and fauna. 'Fish' refers to abundance, comprising both the number and variety of fish. 'Special species' refers to unusual, rare or uncommon species (e.g. turtles or gastropods). 'Water' includes clear, 'blue' or unpolluted underwater conditions. 'Big fish' refers to sightings of sharks, whales or rays, and is an important category only among divers, as these species will seldom be encountered by snorkellers. 'Special events' includes, for example, night dives. 'Visibility' refers to clear waters. 'The first time' was also mentioned by a substantial number of people, indicating the importance of the respondent's initial encounter with the underwater world. 'Distance' means that the diving sites are located in proximity to the hotel, i.e. that only a short boat-ride was involved, which was perceived as positive.

Finally, snorkellers ($n = 111$) and divers ($n = 58$) were asked which kind of species were of importance for their diving experience (see Figure 4.4). Answers indicated that large, colourful fish, the mixture of species, or 'special' species such as barracudas or flying fish are of greatest importance. In this context, one diver's statement that 'it's when you stop seeing the species that they become important for your experience' indicates that at least a share of divers might be well aware of the overall number or composition of species observed.

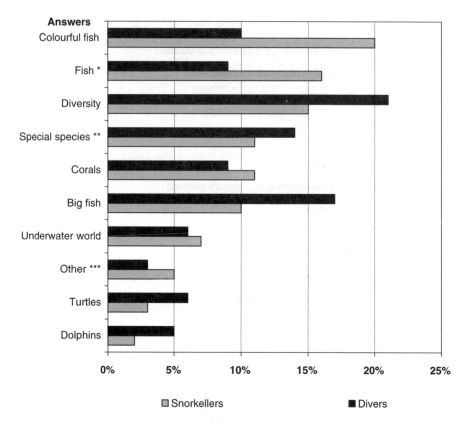

Figure 4.4: Species of importance to the diving experience.

*Including any kind of fish.
**Mentioned were parrot fish (family: Scaridae), lionfish (family: *Scorpaenidae*), lobster (family: *Nephropidae*), clownfish (family: *Pomacentridae*), "killer" whales (*Orcinus orca*), barracudas (family: *Sphyraenidae*), flying fish (family: *Exocoetidae*), angelfish (family: *Pomacanthidae*).
***E.g. shells, gastropods.

Dive Instructors

Interviews with dive instructors were carried out to understand the condition of marine ecosystems in Mauritius from the dive professional's perspective, as well as to quantify diver numbers in a top-down assessment. There was consensus that many reefs are degraded and that fish have become less abundant. Most dive instructors believed that the condition of the marine environment had been better in the past: 'inside the lagoon we had lots of corals. It has gone so fast. Now there are only algae'. Another dive instructor reported that the number of animals on the reef had decreased, although species diversity had remained much the same. Nevertheless, a decade ago more species were sighted per dive, and the dive instructor concluded: 'I cannot promise any encounter with a particular species [anymore].' However, there was also a notion that the quality of the reefs had been improving as the main factors responsible for the present, less favourable conditions had become less problematic. This included the leaching of nutrients from settlements, hotels and sugar plantations; effluents from the textile industry; and pesticides from agriculture. Nevertheless, dive instructors still perceived a number of threats to the marine ecosystem, including spear fishing, net fishing and (over)fishing in general; locals walking on reefs in order to hunt octopus or collect shells; and the large and increasing number of boats, which might spill fuel or cause anchor damage.

Global environmental threats were not seen as particularly problematic for Mauritius, and there was consensus among dive instructors that the 1998 El Niño had little impact on the reefs. Tropical cyclones may be an exception. One dive instructor on the east coast reported that there had been many storms, which can be a substantial problem as they damage the reefs: 'instead of two storms per year, now we get 20. Fortunately, not all of them pass over the island'. Dina, the last serious cyclone passing Mauritius in 2002, did substantial damage to the reefs. The dive instructor also observed patterns of large-scale environmental change, stating that 'a few years ago, I could predict the currents, now I cannot any longer'. However, even though coral cover might have decreased by 25% over the past 10 years in his opinion, re-growth could be seen. He considered that measures taken to protect the environment, such as moorings to reduce anchor damage, were starting to pay off. Provided that the island was not hit by another cyclone, corals would be 'back to normal by next year'. He also thought that damage and re-growth are part of a regular cycle. Similar statements could be heard from a number of dive instructors. In the northwest, dive instructors reported that the lagoon at Grand Baie had been damaged, but was slowly recovering. This might have been the result of putting a stop to problematic human activities, such as sand mining or collecting corals.

Despite their often serious accounts of environmental change, most dive instructors did not think that there were consequences for dive tourism: 'as long as the water is clear, people will continue to dive'. Another dive operator added that '20 fish is enough to make people happy. Wherever you take them, it's beautiful'. He believed that tourists would not be disappointed as long as they see something — and often they might not know what they could have seen: 'When I was a kid, this lagoon was full of shells. Today you'll see nothing. However, the tourists don't see that'. Obviously, in order to evaluate or rank their diving experience, divers will need reference points in time (e.g. to compare the same dive site over several years) and space (e.g. to compare Mauritius dive sites with dive sites elsewhere). If these do not exist, the state of the reef is — within a certain range of environmental parameters — irrelevant. Accordingly, divers commenting on their diving experiences are usually the more experienced ones, who have reference points in space. For example, as one dive instructor reported, some divers compare their diving experiences in Mauritius with other sites they have seen: 'they tell me that the reefs do not have the colours of the Red Sea or the richness of fish of the Maldives'. Such comparisons also indicate that many dive tourists actually have little knowledge of Mauritius and its reefs — indicating a low degree of pre-booking information influencing the destination choice — as the island, according to the dive instructor, is '*not* a 5–6 star diving destination'. As for reference points in time, even fewer visitors might be able to make statements on the quality of the reefs in Mauritius some 5, 10 or even 20 years ago. However, some dive instructors report that there are a number of returning visitors, with divers taking their Open Water certificate in Mauritius coming back after 2 or 3 years. Overall, dive instructors thus observed changes in the marine environment, but in their perception, these changes were not having detrimental consequences for the dive industry.

Only a few dive instructors were willing and/or able to provide statistics on numbers of dive tourists in Mauritius. As a general estimate, one veteran dive instructor with over 20 years of experience in the island estimated that 10% of all tourists come to dive. His estimate was based on the number of licenses sold by the Mauritius Diving School Association (MDSA), of which most dive centres in Mauritius are members. For this study, ten dive centres provided data on the number of divers, varying between 400 and 2200 divers per dive centre per year. In total, 15,000 divers per year were registered, or roughly 1500 per dive centre. Note, however, that some large dive centres were included in this sample, and the island-wide average might thus be lower. Even less reliable were estimates of the number of dives, which varied between three and ten dives per guest over the holiday period.

Economic Importance of Dive Tourism

Regarding the contribution of diving tourism to the economy of Mauritius, some preliminary calculation can be presented. Note that this only includes a rough estimate of the direct contribution of diving tourism, in terms of direct payments to dive centres and not including other associated expenditures, indirect economic or multiplier effects. Results thus need to be seen as conservative. In this sample, 97% of the tourists interviewed were of European origin (including La Reunion), as opposed to 69% according to arrival statistics (in 2004; Government of Mauritius, 2007). As most divers worldwide come from European countries (World Tourism Organization, 2001), the sample may contain a disproportionately large share of dive tourists, which needs to be considered in the calculations. Furthermore, the average length of stay in this study was 15 days, as opposed to about 10 days according to arrival statistics (in 2004; Ministry of Tourism and Leisure, 2005). Assuming, as a conservative estimate, only the European share of the total population of international leisure tourists performs comparable leisure activities (corresponding to 412,500 tourists), a total of 50,000 leisure tourists (12%) would go diving and about 170,000 (41%) would go snorkelling. Regarding the frequency of these activities, divers in this study indicated that they would dive during an average of 7.0 days of their total vacation, while snorkellers reported going snorkelling on an average of 5.9 days of their vacation. Interpolated to the total European leisure tourist population, this would mean, as a broad estimate, that an average tourist accounted for 0.85 diving days and 2.4 snorkelling days during his stay in Mauritius. In total, this corresponds to 350,000 diving days and roughly one million snorkelling days (in 2004). This estimate excludes the non-European share of leisure tourists (34%). Based on these figures, it can be assumed that 0.85 dive days correspond to 1.3 dives, counting every second dive event as being a double-dive. Extrapolating these figures to the European leisure tourist population (412,500), this sums up to a conservative estimate of 536,000 dives in 2004. Diving, at an average price of €30 per dive (taking into account comparably cheaper double-dives), might thus have generated at least €16 million in direct revenues to the Mauritius economy, corresponding to

2.5% of the turnover generated by tourism. However, this estimate only includes direct economic benefits of the European share of international tourists participating in diving activities; it excludes the direct and indirect benefits of snorkelling and other marine environment-based activities, as well as the indirect benefits of diving. Including these might more than double the income generated through marine activities.

These figures can also be compared to data provided by the Ministry of Tourism and Leisure (2003) and the consultancy Deloitte and Touche (2002), with respective estimates of 70,000 and 50,000–100,000 dive tourists. The results of this study are at the lower end of these estimates (50,000 dive tourists), even though 72 dive centres were identified in this study, as opposed to only 39 by Deloitte and Touche (2002). However, the present study might underestimate the share of diving tourists, as only European leisure tourists were considered, leaving roughly one-third of leisure tourists unaccounted for. Business tourists might also go diving at some stage of their visit.

As for snorkelling, 62% of the sample reported participation in these activities, corresponding to at least 255,000 leisure tourists. Snorkelling activities are performed on more than 1.5 million days. The contribution of snorkelling to the Mauritius economy might also be substantial, as snorkellers might hire fins and masks and participate in organised snorkelling trips at a considerable cost. However, no data on the economic benefits generated by these activities exists, and the collection of such data was beyond the scope of this case study. Nor are certain other sectors of the marine tourism industry included in this study. For example, glass-bottom boats are found all around the island, and there are also opportunities for tourists to participate in submarine dives. The submarine company Blue Safari, for instance, had 70,000 guests since 1995, charging Rs 2650 (€82) per adult in 2004. There is also an underwater walk in Grand Baie, which attracted 2550 tourists in 2003. These marine-based activities might contribute considerably to the overall income generated from tourism.

Discussion

As reported earlier in this chapter, the sample used in the survey discussed here consisted almost entirely of European leisure tourists. These are wealthy and highly educated, with 85% of the respondents claiming net annual incomes higher than €20,000, and almost 60% holding university degrees. Travel motives of these tourists are largely based on the 3S (sun, sand, sea) tropical island image; the stated importance of diving and snorkelling as leisure activities is low. However, while 'diving' was mentioned by only 2% of the tourists as an important travel motive (and snorkelling by none), about 25% claim that diving/snorkelling are very important or important leisure activities, and 67% reported going diving and/or snorkelling at some stage of their vacation. Moreover, diving and snorkelling are activities carried out frequently. The high frequency of diving and snorkelling activities, as opposed to the stated importance of diving and/or snorkelling for choosing Mauritius as a destination, indicates that there might be an 'implicit' importance of diving and snorkelling opportunities. In other words, diving and snorkelling opportunities might be considered self-evident in the tourism offering of tropical islands. Consequently, they might have substantial importance for the overall tourism product of Mauritius, even though they are not of primary relevance in travel decisions. This serves to point out a paradox: while it seems no major advantage in terms of marketing that diving and snorkelling opportunities exist, it would be a major disadvantage should tourists find upon arrival that these opportunities did *not* exist.

The perception of healthy marine environments and their importance for travel decisions is far more difficult to evaluate. The study found that of the divers and snorkellers interviewed on the quality of the marine environment ($n = 154$), less than one quarter thought that the coral reefs in Mauritius were in a good and healthy state. Tourist perceptions are confirmed by scientific findings, indicating that many of the reefs in Mauritius are indeed affected by environmental change, although not severely (Ahamada et al., 2004). It needs to be questioned, however, whether tourists are in the position to judge the healthiness of a reef, as their perceptions might rather be based on visible effects such as broken corals, algae growth, or possibly a more general understanding of environmental problems. Hence, while scientists report moderate damage to reefs, not all tourists will note this because they lack the scientific skills and knowledge or the experience of a site over time necessary to evaluate change.

It is clear that in order to make statements on the state of a reef, one needs to have either a more profound environmental knowledge or reference points in time and space, i.e. comparative experiences of reefs in different locations/countries, or in the same location over a period of time. About half of the dive tourists in the survey started diving relatively recently, although the average diving experience of 8.8 years indicates that a proportion of tourists also had practiced diving for a considerable time. Irrespective of experience, divers might possess 'expert knowledge' in the sense that they can judge whether reefs are physically destroyed, whether they are overgrown by algae, or whether there is an abundant fauna. However, more specific aspects of reef biology, such as species diversity, bleached corals versus dead/recovering corals and so on, might presuppose more intimate knowledge, which most of divers in Mauritius are not likely to have. Divers and snorkellers also stated that underwater visibility, broken or dead corals, few species and algae growth negatively influenced their perception of the marine environment. This confirms that perceptions of environmental problems are based on visible, comprehensible parameters (Gössling, 2002). However, it remains unclear when environmental change becomes unbearable, i.e. when negative experiences would start to influence destination choices and word-of-mouth recommendations. For instance, underwater visibility could be 30 m, 20 m or less than 1 m, but it is not clear at which stage visibility will be perceived as no longer satisfactory. It also remains unclear whether there are substitution effects, e.g. whether the experience of a 'special species' (such as a shark) or a special event (such as a night-dive) can outweigh negative perceptions in other areas (such as physically damaged reefs). Likewise, social aspects of diving might sometimes be of importance (Photo 4.3). Musa (2002), for instance, has shown that for divers in Sipadan, Malaysia, social aspects and professional management have substantial importance for the overall diver satisfaction.

Dive instructors reported that tourists often compared Mauritius to other destinations such as the Red Sea or the Maldives, which are generally perceived as 'better' dive sites.

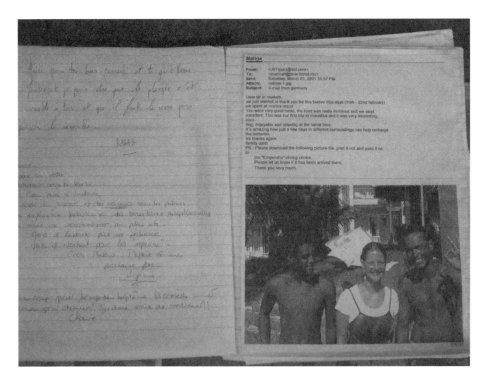

Photo 4.3: Social aspects of diving can be an important part of the dive experience.
(Photograph: Stefan Gössling)

This indicates that there exist reference points in space, at least for some tourists. In the future, with the absolute number of experienced divers increasing, this might have consequences for destination choices. Little is known about reference points in time, i.e. whether divers are returning visitors to Mauritius. Some dive instructors reported, however, that tourists taking a dive certificate in Mauritius are likely to return after a number of years. The motives might rather be social, however, as divers wish to re-visit the place where they took their certificate.

Overall, it seems clear that a few observable environmental parameters shape perceptions of environmental health, including 'visibility', 'colourful reefs', 'variety and number of colourful, rare or charismatic fauna' and 'algae cover'. These findings support evidence from other studies that a healthy reef, clear water and an abundant fish life are some of the most important factors for choosing a dive site (Davis & Tisdell, 1996). It is not clear, however, when negative experiences will start to influence travel decisions. For instance, reefs in Mauritius are moderately affected by environmental change, and almost half of the divers ($n = 43$) and snorkellers ($n = 111$) in the survey were of the opinion that reefs were not in a good and healthy state. Nevertheless, it seems as if current changes do not influence tourist perceptions to a degree where this would result in changing travel behaviour: 36 of 38 divers answering this question would recommend

Mauritius as a moderate-to-very-good place for diving. This might include a comparison with other dive destinations, however. As pointed out earlier, Mauritius is not generally seen as a five-star dive destination. Findings thus indicate that the environmental situation in Mauritius is still acceptable to a degree where this will still result in recommendations. One might thus hypothesise that a theoretical 'damage threshold' is not reached in Mauritius, i.e. a situation in which the damage of a reef becomes so obvious and appalling that tourists would stop recommending the destination and not return themselves. However, it is difficult to establish when such damage thresholds would deter tourists from coming to Mauritius, particularly given the fact that diving and snorkelling seem 'implicit' leisure activities. As future changes in the marine environment are likely to be more substantial, Mauritius and other destinations might thus profit from the fact that most dive tourists appear to be holiday divers, i.e. divers with little knowledge of the state of the local environment, also travelling more or less irrespective of the condition of the marine environment. Divers with intimate knowledge of marine environments, choosing dive locations based on expectations of unique dive experiences (Photo 4.4), might however react more sensitively to environmental change, as they are likely to possess more 'expert knowledge', to have more reference points in time and space, and to also be better informed on the state of the environment at their destinations, for instance through special interest media. In summary, the case study indicates that tourists perceive environmental change negatively, but this does not as yet influence diving experiences, destination choices and recommendations. Thresholds are, however, unknown.

Photo 4.4: Sharks are highly fascinating species for divers. (Photograph: Roger Horrocks)

Conclusions

Marine environments are under increasing pressure through local and global environmental change. A considerable share of coral reefs in the tropics is already dead or severely damaged, and it is likely that this trend will continue in the foreseeable future. Global environmental change, including increasing temperatures, more intense and frequent cyclones, and El Niño effects could have devastating impacts on coral reefs, but it is unclear when and where damages will occur. Dive tourism based on tropical reefs is of growing importance worldwide, generating significant economic benefits in many tropical destinations. The question thus arises of how this special-interest tourism will be affected by environmental change.

A case study in Mauritius revealed that marine ecosystems are moderately affected by local and global environmental change. While coastal zone management has apparently reduced local pollution levels, more frequent and intense cyclones and El Niño phenomena could potentially lead to significant damage of the island's reefs. This raises the question of how tourists will perceive damaged marine environments and whether this has consequences for destination choices. The study found that relatively few environmental parameters appear to be of importance for divers and snorkellers, including undamaged, i.e. physically intact reefs, good visibility, abundance of marine life and colourful or 'special' species, such as turtles or sharks. Even though a minority of divers and snorkellers believes that reefs are in a 'good and healthy state', this does not seem have a negative influence on their diving and snorkelling experiences, and the majority of divers would still recommend Mauritius as a good diving destination. However, the study also indicates that there might be threshold levels where environmental conditions become unfavourable, influencing destination choices. As most tourists appear little informed on local environmental conditions, with diving and snorkelling opportunities being rather implicitly considered as part of 3S holiday experiences, deteriorating environmental conditions might only become important when destinations are no longer recommended. The risk of this happening appears currently rather low in Mauritius, as a large share of divers and snorkellers do not have an intimate knowledge of marine environments and can rather be seen as holiday divers. Consequently, the situation might be fundamentally different in destinations attracting a higher share of more experienced dive tourists, seeking out dive locations because of their unique characteristics.

Overall, the case study has shown that coral reefs in the tropics are affected by both local and global environmental change. Given the seriousness of the problem, the urgency of coastal zone management is unquestioned. However, even if local environmental problems are addressed, extreme weather events such as El Niño phenomena or cyclones are largely uncontrollable, and are likely to have serious consequences for some tropical destinations. Strategies to increase economic dependencies on tourism, as prevalent in virtually all tropical islands, should be evaluated in the light of this.

References

Ahamada, S., Bigot, L., Bijoux, J., Maharavo, J., Meunier, S., Moyne-Picard, M., & Paupiah, N. (2002). Status of coral reefs in the South West Indian Ocean Island Node: Comoros, Madagascar, Mauritius, Reunion and Seychelles. In: C. R. Wilkinson (Ed.), *Status of coral reefs of the World: 2002* (pp. 79–100). Townsville: Australian Institute of Marine Science.

Ahamada, S., Bijoux, J., Bigot, L., Cauvin, B., Kooonjul, M., Maharavo, J., Meunier, S., Moine-Picard, M., Quod, J.-P., & Pierre-Louis, R. (2004). Status of the coral reefs of the South West Indian Ocean island states. In: C. Wilkinson (Ed.), *Status of coral reefs of the World: 2004* (pp. 190–211). Townsville: Australian Institute of Marine Science.

Basson, P. W., Buchard, Jr., J. E., Hardy, J. T., & Price, A. R. G. (1977). *Biotopes of the Western Arabia, marine life and environments of Saudi Arabia.* Dahran, Saudi Arabia: ARAMCO, Department of Loss Prevention and Environmental Affairs.

Bramwell, B. (2004). *Coastal mass tourism: Diversification and sustainable development in Southern Europe.* Clevedon: Channel View Publications.

Buddemeier, R. W., Kleypas, J. A., & Aronson, R. B. (2004). *Coral reefs and global climate change: Potential contributions of climate change to stresses on coral reef ecosystems.* Arlington, VA, USA: Pew Center on Global Climate Change.

Cater, C., & Cater, E. (2007). *Marine ecotourism: Between the Devil and the deep blue sea.* Wallingford: CABI.

Central Intelligence Agency. (2007). The world factbook: Mauritius. https://www.cia.gov/cia/publications/factbook/geos/mp.html. (Accessed 25 January 2007.)

Cesar, H. S. J., & van Beukering, P. J. H. (2004). Economic valuation of the coral reefs of Hawai'i. *Pacific Science, 58,* 231–242.

CHICOP (Chumbe Island Coral Park). (2007). Reef sanctuary. http://www.chumbeisland.com/Reef%20Sanctuary/reef%20sanctuary.html. (Accessed 31 January 2007.)

Cohen, J. E., Small, C., Mellinger, A., Gallup, J., & Sachs, J. (1997). Estimates of coastal populations. *Science, 278,* 1209–1213.

Davis, D., & Tisdell, C. (1996). Economic management of recreational scuba diving and the environment. *Journal of Environmental Management, 48,* 229–248.

Deloitte and Touche. (2002). *Tourism development plan for Mauritius.* Final report. Republic of Mauritius and European Union.

Emmanuel, K. (2005). Increasing destructiveness of tropical cyclones over the past 30 years. *Nature, 436,* 686–688.

Gales, N. J. (Ed.) (2003). *Marine mammals: Fisheries, tourism and management issues.* Melbourne: CSIRO Publications.

Garrod, B., & Wilson, J. C. (2003). *Marine ecotourism: Issues and experiences.* Clevedon: Channel View.

Gössling, S. (2001a). The consequences of tourism for sustainable water use on a tropical island: Zanzibar, Tanzania. *Journal of Environmental Management, 61,* 179–191.

Gössling, S. (2001b). Tourism, environmental degradation and economic transition: Interacting processes in a Tanzanian coastal community. *Tourism Geographies, 3,* 230–254.

Gössling, S. (2002). Human–environmental relations with tourism. *Annals of Tourism Research, 29,* 539–556.

Gössling, S. (2003). Tourism and development in tropical islands: Political ecology perspectives. In: S. Gössling (Ed.), *Tourism and development in tropical islands: Political ecology perspectives* (pp. 1–37). Cheltenham: Edward Elgar Publishing.

Gössling, S., Kunkel, T., Schumacher, K., & Zilger, M. (2004). Use of molluscs, fish and other marine taxa by tourism in Zanzibar, Tanzania. *Biodiversity & Conservation, 13,* 2623–2639.

Government of Mauritius. (2007). Mauritius in figures. http://www.gov.mu/portal/sites/ncb/cso/mif04/index.htm. (Accessed 7 February 2007.)

IUCN/UNEP. (1988). *Coral reefs of the World. UNEP Regional Seas Directories and Bibliographies.* Gland, Switzerland: IUCN and Cambridge: UL/UNEP, Nairobi, Kenya.

Lieseke, E., & Myers, R. (1994). *Coral reef fishes.* London: HarperCollins Publishers.

Lindén, O., & Sporrong, N. (1999). *Coral degradation in the Indian Ocean: Status reports and project presentations.* University of Stockholm, Sweden: CORDIO/SAREC Marine Science Program.

Lindén, O., Souter, D., Wilhelmsson, D., & Obura, D. (2002). *Coral reef degradation in the Indian Ocean: Status report 2002.* University of Kalmar, Sweden: CORDIO.

London, J. B. (2004). Implications of climate change on small island developing states: Experience in the Caribbean region. *Journal of Environmental Management and Planning, 47,* 491–501.

Mauritius Meteorological Services. (2005). Tropical storms/cyclones. http://metservice.intnet.mu/wcygen.htm. (Accessed 18 April 2005.)

Mauritius Tourism Promotion Authority (MTPA) and Ministry of Tourism and Leisure (MTL). (2004). Destination Mauritius 2004. Paphos-Cyprus: Stargazer Trading Co. Ltd.

Ministry of Tourism and Leisure. (2003). *Handbook of statistical data on tourism.* Mauritius: Port Louis.

Ministry of Tourism and Leisure. (2004). Overview of the tourism sector in Mauritius. http://ncb.intnet. mu/mot/overview.htm. (Accessed 1 December 2004.)

Ministry of Tourism and Leisure. (2005). International travel and tourism 2004. http://ncb.intnet.mu/cso/indicate.htm. (Accessed 3 April 2005.)

Mortensen, P. B., Hovland, M., Brattegard, T., & Farestveit, R. (1995). Deep water bioherms of the Scleractinian Coral *Lophelia pertusa (L.)* at 64N on the Norwegian shelf: Structure and associated megafauna. *Sarsia, 80,* 145–158.

Musa, G. (2002). Sipadan: A SCUBA-diving paradise: An analysis of tourism impact, diver satisfaction and tourism management. *Tourism Geographies, 4,* 195–209.

Nicholls, R. J. (2004). Coastal flooding and wetland loss in the 21st century: Changes under the SRES climate and socio-economic scenarios. *Global Environmental Change, 14,* 69–86.

Obura, D. (2005). East Africa summary. In: D. Souter, & O. Lindén (Eds), *Coral degradation in the Indian Ocean. Status report 2005* (pp. 25–31). University of Kalmar, Sweden: CORDIO.

Orams, M. (1999). *Marine tourism: Development, impacts and management.* London: Routledge.

Pauly, D., Christensen, V., Dalsgaard, J., Froese, R., & Torres, Jr. F. (1998). Fishing down marine food webs. *Science, 279,* 860–863.

Pillay, R. M., Terashima, H., Venkatasami, A., & Uchida, H. (2002). *Field guide to corals of Mauritius.* Albion, Mauritius: Ministry of Fisheries, Mauritius and Japan International Cooperation Agency.

Price, A. R. G., Sheppard, C. R. C., & Roberts, C. M. (1993). The gulf: Its biological setting. *Marine Pollution Bulletin, 27,* 9–15.

Talbot, F., & Wilkinson, C. (2001). *Coral reefs, mangroves and seagrasses: A sourcebook for managers.* Townsville: Australian Institute of Marine Science.

Terashima, H., Mosaheb, J. I., Chiranjiwa, N. P., & Vishwanitra, C. (2001). *Field guide to coastal fishes of Mauritius.* Albion, Mauritius: Ministry of Fisheries, Mauritius and Japan International Cooperation Agency.

van Treeck, P., & Schuhmacher, K. (1999). Mass diving tourism — A new dimension calls for new management approaches. *Marine Pollution Bulletin, 37,* 499–504.

United Nations (UN). (2005). Mauritius. http://www.un.org/special-rep/ohrlls/sid/SIDS-states/profiles/mauritius.htm. (Accessed 10 April 2005.)

Veron, J. E. N. (2000). *Corals of the World. Vol. 1–3.* Townsville, Australia: Australian Institute of Marine Science, CRR Old Pty Ltd.

Webster, P. J., Holland, G. J., Curry, J. A., & Chang, H.-R. (2005). Changes in tropical cyclone number, duration, and intensity in a warming environment. *Science, 309,* 1844–1846.

White, A., & Rosales, R. (2003). Community-oriented marine tourism in the Philippines: Role in economic development and conservation. In: S. Gössling (Ed.), *Tourism and development in tropical islands: Political ecology perspectives* (pp. 237–262). Cheltenham: Edward Elgar Publishing.

Wilkinson, C. (Ed.) (2002). *Status of coral reefs of the World: 2002.* Townsville: Australian Institute of Marine Science.

Wilkinson, C. (Ed.) (2004). *Status of coral reefs of the World: 2004.* Townsville: Australian Institute of Marine Science.

Wilkinson, C., Lindén, O., Cesar, H., Hodgson, G., Rubens, J., & Strong, A. E. (1999). Ecological and socio-economic impacts of 1998 coral mortality in the Indian Ocean — and ENSO impact and a warning for future change? *Ambio, 28,* 188–196.

World Tourism Organisation. (2001). *Tourism 2020 vision. Vol. 7. Global forecasts and profiles of market segments.* Madrid: WTO.

Chapter 5

Vulnerability of Marine Mammals to Diving Tourism Activities

Susanna Curtin and Brian Garrod

Introduction

Tourists are increasingly seeking out interactions with marine mammals, including various cetacean species (whales, dolphins and porpoises) and pinnipeds (sea lions and seals). These interactions can take place in captivity, semi-captivity or in the wild (Orams, 1999). In the wild, such encounters tend to take place within the context of a scuba-diving session or, increasingly, as part of a specialist 'swim-with' boat tour. During such tours, partici-pants are usually equipped with snorkel, mask and fins, and then dropped into the water alongside the animals. A number of negative impacts on the behaviour and physiology of marine mammals are thought to result from these activities and, in some parts of the world, various regulations and codes of conduct have been introduced in an attempt to manage such interactions. For example, in some instances the use of 'mermaid' lines is required. Mermaid lines are ropes of approximately 15 m length which are trailed out in the water behind the tour boat, along which divers are stationed at regular intervals (Photo 5.1). These enable swimmers to remain in contact with the vessel for safety reasons. They also make their movement more predictable, enabling the marine mammals to carry out the encounter more on their own terms. This chapter will review the scientific evidence on the vulnerability of free-ranging marine mammals to diving activities and assess the adequacy of the management policy response. Conclusions and recommendations for the improved management of interactions between human divers and marine mammals will then be drawn from this analysis.

The desire to encounter and interact with free-ranging marine mammals is intensifying in many tourist locations around the world. The reason for this escalation in demand has yet to be fully explained by the literature. Indeed, research on tourism motivations for diving

New Frontiers in Marine Tourism: Diving Experiences, Sustainability, Management
Copyright © 2008 by Elsevier Ltd.
All rights of reproduction in any form reserved.
ISBN: 978-0-08-045357-6

Photo 5.1: Dolphin swim with ropes, Port Phillip Bay, Victoria, Australia (Photograph: Carol Scarpaci, with thanks to the Earthwatch Volunteers).

and swimming with marine mammals in the wild is still in its infancy. However, there do seem to be a number of forces at work which instil in people a strong desire for interaction with marine mammals. Prominent among these is the social representation of marine mammals in the popular media and the tendency for tour operators to draw upon these popular images in the development of new products and the marketing of tourism attractions (Photo 5.2). It is clear, nevertheless, that marine mammals are poorly understood by the public at large, with a prevalence of utilitarian attitudes towards marine mammal species and a strong predisposition to interpret their behaviour anthropomorphically (Amante-Helweg, 1996; Barney, Mintzes, & Yen, 2005).

In 2003, the British Broadcasting Corporation (BBC) surveyed 20,000 Britons asking them to vote on the 50 things they thought people should do in their lifetime; swimming with dolphins ranked first (British Broadcasting Corporation, 2003). Cloke and Perkins (2005, p. 910) suggest that this is because they are subject to a range of "anticipatory knowledge and expectations" following exposure to powerful image constructions. Cetaceans, particularly dolphins, are frequently portrayed as mythical, intelligent, playful and sociable creatures which respond to human interaction (Carwardine, Hoyt, Fordyce, & Gill, 1998; Liddle, 1997). This depiction is repeated and confirmed through popular representations in art, literature and the media. It is therefore little wonder that the notion of

Photo 5.2: Snorkeller with humpback whale (*Megaptera novaeangliae*) (Photograph: Scott Portelli, with thanks to WhaleSwim Adventures www.whaleswim.com).

diving and swimming with dolphins as an exhilarating and unforgettable experience is firmly embedded in the tourist psyche. Major tour operators such as Thomson (2005) have been quick to respond to tourist demands and promote swimming with dolphins as a number-one, 'must-do' tourist activity. Indeed, even the briefest survey of tour operators' holiday brochures and web sites confirms that there is no shortage of enthusiasm on the part of the tourism suppliers to respond to this groundswell in demand.

Despite this advertising hype and the growth of new opportunities to develop tourism experiences based on interacting with marine mammals, Valentine, Birtles, Curnock, Arnold, and Dunstan (2004) maintain that the industry must ensure that marketing does not promote unrealistic expectations. In reality, satisfying tourist experiences cannot always be guaranteed. Amante-Helweg (1996) interviewed 306 people during swim-with-dolphins tours in the Bay of Islands, New Zealand, and found that 53% did not actually get to swim with dolphins. This did not, however, necessarily reduce their satisfaction with the trip. Conversely, Constantine and Baker's (1997) research on swim-with-dolphin tours in the same area found that only 60% of swim attempts with bottlenose dolphins and only 31% of swim attempts with common dolphins were actually 'successful' (success being defined as at least one dolphin being within five metres of a swimmer). The research also found that 48% of 'sustained encounters' with dolphins lasted an average of 4.2 min, while 24% lasted an average of 5.3 min. A study by Scarpaci, Dayanathi, and Corkeron (2003) of swim-with-dolphin tourism in Port Phillip Bay, Australia, meanwhile, found an average swim time by individual swimmers of just 3 min. Even for those who do actually get to swim with dolphins, therefore, the experience can be surprisingly ephemeral. Moreover, the embodied experience of swimming in sometimes cold, choppy and deep water requires a certain level of skill and spirit of adventure which tourists can find somewhat disturbing, especially in more remote and wild locations (Curtin, 2006).

There are a number of tourism destinations which are renowned for their opportunities to encounter marine mammals. Kaikoura in New Zealand is the best example of a destination that has had its existence transformed through marine mammal tourism based on a variety of cetacean species such as the sperm whale (*Physeter macrocephalus*), southern right whale (*Eubalaena australis*), humpback whale (*Megaptera novaeangliae*), dusky dolphin (*Lagenprhynchus obscurus*), Hector's dolphin (*Cephalorhynchus hectori*) and New Zealand fur seal (*Arctocephalus fosteri*). Other important destinations include the Galapagos Islands, where tourists can interact in the water with Californian seal lions (*Zalophus californianus*); Hawaii, where there are opportunities to encounter spinner dolphins (*Stenella longirostris*); Baja California in Mexico, where there are California sea lions (*Zalophus californianus*), bottlenose dolphins (*Tursiops truncatus*), common dolphins (*Delphinus delphis*), grey whales (*Eschrichtius ributus*), fin whales (*Balaenoptera physalus*), humpback whales (*Megaptera novaeangliae*) and blue whales (*Balaenoptera musculus*); the Canary Islands, which offers encounters with dense-beaked whales (*Mesoplodon densirostris*); and the Australian Great Barrier Reef, where tourists can interact with dwarf minke whales (*Balaenoptera bonaerensis*).

While there have been quite a few studies which indicate how tourists benefit from these enriching close encounters (see Box 5.1), there is also widespread concern about the consequences that these interactive tourist activities can have on marine mammals. In responding to the rapid growth in demand for diving and swim-with opportunities, operators and managers are faced with immense risks as "the subsequent impacts of these current levels of interaction with marine wildlife species remain unknown" (Wilson & Garrod, 2003, p. 9). Even tourists themselves indicate a concern for the impacts of diving and swimming with marine mammals associated with inappropriate behaviour on the part of tour providers and tourists, particularly those who try to chase or otherwise harass marine mammals (Valentine et al., 2004).

Box 5.1: How tourists benefit from encounters with marine mammals.

There is no doubt that marine mammals, and particularly dolphins, have a widespread contemporary appeal among tourists. Why this is should be so remains a moot point (Bulbeck, 2005). However, the fascination humans clearly hold for marine mammals has turned into a rapidly expanding, worldwide tourist activity, with a proliferation of opportunities to swim with wild cetacean populations throughout the world. While the intrusion of tourists into vulnerable marine settings has the potential to cause disturbance and long-term impacts on marine mammal populations, there is little doubt that the activity provides profound psychological benefits for tourists.

Firstly, close encounters with marine mammals have the ability to enhance tourist satisfaction and generate feelings or exhilaration caused by "the thrills and excitement of the moment" set in the "peace and tranquility of nature" (Muloin, 1998, p. 207). In certain situations, encounters with marine mammals have the ability to exceed all expectations. For example, Valentine et al. (2004) found a positive correlation between the closeness of a minke whale and the rating of overall satisfaction given that a high number of tourists did not expect to ever experience being so close to whales. This rendered the experience a 'once in a lifetime opportunity'.

Intrinsically motivated encounters with wild animals have long been recognised as a trigger for a heightened human experience. DeMares and Krycka (1998) found that respondents who had had a significant encounter with a whale or dolphin described emotions attributed to the notion of a 'peak experience', first espoused by Maslow (1968), in which they describe feelings of connectedness to self and life, harmony and aliveness, joy, exhilaration and excitement. This heightened state of well-being could be later remembered, re-lived and re-told in their everyday lives to help overcome or alleviate the tedium and disappointments of everyday existence; to reduce stress and to provide an emotional boost (DeMares & Krycka, 1998). For the human participant, therefore, there is a feeling of being permanently changed or enlightened by the experience.

During an encounter with cetaceans, many humans experience an immediate reduction in stress (Webb & Drummond, 2001; Bentrupperbäumer, 2005), as well as a sense of wonderment and a feeling of inner harmony and 'flow' (Csikszentmihalyi, 1990), where the awareness of self, particularly the ego, falls away and thoughts can run freely and creatively. Cloke and Perkins (2005, p. 907) refer to this cetacean-triggered peak experience as a "trophy moment" brought about "by the liminal and imaginative encounter" where the place becomes the stage and the cetaceans and the swimmer, the performance. Narratives depicting how tourists experienced swimming with dolphins in Kaikoura varied according to age, gender and adventurous, but Cloke and Perkins found that accounts were consistently very emotional. The participatory practice of swimming with cetaceans, rather than merely observing them, allows an active, embodied experience and a close, relational and spiritual encounter with an 'animal-other' which blurs the human–nonhuman divide in a "gleeful co-haunting whereby a spontaneous playfulness and corporeal connectivity transmutes the tourist experience into something more cosmic and spiritually instinctive" (Cloke & Perkins, 2005, p. 918). This is especially the case where eye contact is made or where the dolphin initiates the contact. DeMares and Krycka (1998, p. 169) explain that it is eye contact which determines 'connectedness' in the dolphin encounter as "one finds connection with another being when one sees oneself reflected in the other being's eyes".

Other researchers have identified the human need to be part of nature as an important determinant of the demand for close-up wildlife encounters (Bentrupperbäumer, 2005). As economic and social 'progress' had led us to lead lifestyles that are more urbanised and less directly connected to nature, so such needs have become increasingly unmet in our daily lives. Wildlife tourism, therefore, represents a means by which such needs can be satisfied. This perspective, sometimes known as the 'biophilia hypothesis' (Wilson, 1984) argues that humans have an inescapable need for contact with nature, although whether this need is innate to humans or learned through human experience remains a matter of some dispute (Knopf, 1987).

Finally, an increasingly important theme in research into the motivations for humans to seek interactions with wildlife is that of affiliation with animals (Bentrupperbäumer,

(Continued)

2005). Research has tended to focus mainly on the human desire for companionship that is often achieved through us keeping pets, there being notable psychological benefits to such relationships in the form of decreased levels of depression, decreased stress levels, reduced feelings of loneliness, and so on. It can be argued that such benefits can also be captured through interaction with wild animals. Other studies (e.g. Reynolds & Braithwaite, 2001; Tremblay, 2002) suggest that humans tend to be attracted to particular kinds of animals, particularly those that have a similar physiology to humans; appear to behave in human-like ways; hold aesthetic appeal in terms of colour, movement, shape and texture (the 'cute-and-cuddly' factor); and/or are rare or endangered (emphasising the unusual nature of such species, as well the degree of sympathy humans can feel for remaining members). Species that are strong in such attributes are sometimes known as 'charismatic megafauna' (Garrod & Wilson, 2004, see also Cater, Chapter 3, this volume) and the various species of marine mammal that are the subject of this chapter would certainly appear to match these criteria very well. A study by Woods (2000) ranked dolphins second in a list of young Australians' favourite animals. Whales ranked 10th most favourite while seals were 21st on the list. The domestic dog was ranked number one.

Research into the human dimension of swimming and interacting with cetaceans is still in its infancy. However, the limited number of studies already conducted suggests that the dynamics of the encounter become a cherished life experience, ranked in the mind of the human participant as among life's most memorable experiences.

There are serious concerns about the conservation status of many of the species that are the focus of interactive tourism programmes, and the potential for disturbance of their natural behavioural patterns is considered to be substantial (Orams, 2004). Dive-with and swim-with activities target at a number of marine mammal species worldwide and new programmes are initiated on a regular basis (Samuels, Bejder, Constantine, & Heinrich, 2000, 2003). This rapidly developing industry has attracted an amount of research and this has documented behavioural responses indicating possible negative impacts on the marine mammals involved, as well as potentially dangerous implications for divers and swimmers.

The Impact of Swimming with Free-Ranging Whales and Dolphins

The Whale and Dolphin Conservation Society (WDCS), a major non-government organisation interested in the conservation of cetacean species and based in the UK, does not condone tour programmes that offer diving and swimming with wild cetaceans and nor does it include such tours on its list of recommended cetacean tour operators (WDCS, 2005). This judgment was made on two main grounds. First, it is very difficult to ensure, even with responsible tour operators, that such encounters takes place on the whales' or dolphins' own terms. Secondly, the safety of the divers or swimmers cannot be guaranteed. Cetaceans, in spite of their 'human-friendly' portrayal, are large, powerful and unpredictable animals, which are capable of injuring people either by accident or, if they feel threatened, on purpose (Kirkwood et al., 2003; Orams, 1997). While there is a wealth of studies that show how the presence of tour vessels affect the behaviour of a range of different marine mammal species (see Lusseau & Higham, 2004, for a comprehensive review), research projects based on the responses of mammals when swimmers are present are still relatively few and far between. This is probably because the swim-with industry is a rather more recent tourism phenomenon. Meanwhile those looking specifically at the impacts of scuba divers are, to the authors' knowledge, non-existent. In view of the perhaps even greater potential that scuba diving has to impact adversely on marine mammals, for example through the potential to follow the animal under the surface of the water and to remain there longer than a swimmer or snorkeller would be able to, this is a serious gap in scientific knowledge. Some insights on the likely impacts of scuba diving on marine mammals can, nevertheless, be inferred from the studies that have been carried out on snorkellers and swimmers.

At least four seal species, namely Australian fur seals (*Arctocephalus pusillus*), New Zealand fur seals (*Arctocephalus fosteri*), Californian sea lions (*Zalophus californianus*) and grey seals (*Halichoerus grypus*), and 20 cetacean species are targeted by swim-with activities in various parts of the world. Dolphin species that are the focus of swim-with tours include the Atlantic spotted (*Stenella frontalis*), bottlenose (*Tursiops truncates*), common (*Delphinus delphis*), dusky (*Lagenprhynchus obscurus*), Hector's (*Cephalorhynchus hectori*), humpback (*Sousa teuszii*), Risso's (*Grampus griseus*), rough-toothed (*Steno bredanensis*), spinner (*Stenella longirostris*), striped (*Stenella coeruleoalba*) and tucuxi (*Sotalia fluvaitilis*). Whale species subject of swim-with tours include pilot (*Globicephala melas* and *Globicephala macrorhynchus*), false killer (*Pseudorca crassidens*), killer (*Orcinus orca*), minke (*Balaenoptera acutorostrata*), dwarf minke (*Balaenoptera bonaerensis*), sei (*Balaenoptera borealis*), dense-beaked (*Mesoplodon densirostris*) and sperm (*Physeter macrocephalus*) (Samuels et al., 2000). Some of these locations also offer opportunities to scuba dive with such species, while in other locations scuba diving with marine mammals is restricted by local regulations or national legislation. Table 5.1 provides some examples of organised tours in various parts of the world which involve people snorkelling and/or scuba diving with free-ranging marine mammals.

Potential impacts vary depending not only on the species concerned but also on the context in which the encounter takes place. Some involve free-ranging cetaceans that are 'lone or sociable' (Orams, 1997), others occur in food-provisioned locations (Samuels & Bejder, 2004). Some are with habituated animals (Orams, 1995; Weir, Dunn, Bell, & Chatfield, 1996), while others with non-habituated individuals (Samuels et al., 2000). Clearly, a one-time, chance encounter between tourists and an individual marine mammal is unlikely to have a major impact on the latter. However, the nature of the swim-with industry is such that specific communities and animals are repeatedly sought out for prolonged and close-up encounters (Samuels et al., 2000). Therefore, targeted animals are potentially at risk from the cumulative pressures of tourism. These situations can lead to chronic interactions that may compromise free-ranging marine mammals by disrupting natural behaviour such as maternal care, breeding, feeding and resting. All of these may ultimately result in decreased survival rates or reduced reproductive success. Furthermore, the very presence of swim-with operations increases the risk of vessel strikes, entanglement or harassment (Spradlin, Terbush, & Smullen, 1998). For a résumé of individual impact studies of swim-with activities see Table 5.2.

Table 5.1: Selected examples of swim-with free-ranging cetaceans and pinniped tours from around the world.

Location	Species involved	Notes
Cairns, Great Barrier Reef, Australia	Dwarf mink whales	Snorkelling and scuba tours
Porgy Bay, Bimini, Bahamas	Atlantic spotted and bottlenose dolphins	Human–dolphin 'connection program' includes swimming with wild dolphins
Marsa Alam, Red Sea, Egypt	Spinner dolphins	Snorkelling tours
Gansbaai, South Africa	Cape fur seas	Offered as part of an 11-day cage-diving tour focusing on sharks
Sodwana Bay, South Africa	Southern right and humpback whales	Scuba-diving with whales
Azores	Common dolphin, bottlenose dolphin, Risso's dolphin, spotted dolphin	Snorkelling tours
Tonga	Humpback whales	Snorkelling tours
Baird Bay, South Australia	Sea lions	Snorkelling tours
Bay Islands, Honduras	Bottlenose dolphins	Diving, snorkelling and swimming. Also a six-day 'dolphin scuba camp' for children
Akaroa, New Zealand	Hector's dolphin	Snorkelling tours
Cancun, Mexico	Bottlenose dolphins	Snorkelling and scuba diving tours
Panama City, Florida	Bottlenose dolphins	Snorkelling tours
Port Phillip Bay, Australia	Bottlenose dolphins and Australian fur seals	Snorkelling tours
Bay of Islands, New Zealand	Bottlenose and common dolphins	Snorkelling tours
Kaikoura, New Zealand	Dusky dolphins and New Zealand fur seals	Snorkelling tours
Rockingham, Bunbury and Mandurah, Western Australia	Bottlenose dolphins	Snorkelling tours

The ultimate goal of these impact studies is to determine the long-term responses that have a biological significance for the animals: in other words, how much energy is lost as a result of disturbance by swimmers. Energy loss may be direct, for example through the animal adopting avoidance behaviour, or indirect, for example by the animal being disturbed from feeding activities. Many impact studies look purely at the observable, short-term responses on the part of marine mammals. Measurable short-term responses include the following: vocal behaviour; non-vocal behaviour such as surfacing, ventilation and dive patterns; swim speed, course and orientation; group dispersion or cohesion; behavioural states and activity budgets (i.e. how much time is spent foraging, resting and socialising with members of the same species). However, it must be recognised that no real understanding presently exists of how these short-term responses are linked to long-term consequences (Bejder & Samuels, 2004). Indeed, both Lay (2000) and Orams (2004) highlight the need to consider the long-term effects of stress responses in cetaceans given that the relationship between stress and general health in other (non-marine) mammal species is well-documented. Such studies show that prolonged stress as a result the undue attentions of tourists has a very real potential to impact upon reproductive and immune systems. However, it is extremely difficult to gauge the levels of stress induced in marine mammals mainly because stressors tend to be either cumulative or delayed in the expression of their effects (Frohoff, 2004).

The nature of the linkage between short-term and long-term impacts is especially pertinent in the case of dusky dolphins (*Lagenprhynchus obscurus*), where they are under constant demand. Yin (1999) and Barr and Slooten (1998) found it very difficult to determine whether boats and swimmers affect dolphin behaviour when the length of time between successive encounters was so brief. Marine mammals typically take time to adjust and assume 'normal' behaviours after an encounter with humans, implying that almost all of the observations made by researchers represent modified behaviour. Similarly, research that adopts an observational platform aboard a commercial tour boat may only include dolphins that are tolerant of approaches (Bejder & Dawson, 1998), making before-and-after comparisons impossible (Wursig, 1996; Yin, 1999). This is a major concern as most of these studies occur after tourism development has taken place and are reactive as opposed to proactive. There are few destinations which embark on impact studies prior to development (Orams, 2004). In such cases, baseline data will simply be unavailable or unobtainable, and this prevents comparison of behaviour under experimental situations, such as in the presence of tourists, with behaviour prior to the commencement of anthropogenic activity or undisturbed conditions. Clearly a prerequisite for recognising 'disturbed behaviour' is a comprehensive inventory of 'normal' behaviour (Bejder & Samuels, 2004).

Unfortunately, even assessing normal behaviour is logistically challenging as cetaceans are wide-ranging and spend the majority of their time under the water in an environment which is difficult for humans to penetrate. This means that locating, following, observing and understanding dynamic behaviours are all fraught with difficulty (Lusseau & Higham, 2004). Quantifying the impacts of tourist encounters is compounded by the complexity and dynamic nature of the marine environment, as well as the marine mammals themselves, which present several methodological obstacles. Being able to recognise and study individuals, usually by photo-identification, is imperative to swim-with impact studies which are based purely on observation. Indeed, as Altmann (1974) indicates, an observer cannot monitor all the behaviour of all the individuals within a group. However, some cetaceans are found in groups over one hundred strong, making the recognition of individuals within the group extremely difficult (Mann, 1999).

Research is further complicated by the fact that marine mammal behaviour is often subtle, highly complex and dependent upon context (Mann, 2000). For instance there are

Table 5.2: Review of impact studies on swim-with activities.

Author(s)	Species	Key findings	Location
Arnold and Birtles (1998, 1999)	Dwarf minke whales	Whales initiated encounters with boats and swimmers, even slowing down and maintaining their position. Encounters often lasted an hour or more. Whales only exhibited disturbance behaviours when swimmers attempted to touch them.	Great Barrier Reef, Australia
Barr (1997)	Dusky dolphins	Dolphins were accompanied by tour vessels during 72% of the observation time. This resulted in an observed increase in aerial activity and the formation of tighter groups.	Kaikoura, New Zealand
Barr and Slooten (1998)	Dusky dolphins	10% of vessels approaching dolphins violated national Marine Mammal Protection Regulations.	Kaikoura, New Zealand
Bejder, Dawson and Harraway (1999)	Hector's dolphins	43% of in-water encounters were at least 'potentially disturbing', i.e. dolphins moved more than 200 m away within 5 min of an approach by swimmers. Dolphins were more tightly bunched when vessels were in the area.	Kaikoura, New Zealand
Constantine (1995, 1999, 2001, 2002)	Bottlenose dolphins	Method of placement of swimmers in the water affected dolphin responses. Tour operator success with swim attempts decreased from 48% to 31% between 1994/1995 and 1997/1998. Avoidance by dolphins of swim attempts increased from 22% to 31% over the same period. During swim attempts, juvenile dolphins were more likely to respond than adults. Estimated that the average dolphin was exposed to 31 swim attempts per year, a level of exposure which suggests that dolphins have become sensitised to swim attempts.	Bay of Islands, New Zealand

Reference	Species	Findings	Location
Constantine and Baker (1997)	Common and bottlenose dolphins	Differences detected between the species. Thirty-two percent of vessel approaches to bottlenose dolphins resulted in changes in group activity with feeding being the activity least likely to be disrupted and socialising most likely. Fifty-two percent of approaches to common dolphins were more likely to change resting behaviour as opposed to socialising behaviour. The 'line-abreast' (parallel) strategy of swimmer placement resulted in the lowest rate of avoidance but also the lowest rates of swim success as dolphins could continue past. In contrast, 'in-path' placement resulted in the highest rate of avoidance.	Bay of Islands, New Zealand
Constantine, Brunton and Baker (2003)	Bottlenose dolphins	Dolphins rested less and milling behaviour increased in the presence of boats. The change from discrete to staggered departure time and an increase in the number of departures was also related to decreased resting behaviour. The 'line-abreast' method of placing swimmers in the water was found to reduce avoidance behaviour.	Bay of Islands, New Zealand
Constantine and Yin (2003)	Bottlenose dolphins	Found that over time, the bottlenose dolphins in the Bay of Islands, New Zealand, have been interacting with swimmers less and avoiding them more.	Bay of Islands, New Zealand
Courbis (2004)	Spinner dolphins	Spinner dolphins in Hawaii were avoiding important areas for resting, nursing, socialising and mating because of the increased presence of swimmers in the water.	Hawaii

(Continued)

Table 5.2: *Continued*

Author(s)	Species	Key findings	Location
Forrest (1999)	Spinner dolphins	Resting and socialising were being disrupted due to the presence of increasing numbers of swimmers and kayakers.	Hawaii
Green and Calvez (1999)	Spinner dolphins	Changes to diurnal activity were found. In the morning dolphins were interactive with swimmers, while later on in the day there were many tourists and boats and the dolphins tended to avoid them.	Hawaii
Lusseau (2003)	Bottlenose dolphins	Dolphins were more sensitive to boats when they were resting and socialising.	Milford Sound, New Zealand
Mann and Smuts (1999)	Bottlenose dolphins	Studied provisioned wild dolphins in a human interaction area near the shore. Echelon swimming (i.e. the energetic benefits from swimming in contact with or in the slip stream of its mother) was common away from food-provisioned areas but the proportion of time calves spent in echelon-swim position decreased when the dolphins were in the provisioned-food area. Away from shore, mothers foraged and socialised more often than they did in the food-provisioned area.	Monkey Mia, Western Australia
Ritter and Brederlau (1999)	Beaked whales and sei whales	Recorded 38% of in-water encounters to be intense. Whales appeared to be highly curious and did not generally attempt to avoid swimmers.	The Canary Islands
Scarpaci, Bigger, Corkeron, and Nugegoda (2000)	Bottlenose dolphins	Whistle reproduction was found to be significantly greater in the presence of commercial swim-with boats, regardless of the dolphin's behavioural state prior to the arrival of the boats. This may indicate that social cohesion is affected by approaches.	Port Philip Bay, Australia

Reference	Species	Findings	Location
Weir et al. (1996)	Common and bottlenose dolphins	Sixty percent of swim attempts were successful but in only 17% of swims did dolphins interact with swimmers. In 33% of swims, dolphins responded to swimmers by avoidance or no change in behaviour. Extended observations revealed certain pods being disturbed for hours at a time without respite and in some cases dolphins were hemmed in by more than 20 boats.	Port Philip Bay, Australia
Yin (1999)	Dusky dolphins	Whistle rate increased when swimmers entered the water. Dolphins were more active and travelled further during the early afternoon sessions usually at a time when they normally rested.	Kaikoura, New Zealand

variations in cetacean behaviour depending on species, age, gender, reproductive status, individual characteristics and levels of habituation (Bejder & Samuels, 2004). In addition, spatial and temporal discontinuities and levels of natural variation compound accurate analysis of cause and effect (International Fund for Animal Welfare, 1995). There is the potential impact of the researcher, as most research on cetaceans is carried out from a vessel or with scuba equipment, and thus the presence of the researchers themselves may influence behaviour (Orams, 2004). Similar concerns prevail in the literature on the impacts of tourism on seal behaviour (Westcott & Stringell, 2003). Finally, as Samuels et al. (2000) point out, it is often difficult to disassociate cetaceans' responses to swimmers from their responses to the vessels bringing the swimmers to them.

The Impacts of Swimming with Seals and Sea Lions

Swimming with seals can be an integral part of a dolphin-swim tour because both encounter and success rates for seal swims tend to be more reliable. Sometimes encounter and swim success rates are even 100% for seals (Scarpaci et al., 2005). Swimming with seals thus provides an alternative activity that tourists can do in the event that cetaceans are not sighted. Because seals and sea lions are capable of hauling themselves out of the water, encounters with seals can be very close-up and sustained (Photo 5.3). The swim time with seals also tends to be significantly greater than for dolphin swims. For example, a study of swim-with operations targeted on Australian fur seals in Port Phillip Bay, Australia (Scarpaci et al., 2005) suggested that the average swim time for seals was 21.5 min, as opposed to only 2.6 min for swims with dolphins in the Bay.

There has, however, been less research conducted on the impact of swimming with seals and in many locations no regulations exist. What research does exists tends to suggest that seals are more likely to stay close to swimmers and that swimmers can actually swim towards seals, in contrast to the case with dolphin swims where swimmers tend to be placed parallel or 'line abreast' to moving dolphins. Scarpaci et al. (2005) are concerned that the lack of regulations or permits for seal swims gives the impression to tour operators that any behaviour is acceptable and also that their behaviour does not impact in any way on their ability to continue to conduct seal swims in the future. Tour operators tend to assume that the fact that the seals remain present in the area is an indication that tourist interaction is not impacting upon them. Surprisingly, however, little research interest seems to have been directed at whether seals are equally more tolerant of scuba divers.

Richardson, Greene, Malme, & Thomson (1995) report short-term disturbance on New Zealand fur seals (*Arctocephalus fosteri*), mostly in terms of temporary displacement from haul-out sites or increased vigilance by sitting up or moving away from the source of disturbance. Orsini, Shaughnessy, and Newsome (2006) notes similar impacts in respect of hauled-out Australian sea lion (*Neophoca cinera*) being approached by tourists. Seals have been known to become habituated to the presence of tour boats but this tends to depend on the reproductive status, age and experience of the individual animals concerned. In New Zealand, increasing number of tourists in Kaikoura has resulted in increased pressure on the seals found along exposed highways and viewing areas. In addition to land-based tour operators there are boat-based operators, with a maximum allowance of 154 trips per week. The cumulative effect of these boat tours, coupled with the disturbance along the

Photo 5.3: Tourists swimming with Australian fur seals (*Arctocephalus pusillus*) at Chinaman's Hat, Port Phillip Bay, Victoria, Australia (Photograph: Carol Scarpaci, with thanks to the Earthwatch Volunteers).

shoreline, is presently unknown. Seals hauled out along this coast have been subjected to close approaches by land-based visitors, but when attempting to avoid the disturbance by entering the sea they have then encountered guided swim-with-seal tourists. Constantine (1999) warns that such persistent disturbance could result in aggressive responses by the animals, such as charging and biting. This type of disturbance has also been shown to affect reproduction. Lidgard (1996) noted a preference by seals to give birth in areas of low disturbance. Females in areas of high disturbance often give birth later in the season and had a shorter lactation period and subsequent reduced growth rate for pups. Similar research on harbour seals (*Phoca vitulina*) in California found that females hauling out at disturbed sites had lower pup production and higher pup mortality than those at non-disturbed sites (Allen & King, 1992).

It is clear that there are considerable issues with regards to the swim-with industry and that impact studies are still in their infancy. Despite this, Samuels et al. (2000) suggest that sufficient information is in fact available on cetaceans to make management recommendations to the industry and to government bodies. Constantine's work on bottlenose dolphins in the Bay of Islands, New Zealand, represents the most prolonged study of swim-with programmes (covering the period 1995 to the present). Her findings have proved critical in implementing appropriate management plans that take a long-term and precautionary perspective.

Management of Swimmers

There are a number of important conditions recommended in the context of marine mammal swim-with tourism that endeavour to lessen its negative impacts. A number of restrictions are enforced in various locations (notably Queensland, Australia; Western Australia; New Zealand and the USA). Scarpaci et al. (2003, 2004) note that these include regulations governing the type of approach (i.e. how the tour boat approaches the animals), how swimmers are placed in the water; the length of swim time; the total time the boat is in close proximity to the dolphins; the number of swimmers in the water at any one time; and the insistence that swims do not take place in the presence of 'foetal fold' calves (a foetal fold calve is defined an individual that was closely associated with a fully grown dolphin and was either one-third the size of its accompanying adult or had visible foetal folds). In some cases, it is illegal for tourists to swim freely with whales or dolphins (Arnold & Birtles, 1999). Instead swimmers are instructed to hold on to a mermaid line at all times. This enables the cetacean to decide on the length and intensity of the encounter it desires, and prevents swimmers from harassing marine mammals (Valentine et al., 2004). It also helps to ensure the safety of swimmers while in the water (Scarpaci et al., 2004).

How vessels approach marine mammals is also sometimes stipulated. In New Zealand, it is illegal to cut across the path of travel of a cetacean. A parallel (or 'line-abreast') strategy is the only approach that provides the mammals with a voluntary choice whether or not to interact with either the tour boat or swimmers placed in the water. This contrasts with a direct approach, when a tour vessel manoeuvres directly into the pod, or a 'J' approach, when a vessel begins by travelling parallel to the movement of the dolphins but then passes them at a distance and turns directly into their path.

Constantine (1995) found that the manner in which swimmers were placed in the water had a significant influence on how bottlenose and common dolphins responded. For example, if swimmers were placed directly in the path of the dolphins' travel, or deposited directly into the pod of dolphins as they were grouping, the dolphins were more likely to avoid the swimmers than when they were placed parallel to the dolphins' line of travel. Later, both Constantine and Baker (1997) and Weir et al. (1996) found that the approach techniques which afford the greatest swim success also caused the highest level of avoidance deemed to be symptomatic of disturbance or stress. The line-abreast strategy resulted in the lowest rate of avoidance by the dolphins but also has a lower rate of sustained interaction (Constantine, 1999). Clearly, it is a question of ensuring that dolphins' well-being is put before maximising swim success. Other methods to reduce impacts include safeguarding dolphins' midday rest periods (Yin, 1999), turning off boat engines when the dolphins were present (Barr, 1997) and the instigation of protected areas where dolphins can take refuge (Samuels et al., 2000). In view of Weir et al.'s (1996) observations of pods of dolphins being disturbed for hours at a time without respite and being hemmed in by several boats, the latter point of creating protected zones is worthy of further attention.

In their study of the bottlenose dolphins in Doubtful Sound, Lusseau and Higham (2004) suggest that a delineation of multi-levelled marine sanctuaries may be an effective approach to managing the impacts of tourism on cetaceans by decreasing the probability of anthropogenic impacts. The establishment of sanctuaries usually relies on abundance information and tends to be in locations where the highest numbers of animals are present.

Of course there is a commercial dilemma involved here, as these are likely to be areas where interaction can be more guaranteed and are therefore likely to attract commercial tours. The only way to appease all parties and to achieve acceptance and adherence is thus to establish a compromise which protects the dolphins as well as meeting the needs of the local communities and operators who benefit from tourist interactions. To that end, multi-level marine sanctuaries may be the answer. Here, various regulations are imposed within specific zones. For example, Lusseau (2003) discovered that bottlenose dolphins (*Tursiops truncatus*) were particularly vulnerable to disturbance when they were socialising and resting, so tourist interactions would be totally eliminated in zones that are mainly used by the dolphins for these purposes. Lusseau and Higham (2004) also propose a second level of restriction, which are zones that are only accessible to researchers and permitted operators and thereby afford some degree of protection.

Adherence to these restrictions, even when licences and permits are dependent upon compliance, cannot however be guaranteed (Orams, 2004). Owing to the remoteness of some locations, enforcement of regulations and policing activities is difficult and expensive (Lusseau & Higham, 2004). Whereas permit holders understand the regulations, non-permitted marine-tour operators and private recreational vessels are seldom aware of any restrictions and may therefore "impose themselves upon the animals in an inappropriate way" (Orams, 2004, p. 24). Prosecution of non-permitted operators can only occur where intentional interactions with dolphin schools can be demonstrated. Without policing, even permits become a weak management tool as permit holders frequently complain that any operator can freely access the site without repercussions. On top of this, permit holders can find themselves at a commercial disadvantage because they are bound to national responsibilities, an extra level of management, and are prevented from expanding the number of boats and/or trips. Lastly, Scarpaci et al. (2004) found that any ambiguity in the regulations meant a lack of compliance and that operators are more likely to adhere to conditions that are easily quantified.

Conclusions

While some attempts have been made to help lessen the impacts, Gales (1999) confirms that the management of commercial swim-with-dolphin programmes has proceeded without clear scientific guidance. Present regulations and conditions that attempt to reduce impacts may, in the long term, be totally inadequate given that the demand and growth of this industry has significantly outstripped the ability of scientists to develop and implement research methods that provide a sound basis for management policies. Current understanding of the effects of swim-with activities on free-ranging marine mammals is far from satisfactory. Meanwhile scientific knowledge on the impact of scuba-diving tourism operations is effectively absent. Clearly there is a need for baseline and longitudinal data on which to measure the limits of acceptable change and to propose suitable protection for marine mammal species that are the subject of attention by tourism operators. Such research needs to be both species-specific and location-specific, given that generic management policies for marine mammal tourism are seldom appropriate (International Whaling Commission, 2000; Orams, 2004). Such research needs to investigate scuba-diving activities as well as swim-with programmes. Until these findings are at hand, providing protected areas is the only convincing solution to ensure that marine mammals can have some respite from tour vessels so that they can rest and resume their 'normal' behaviours.

It could be that diving and swimming with marine mammals represent 'a step too far' in the portfolio of wildlife tourism products. Intrusive tourist activity is not condoned by the Travel Foundation (2006), which stipulates that free contact between visitors and wildlife should be actively discouraged. In the context of marine-based wildlife interactions, they recommend that operators and regulators uphold a policy of wildlife approaching humans rather than humans approaching wildlife, so as to avoid stressing animals. This requires maintaining a safe distance for the visitor and animal alike, so that the latter remain undisturbed while the former gain a satisfying tourism experience. This 'look, but don't touch' policy is based on the concept of sustainable wildlife watching, as opposed to the current demand for close-up, personal encounters with marine mammals.

References

Allen, S. G., & King, M. C. (1992). Tomales Bay harbor seals: A colony at risk. In: *Proceedings of the third biennial state of the Tomales Bay conference* (pp. 35–39). Inverness: Inverness Foundation, California.

Altmann, J. (1974). Observational study of behaviour: Sampling methods. *Behaviour, 49*, 227–267.

Amante-Helweg, V. (1996). Ecotourists' beliefs and knowledge about dolphins and the development of cetacean ecotourism. *Aquatic Mammals, 22*, 131–140.

Arnold, P. W., & Birtles, R. A. (1998). *Towards sustainable management of the developing dwarf minke whale tourism in Northern Queensland.* International Whaling Commission Scientific Committee, SC/50/WW1.

Arnold, P. W., & Birtles, R. A (1999). *Towards sustainable management of the developing dwarf minke whale tourism in Northern Queensland.* CRC Reef Research Centre, Great Barrier Reef Marine Park. Report No. 27.

Barney, E. C., Mintzes, J. J., & Yen, C. F. (2005). Assessing knowledge, attitudes and behaviour toward charismatic megafauna: The case of dolphins. *Journal of Environmental Education, 36*, 41–55.

Barr, K. (1997). *The impacts of marine tourism on the behaviour and movement patterns of dusky dolphins (Lagenorhynchus obscurus) at Kaikoura, New Zealand.* MSc Thesis. Dunedin, New Zealand: University of Otago.

Barr, K., & Slooten, E. (1998). *Effects of tourism on dusky dolphins at Kaikoura.* International Whaling Commission Scientific Committee, SC/50/WW10.

Bejder, L., & Dawson, S. M. (1998). *Responses by Hector's dolphins to boats and swimmers in Porpoise Bay, New Zealand.* International Whaling Commission Scientific Committee, SC/50/WW11.

Bejder, L. S., Dawson, S. M., & Harraway, J. A. (1999). Responses by Hector's dolphins to boats and swimmers in Porpoise Bay, New Zealand. *Marine Mammal Science, 15*, 738–750.

Bejder, L., & Samuels, A. (2004). Evaluating the effects of nature-based tourism on cetaceans. In: N. Gales, M. Hindell, & R. Kirkwood (Eds), *Marine mammals, fisheries, tourism and management issues* (pp. 229–256). Collingwood: CSIRO Publishing.

Bentrupperbäumer, J. (2005). Human dimension of wildlife interactions. In: D. Newsome, R. Dowling, & S. Moore (Eds), *Wildlife tourism.* Clevedon: Channel View.

British Broadcasting Corporation. (2003). *Fifty things to do before you die* (accessed 29 November 2006: http://news.bbc.co.uk/i/hi/programmes/breakfast).

Bulbeck, C. (2005). *Facing the wild: Ecotourism, conservation and animal encounters*. London: Earthscan.

Carwardine, M., Hoyt, E., Fordyce, R. E., & Gill, P. (1998). *Whales & dolphins: The ultimate guide to marine mammals*. London: Harper Collins.

Cloke, P., & Perkins, H. C. (2005). Cetacean performance and tourism in Kaikoura, New Zealand. *Environment and Planning D: Society and Space, 23*, 903–924.

Constantine, R. L. (1995). *Monitoring the commercial swim-with-dolphin operations with the bottlenose (Tursiops truncates) and common dolphins (Delphinus delphis) in the Bay of Islands, New Zealand*. Masters Thesis. University of Auckland, New Zealand.

Constantine, R. (1999). *Effects of tourism on marine mammals in New Zealand*. Science for Conservation: 106. Wellington, New Zealand: Department of Conservation.

Constantine, R. (2001). Increased avoidance of swimmers by wild bottlenose dolphins (*Tursiops truncatus*) due to long-term exposure to swim-with-dolphin tourism. *Marine Mammal Science, 17*, 689–702.

Constantine, R. L. (2002). *The behavioural ecology of bottlenose dolphins (Tursiops truncates) of Northeast New Zealand: A population exposed to tourism*. PhD Thesis, University of Auckland, New Zealand.

Constantine, R., & Baker, C. S. (1997). *Monitoring the commercial swim-with-dolphin operations in the Bay of Islands*. Science for Conservation: 56. Wellington, New Zealand: Department of Conservation.

Constantine, R., Brunton, D. H., & Baker, C.S. (2003). Effects of tourism on behavioural ecology of bottlenose dolphins in Northeast New Zealand. DOC Science Internal Series 153. Wellington, New Zealand: Department of Conservation.

Constantine, R. L., & Yin, S. (2003). Swimming with dolphins in New Zealand. In: T. Frohoff & B. Peterson (Eds), *Between species* (pp. 257–263). San Francisco, CA: Sierra Club Books.

Courbis, S. S. (2004). *Behaviour of Hawai'ian spinner dolphins (Stenella longirostris) in response to vessels/swimmers*. Masters Thesis, San Franciso State University, CA.

Csikszentmihalyi, M. (1990). *Flow: The psychology of optimal experience*. New York: Harper & Row Publishers.

Curtin, S. C. (2006). Swimming with dolphins: A phenomenological exploration of tourist recollections. *International Journal of Tourism Research, 8*, 301–315.

DeMares, R., & Krycka, K. (1998). Wild animal triggered peak experiences: Transpersonal aspects. *Journal of Transpersonal Psychology, 30*, 161–177.

Forrest, A. M. (1999). The Hawaiian spinner dolphin, *Stenella longirostris*: Effects of tourism. In: K. M. Dudzinski, T. G. Frohoff, & T. R. Spradlin (Eds), *Wild dolphin swim program workshop*, 13th biennial conference on the biology of marine mammals, Maui, Hawaii, November 1999.

Frohoff, T. G. (2004). Stress in dolphins. *Encyclopaedia of animal behaviour* (pp. 1158–1164). Westport, CT: Greenwood Press.

Gales, N. (1999). An overview of the management of commercial swim-with-dolphin programs in Australia. In: K. M. Dudzinski, T. G. Frohoff, & T. R. Spradlin (Eds), *Wild dolphin swim program workshop*, 13th biennial conference on the biology of marine mammals, Maui, Hawaii, November 1999.

Garrod, B., & Wilson, J. C. (2004). Nature on the Edge? Marine ecotourism in peripheral coastal areas. *Journal of Sustainable Tourism, 12*, 95–120.

Green, M., & Calvez, L. (1999). Research on Hawaiian spinner dolphins in Kealakekua Bay, Hawaii. In: K. M. Dudzinski, T. G. Frohoff, & T. R. Spradlin (Eds), *Wild dolphin swim program workshop*, 13th biennial conference on the biology of marine mammals. Maui, Hawaii, November 1999.

International Fund for Animal Welfare. (1995). *Report of the workshop on the scientific aspects of managing whale-watching*. International Fund for Animal Welfare (IFAW), Tethys and Europe Conservation, Montecastello di Viblo, Italy 30th March–4th April 1995.

International Whaling Commission. (2000). *Report of the scientific committee, 52nd meeting of the International Whaling Commission,* Adelaide, June 2000.

Kirkwood, R., Boren, L., Shaughnessy, P., Szteren, D., Mawson, P., Huckstadt, L., Hofmeyr, G., Oosthuizen, H., Schiavani, A., Campagna, C., & Berris, M. (2003). Pinniped-focused tourism in the southern hemisphere: A review of the industry. In: N. Gales, M. Hindell, & R. Kirkwood (Eds), *Marine mammals, fisheries, tourism and management issues* (pp. 257–276). Collingwood: CSIRO Publishing.

Knopf, R. (1987). Human behavior, cognition, and affect in the natural environment. In: D. Stokols, & I. Altman (Eds), *Handbook of environmental psychology.* Vol. 2 (pp. 783–826). New York: John Wiley & Sons.

Lay, D. C. (2000). Consequences of stress during development. In: G. P. Moberg, & J. A. Mench (Eds), *The biology of animal stress: Basic principles and implications for animal welfare* (pp. 249–267). Wallingford: CABI Publishing.

Liddle, M. (1997). *Recreational ecology.* London: Chapman & Hall.

Lidgard, D. C. (1996). *The effects of human disturbance on the maternal behaviour and performance of grey seals (Halichoerus grypus) at Donna Nook, Lincolnshire, U.K.* Preliminary Report to the British Ecological Society, UK.

Lusseau, D. (2003). Effects of tour boats on the behaviour of bottlenose dolphins: Using Markov chains to model anthropogenic impacts. *Conservation Biology, 17,* 1785–1793.

Lusseau, D., & Higham, J. E. S. (2004). Managing the impacts of dolphin-based tourism through the definition of critical habitats: The case of bottlenose dolphins in Doubtful Sound, New Zealand. *Tourism Management, 25,* 657–667.

Mann, J. (1999). Behavioural sampling methods for cetaceans: A review and critique. *Marine Mammal Science, 15,* 102–122.

Mann, J. (2000). Unravelling the dynamics of social life. In: J. Mann, R. C. Connor, P. L. Tyack, & H. Whitehead (Eds), *Cetacean societies: Field studies of dolphins and whales* (pp. 45–64). Chicago: University of Chicago Press.

Mann, J., & Smuts, B. (1999). Behavioural development in wild bottlenose dolphin newborns *Tursiops sp. Behaviour, 136,* 529–566.

Maslow, A. (1968). *Towards a psychology of being.* New York: Van Nostrand Reinhold.

Muloin, S. (1998). Wildlife tourism: The psychological benefits of whale watching. *Pacific Tourism Review, 2,* 199–213.

Orams, M. B. (1995). Towards a more desirable form of ecotourism. *Tourism Management, 16,* 3–8.

Orams, M. B. (1997). Historical accounts of human–dolphin interaction and recent developments in wild dolphin based tourism in Australasia. *Tourism Management, 18,* 317–325

Orams, M. (1999). *Marine tourism: Development, impacts and management.* London: Routledge.

Orams, M. B. (2004). Why dolphins may get ulcers: Considering the impacts of cetacean-based tourism in New Zealand. *Tourism in Marine Environments, 1,* 17–28.

Orsini, J.-P., Shaughnessy, P. D., & Newsome, D. (2006). Impacts of human visitors on Australian sea lions (*Neophoca cinerea*) at Carnac Island, Western Australia: Implications for tourism management. *Tourism in Marine Environments, 3,* 101–115.

Reynolds, P. C., & Braithwaite, R. W. (2001). Towards a conceptual framework for wildlife tourism. *Tourism Management, 22,* 31–42.

Richardson, W. J., Greene, C. R., Malme, C. I., & Thomson, D. H. (1995). *Marine mammals and noise.* San Diego, CA: Academic Press.

Ritter, F., & Brederlau, B. (1999). Behavioural observations of dense beaked whales (*Mesoplodon densirostris*) off La Gomera, Canary Islands (1995–1997). *Aquatic Mammals, 25,* 55–61.

Samuels, A., & Bejder, L. (2004). Chronic interaction between humans and free-ranging bottlenose dolphins near Panama City Beach, Florida, USA. *Journal of Cetacean Research Management, 6,* 69–77.

Samuels, A., Bejder, L., Constantine, R., & Heinrich, S. (2003). Swimming with wild cetaceans, with a special focus on the Southern Hemisphere. In: N. Gales, M. Hindell, & R. Kirkwood (Eds), *Marine mammals, fisheries, tourism and management issues* (pp. 277–303). Collingwood: CSIRO Publishing.

Samuels, A., Bejder, L., & Heinrich, S. (2000). *A review of the literature pertaining to swimming with wild dolphins*. Marine Mammal Commission, Bethesda, Maryland, US. Contract Number T74463123.

Scarpaci, C., Bigger, S. W., Corkeron, P. J., & Nugegoda, D. (2000). Bottlenose dolphins (*Tursiops truncatus*) increase whistling in the presence of "swim-with-dolphin" tour operations. *Journal of Cetacean Research and Management, 2*, 183–185.

Scarpaci, C., Dayanathi, D., & Corkeron, P. J. (2003). Compliance with regulations by 'swim-with dolphin' operators in Port Phillip Bay, Victoria, Australia. *Environmental Management, 31*, 324–347.

Scarpaci, C., Dayanathi, D., & Corkeron, P. J. (2004). No detectable improvement in compliance to regulations by 'swim-with dolphin' operators in Port Phillip Bay, Victoria, Australia. *Tourism in Marine Environments, 1*, 41–48.

Scarpaci, C., Nugegoda, D., & Corkeron, P. J. (2005). Tourists swimming with Australian fur seals (*Arctocephalus Pusillus*) in Port Phillip Bay, Victoria, Australia: Are tourists at risk? *Tourism in Marine Environments, 1*, 89–95.

Spradlin, T. R., Terbush, A. D., & Smullen, W. S. (1998). NMFS update on human/dolphin interactions in the wild. *Soundings, 23*, 25–27.

Thomson. (2005). *Top 10 'must do' things'* Thomson' (TUI) In-flight Brochure.

Travel Foundation. (2006). Guide to good practice for wildlife tourism (accessed 29 November 2006: https://taw.bournemouth.ac.uk/exchweb/bin/redir.asp?URL=http://www.thetravelfoundation.org.uk/tools_training_guidelines.asp).

Tremblay, P. (2002). Tourism wildlife icons: Attractions or marketing symbols? *Journal of Hospitality and Tourism Management, 9*, 164–180.

Valentine, P. S., Birtles, A., Curnock, M., Arnold, P., & Dunstan, A. (2004). Getting closer to whales: Passenger expectations and experiences and the management of swim with dwarfe minke whale interactions in the Great Barrier Reef. *Tourism Management, 25*, 647–655.

Webb, N. L., & Drummond, P. D. (2001). The effect of swimming with dolphins on human well-being and anxiety. *Anthrozoos, 14*, 81–85.

Weir, J., Dunn, W., Bell, A., & Chatfield, B. (1996). *An investigation into the impact of "dolphin-swim ecotours" in Southern Port Phillip Bay*. Hampton, Victoria, Australia: Dolphin Research project Inc.

Westcott, S. M., & Stringell, T. B. (2003). *Grey seal distribution and abundance in north wales*. Marine Monitoring Report No.13. Countryside Council for Wales.

Whale and Dolphin Conservation Society. (2005). The Whale and Dolphin Conservation Society (WDCS) (accessed 20 June 2005: http://www.wdcs.org/dan/publishing.nsf/allweb).

Wilson, E. O. (1984). *Biophilia*. Cambridge: Harvard University Press.

Wilson, J. C., & Garrod, B. (2003). Introduction. In: B. Garrod, & J. C. Wilson (Eds), *Marine ecotourism: Issues and experiences* (pp. 1–11). Clevedon: Channel View Publications.

Woods, B. (2000). Beauty and the beast: Preferences for animals in Australia. *Journal of Tourism Studies, 11*, 25–35.

Wursig, B. (1996). Swim with dolphin activities in nature: Weighing the pros and cons. *Whalewatcher, 30*, 11–15.

Yin, S. E. (1999). *Movement patterns, behaviours, and whistle sounds of dolphin groups off Kaikoura, New Zealand*. Masters Thesis, Texas: A&M University.

Chapter 6

Environmental Management and Education: The Case of PADI*

Anna Lindgren, Jessica Palmlund, Ida Wate and Stefan Gössling

Introduction

Diving tourism has been characterised by rapid growth over the past 15 years, and there are now estimated to be several million active divers worldwide (e.g. World Tourism Organization (WTO), 2001). In a number of dive destinations this has caused increasing pressure on the marine environment. Divers are rarely the sole cause for environmental change in marine ecosystems but as reported in numerous publications, they can be significant factors of disturbance and damage (e.g. Barker & Roberts, 2004; Hawkins & Roberts, 1993; Hawkins et al., 1999; Shackley, 1998; Tratalos & Austin, 2001; Zakai & Chadwick-Furman, 2002). Dive centres, usually including a dive school and a tour-operator business, have a central function in the management of diver behaviour. They provide information on environmentally harmful activities. They are also in a position to actively influence diver behaviour under water, both through the training of divers and intervention by dive leaders (Barker & Roberts, 2004; Medio, Ormond, & Pearson, 1997). However, this often means that a balance has to be achieved between economic and ecological goals, i.e. the maximisation of diver numbers is to some extent at odds with the minimisation of environmental impacts. In adding to discussions of corporate social responsibility (Townsend, Chapter 7, this volume), regulation (Barker & Roberts, Chapter 9, this volume) and education as conservation tool (Townsend, Chapter 10, this volume), this chapter discusses corporate perspectives on environmental responsibility. Based on an assessment of

*None of the authors has at any time worked for or is currently working for PADI or other dive organisations. The chapter has been written without the knowledge, consent or cooperation of PADI, and the views presented are entirely our own.

the integration of environmental aspects in educational materials by the Professional Association of Diving Instructors (PADI), the world's largest dive organisation, as well as a discussion of the understanding of dive operators and dive organisations of environmental management, the chapter outlines structural weaknesses of the current diver-certification system, and makes recommendations for improvements.

Environmental Impacts of Diving

Diving is seldom the only factor affecting the state of marine environments, and it is arguably of secondary importance in comparison to other impacts (Rouphael & Hanafy, 2007). Coral reefs, for instance, are threatened by sediments, chemicals and sewage, destructive fishing practices and engineering modification of shorelines, as well as various dimensions of climate change including sea-level rise, increasing seawater temperatures and the potentially negative consequences of more acidic waters (Wilkinson, 2004; see also Gössling et al., Chapter 4 this volume). These environmental changes pose serious threats to marine environments, with about one quarter of the world's coral reefs being under imminent risk of collapse through human activities and another 26% being under longer-term threats (Wilkinson, 2004).

Diving has become a global activity, with virtually no marine environments left unvisited by divers, even though dive activities are evidently focused on tropical waters and coral reef ecosystems. Marine ecosystems can be affected by a single careless diver, if he or she walks on or breaks corals, but problems seem to aggregate in spots where diving is concentrated and where disturbances and damage add together, resulting in measurable impacts. For instance, Walters and Samways (2001) report that Sodwana Bay, South Africa receives 80,000 dives per year, while Zakai and Chadwick-Furman (2002) even give figures of 250,000 dives per year on a 12 km stretch of coastline at Eilat on the Red Sea, with the most heavily visited sites receiving 30,000 dives per year. Tratalos and Austin (2001) estimate that sites in Grand Cayman see up to 17,800 divers per year. At the same time it has been estimated that, for some coral reefs, considerably fewer dives per year (4000–6000) can cause significant changes in marine environments (e.g. Dixon, Fallon Scura, & van't Hof, 1993; Hawkins et al., 1999; see also van Treeck and Eisinger, Chapter 8, this volume).

The scientific literature lists a considerable number of diver-related impacts. These might not always be the primary reason for environmental degradation in a given area, but they might combine with other impacts. In areas where diver activities are concentrated, such impacts may themselves be significant factors of environmental change. Table 6.1 provides an overview of the impacts divers can have on marine environments, including breakage of corals caused by kicking with fins, touching with hands, holding onto substrate with hands or resting against substrate with knees; contact with gear; trampling; or indirect damage caused by anchors. Other diver-related impacts include the raising of sediments through fins, behavioural change and altered feeding habits of marine fauna (e.g. stingrays and sharks), as well as skin abrasion (e.g. stingrays), and disturbances caused by diving with marine mammals (see Curtin and Garrod, Chapter 5, this volume). While never investigated scientifically, the collection of marine organisms such as crustaceans

Table 6.1: Impacts of diving on marine environments.

Impact	Source
Breakage, degradation of corals	Barker and Roberts (2004), Garrabou, Sala,
• Kicking with fins	Arcas, and Zabala (1998), Hawkins et al.
• Touching with hands	(1999), Muthiga and McClanahan (1997),
• Holding onto substrate with hands	Rouphael and Inglis (1995, 1997, 2001,
• Resting against substrate with knees	2002), Roberts and Harriott (1994), Talge
• Contact with gear	(1992), Tratalos and Austin (2001), Zakai
• Trampling (reef flats)	and Chadwick-Furman (2002)
• Anchor damage	
Raising of sediments	Zakai and Chadwick-Furman (2002)
Behavioural change, altered feeding	Shackley (1998), Cater (Chapter 3, this
habits (stingrays, sharks)	volume)
Skin abrasion (stingrays)	Shackley (1998)
Diving with marine mammals	Curtin and Garrod (Chapter 5, this volume)

(for seafood) or ornamental shells (for souvenirs) might also be counted as a diving-related environmental change, even though these activities tend to be confined to commercial diving and the sale of marine species (see Gössling, Kunkel, Schumacher, & Zilger, 2004). Likewise, there might also be various boat-related impacts, such as spills of engine residues that are, to our knowledge, not dealt with in the scientific literature. More generally, *in situ* studies have shown that impacts of diving are complex and site-specific, depending on disturbance regimes, reef structure, and the specific characteristics of reef communities (Hawkins et al., 1999).

The above list of diver-related environmental impact studies indicates that research has so far been site-specific. As climate change already affects marine environments, and will become increasingly important for marine ecosystems in the future (see Wilkinson, 2004), tourism's contribution to climate change should be added to the list as an important global factor of environmental change to which tourism contributes (Gössling, 2002; Gössling, Borgström-Hansson, Hörstmeier, & Saggel, 2002). Diving tourism in particular appears to be energy-intense (see Box 6.1), resulting in fundamentally unsustainable emissions of greenhouse gases if calculated on a per-diver basis.

Environmental management could help to address the problems outlined above. Dive organisations can promote environmental awareness in general terms, for instance on their websites and in their marketing materials, by pointing out the critical state of marine environments, and by involving their members in pro-environmental actions. Dive organisations can also incorporate environmental issues in the curricula of both dive instructors and divers. This can be done through various measures and on several educational levels. First, the need for environmental action can be addressed in a general way in diver education. This can create *awareness* of the need for action among the members of dive organisations. Second, the individual environmental *knowledge* of dive instructors and divers can help to minimise impacts, as divers will know which actions cause harm to marine ecosystems and

Box 6.1: Diving and climate change

It is now widely recognised that tourism transport accounts for a large and growing share of greenhouse gas emissions in industrialised countries. Recent mobility studies all indicate that there are huge gaps between current mobility trends and sustainable transport scenarios (e.g. Åkerman & Höjer, 2006; Bows, Anderson, & Upham, 2006; Peeters, van Egmond, & Visser, 2004). In particular, long-distance travel has been shown to entail substantial energy use (see Gössling et al., 2002). This box provides an estimate of an individual dive holiday's contribution to climate change.

Transport to Destination

Cater (Chapter 3, this volume) suggests that divers move through a travel career, which includes seeing a number of 'must-do' dive destinations around the world. Websites such as Cyber Diver (2006) or Scuba Travel (2006a, 2006b), provide rankings of the top dive sites worldwide. According to these websites, top dive sites are to be found in Australia, Belize, Ecuador, New Guinea, Fiji, Mozambique, Egypt, Maldives, Costa Rica, Micronesia, Malaysia, Hawaii and Indonesia. These locations might not be representative of the most popular global destinations (in terms of visitor numbers), but they indicate the predominance of tropical destinations. Divers, on the other hand, are mostly registered in Western countries. Consequently, for the majority of divers, visiting top diving sites involves long-haul travel. For instance, out of the 100 best dive sites in the world as suggested by UK-based Scuba Travel (2006b), only five are located in Europe, while the broad majority is located in remote areas involving return travel distances exceeding 20,000 passenger km (pkm). Calculating two examples, a return distance of 4,000 pkm (corresponding to a trip from the UK to Egypt), and 30,000 pkm (corresponding to a trip from the UK to Australia) indicates that emissions caused by transport to the destination can vary between 2.1 and 12.9 t CO_2-equivalent (calculation: www.atmosfair.de). If divers carry on diving equipment, this might add on the weight of the aircraft and lead to higher fuel use. On the distance from the UK to Australia, 1 kg of additional weight will lead to additional fuel use of approximately 0.7 kg (return flight; Paul Peeters, pers. comm. NHTV Breda), corresponding to emissions of almost 6 kg CO_2-equivalent.

Emissions on Site

At the destination, divers will cause additional emissions through their stay in various accommodation establishments, transports and activities (including dive trips). Generally, energy use in different accommodation categories varies widely, with reported average energy consumption values of 25 (bed-and-breakfast establishments) to 325 (upper-class hotels) MJ/guest night (Bohdanowicz & Martinac, 2006; Gössling, 2002). Depending on how energy is generated, corresponding emissions will be in the order of up to 50 kg CO_2 per guest night. Local transport by car, bus, etc can add on the total carbon emissions caused by the dive holiday (see Gössling et al., 2002), but are here deemed minor in comparison to the trip by air, accommodation and activities, the latter primarily including dive trips.

While the dive trip would theoretically include the filling of tanks (compressors) and other energy use, the focus here is on the trip by boat. Emissions will be affected by various factors, including boat size, engine type (horse power and fuel type, i.e. diesel or petrol), vessel type, distance travelled, and, for the calculation of per-tourist emissions, the number of divers onboard. Clearly, these parameters can vary widely, and any calculation can thus only be an estimate of a likely combination of these. Regarding fuel use of boats, the scientific literature does not provide much information. Byrnes and Warnken (2006) estimate that emissions caused by Australian tour boat operators are in the order of 70,000 t CO_2-equivalent per year. Calculated per tourist, this translates into 61 kg of CO_2-equivalent if the boat uses a diesel engine, or 27 kg CO_2-equivalent if the boat uses a petrol engine. However, Byrnes and Warnken (2006) calculate these average values based on an assessment of trips with multiple purposes such as fishing, diving, cruises, etc and it remains unclear whether there are large differences between these categories.

During a dive holiday, tourists are likely to visit several dive locations, and the total amount of emissions will be a function of the number of trips and the boat-specific characteristics as outlined above. Gössling et al. (Chapter 4, this volume) found in their case study of divers in Mauritius that divers participated in dive activities on an average of 7 out of 15 days of stay. These divers mostly fell in the category of holiday divers, i.e. they did not choose Mauritius particularly for the purpose of diving, nor did they go on holiday with the primary purpose of diving. Using the Byrnes and Warnken (2006) values for the calculation of emissions, and an estimated number of seven trips per diver, boat travel to dive sites would account for per diver emissions of between 0.2 and 0.4 t of CO_2-equivalent.

While these calculations can only be indicative, they nevertheless show that a dive holiday may cause emissions anywhere in the range of 2.3–13.3 t CO_2-equivalent, the major share of this attributed to air transport. Note that this calculation is conservative and not based on a lifecycle approach, which might increase emissions substantially. Emissions caused by a dive holiday can be compared to sustainable *annual* emissions of about 3.5 t CO_2 (global per capita average), indicating that dive holidays are highly energy-intense. On a per-capita basis, dive holidays thus contribute significantly to global warming, which in turn is one of the major threats to coral reefs. This two-way relationship has been rarely discussed in the dive literature, even though it sheds new light on the conservation value of diving. While diving might locally contribute to the preservation of marine ecosystems (e.g. White & Rosales, 2003), it might globally be one of the least sustainable forms of tourism from a climate-change perspective.

can try to avoid them. Divers with greater environmental knowledge are also likely to be more interested in *behaving* in appropriate ways (Cottrell & Meisel, 2004). Finally, reducing diver-related damage in marine ecosystems will demand *practical skills,* such as the ability to maintain buoyancy. Divers occupied with managing their own problems under water (checking air supplies, depth, buoyancy, etc.) are less likely to control their impacts, such as kicking with fins or contact of substrate with gear. This is confirmed by Walters and Samways (2001), who report that photographers are far more likely to cause damage to reefs than other divers, probably because they are more focused on their photographic motives than the consequences of their movements for the surrounding environment. Note that the management of practical skills also has a safety dimension (cf. Coxon et al., Chapter 11, this volume). This indicates that the environmental management of dive activities should address at least four different aspects: awareness, knowledge and behaviour, as well as practical skills. It should also include both local and global perspectives on environmental change. In addition, environmental management of dive activities needs to be considered at various organisational levels such as dive organisations, their respective dive centres, tour operators offering dive holidays, and individual divers.

Environmental Management in the Dive Industry

Environmental management comprises any policy, strategy, communication, or other tools to achieve greater sustainability (e.g. Ammenberg, 2004). Organisations making the decision to engage in environmental management move through a process of assessment, implementation and monitoring in a continuous cycle of improved performance, indicating that environmental management needs to be based on long-term commitment. Ideally, this will generate direct and indirect economic benefits for the organisation, for instance through reduced resource use or a more positive public image, which can in turn sharpen the competitive edge of the organisation (e.g. Lynes & Drenge, 2006).

Environmental management in the dive industry is understood to contain policies, communication, education and actions that can help to avoid or minimise environmental impacts in marine environments. Environmental management in the dive industry is different from management in many other service sectors because production and consumption occur at the same time, with individual divers directly causing the environmental damage. The exception to this might be boat-related damage, as well as purchases of diving gear and equipment by dive organisations or dive centres (which might be produced in environmentally harmful ways). Environmental management thus needs to focus primarily on clients, rather than the performance of the dive centre itself, and seek to involve divers in the management process.

The global diving industry is structured through various international umbrella organisations such as the Professional Association of Diving Instructors (PADI), the National Association of Underwater Instructors (NAUI), the National Association of Scuba Diving Schools (NASDS), Scuba Schools International (SSI), and the Confédération Mondiale des Activités Subaquatiques (CMAS), as well as their national and regional branches. Furthermore, there is a range of national diving organisations including, for example, Verband Deutscher Sporttaucher (VDT, Germany) and the British Sub Aqua Club (BSAC, UK). International dive organisations cooperate with individual dive centres, which operate under their rules and conditions. The dive centres are in return mandated to certify individual divers, who pay the dive centres for the training courses and examinations.

Given the structure of the dive industry, environmental management can theoretically be integrated across various organisational levels. First of all, dive organisations can point

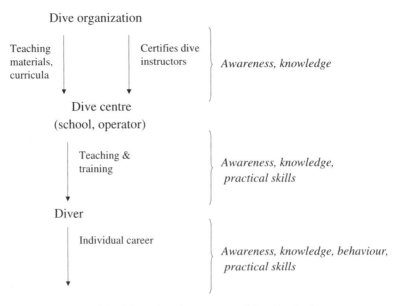

Figure 6.1: Educational structure of the dive industry.

out the rapid rate of change in marine environments, and inform their members as well as the public about the underlying reasons of change. Dive organisations can thus raise awareness of the need of environmental management, as well as lobby on regional, national and supranational levels for pro-environmental action. Secondly, dive organisations provide educational materials for dive schools and decide on the curricula for dive instructors. They can thus decide whether environmental management should become a mandatory element of diver education, and how it should be prioritised in comparison to other issues such as dive physics, gear handling, first aid and communication. Dive organisations also make decisions on the importance of environmental knowledge and the level of depth of this knowledge. Finally, they can prioritise practical skill training, raising awareness or the acquisition of knowledge.

Figure 6.1 shows that dive instructors are central in the educational process. Dive instructors receive their teaching licenses through dive organisations, and their awareness and environmental knowledge as well as their perception of the importance of environmental management is to some degree shaped by the curricula of dive organisations. Divers, on the other hand, go through an educational process that is based on educational materials provided by dive organisations as well as theoretical and practical training provided by dive centres. The framework of this education in terms of length of training, maximum student group size, content and emphasis is set by dive organisations, but the outcome of the training will primarily depend on the individual dive instructor, his or her knowledge, and his or her interpretation of and emphasis on different parts of the educational process. The behaviour of divers in marine environments will thus ultimately depend on the theoretical and practical training they have received, and ultimately, when they are diving, the control and intervention of dive guides. Environmental awareness, knowledge and behaviour, as well as practical skills, will then continue to change through the diver's career. For example, upon completion of the first diver certificate, a diver might learn to control buoyancy to some extent, depending on the frequency and intensity of subsequent practice. Likewise, environmental knowledge and behaviour will develop depending on new theoretical knowledge acquired through books and other media, or information provided by dive instructors and fellow divers. The knowledge base can also deteriorate, as might happen in the case of holiday divers who do not seek to renew or update their theoretical and practical diving knowledge.

Case Study: PADI

To understand better how environmental management is currently considered by dive organisations and incorporated in the educational process, a study was carried out focusing on PADI, the world's largest dive organisation. PADI is, according to the organisation, represented in 180 countries, has more than 100,000 members and represents about 60% of the dive companies (schools and operators) worldwide. According to the organisation, three out of five divers in the world are certified by PADI, totalling more than one million divers (PADI, 2006a).

To assess the degree of integration of environmental management by PADI, a content analysis of the organisation's educational material, as well as other course literature, was carried out. Educational materials were searched for keywords of relevance in the context of marine environmental management (i.e. 'biology', 'buoyancy', 'disturbance', 'ecology', 'environment', 'fauna', 'marine life', 'impacts'), and whenever such keywords were found, sections were critically evaluated with respect to the quantity, quality and character of the information provided. Likewise, the structure of the teaching hierarchy was critically assessed, along with an evaluation of course contents and preconditions for diver examination. Furthermore, semi-structured interviews with two dive master students, three dive instructors, and one representative of PADI's board of directors (PADI Nordic) were carried out. All interviews were recorded and afterwards transcribed. Of the three dive instructors, two worked for PADI, and one had worked for both NAUI and CMAS. The interview subjects had varying degrees of experience, both in terms of the number of years they had worked within the respective organisations, as well as their working experience in Sweden and abroad. However, two of the dive instructors reported to have been diving worldwide, and one in the Nordic countries. All had more than a decade of diving experience. Interview participants were identified randomly by contacting various dive centres in the Swedish cities of Malmö, Lund and Helsingborg. While the focus of the study was the Swedish dive market, interviewees with experience abroad also provided their perspectives on how diving is organised in the countries in which they had worked (e.g. Portugal and Thailand). Questions addressed the overall integration of environmental management in diver education, respondents' understanding of what constitutes environmental problems, as well as their knowledge of these issues. It should be noted that aspects of safety and social and environmental standards are generally of great importance in Scandinavia, and the results do not necessarily represent the perception of dive instructors elsewhere. Interviews were evaluated through comparative analysis.

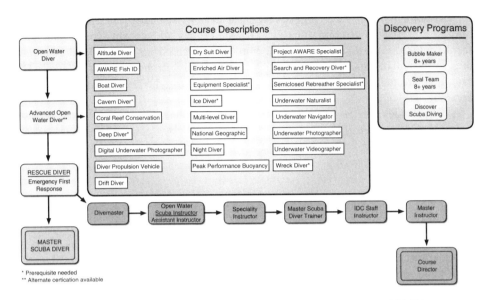

Figure 6.2: PADI courses and educational hierarchy (PADI, 2006b).

Teaching Materials

The educational system of PADI is created as a career ladder consisting of about 40 different modules (Figure 6.2). Novice divers will begin with the Open Water Diver course (delivering basic diving skills, with a maximum dive depth of 18 m). The Open Water Diver certificate is based on five lessons in class, five lessons in a pool and four dives in natural water bodies. The course, like all PADI courses, is performance based, i.e. there are no rules over which period of time the certificate should be taken, even though PADI recommends 31 h (PADI, 2003a). Open Water Diver certificate holders can then participate in speciality courses (see Figure 6.2) or continue up the career ladder by taking the Advanced Open Water Diver certificate. This includes a deep dive and a navigator dive, plus three dives (of the participant's free choice) from the following: altitude diving, AWARE fish identification, boat diving, deep diving, diver propulsion vehicle use, drift diving, dry suit diving, multi-level and computer diving, night diving, peak performance buoyancy, search and recovery, underwater nature study, underwater navigation, underwater photography, underwater videography and wreck diving. The Advanced Open Water Diver certificate enables divers to dive up to 40 m in depth and takes 15 h to complete (recommended minimum time). Finally, divers holding both the Open Water and Advanced Open Water certificates can continue with the Rescue Diver module. These three first courses are non-professional, and can be complemented with a total of 24 speciality courses. With a minimum number of five speciality diver certificates (recommended time of 2–24 h per course) and 50 logged dives, divers can achieve the rank of Master Scuba Diver.

The hierarchy then continues on the professional level, including the Dive Master and various Dive Instructor level certificates. To begin the Dive Master course, the student has to undertake a minimum of 20 logged dives. The Dive Master certificate enables the holder to assist in education of non-professional divers. Finally, to enter the Open Water Scuba Instructor Program, a diver needs a minimum of 60 logged dives, with at least 100 logged dives by the end of the course (the certificate of Assistant Instructor is then awarded). Dive instructors are trained and examined by Course Directors, the highest rank in the PADI hierarchy.

PADI provides dive manuals for each level of dive education, out of which three are evaluated below in respect of their consideration of environmental management: the Instructor Manual, the Open Water Diver Manual and the Advanced Open Water Manual (PADI, 2003a, 2005).

Instructor Manual

The Instructor Manual assessed for the purpose of this chapter was printed in 2003, but updated by a number of PADI Training Bulletins (providing updates on the Instructor Manuals) through to the fourth quarter 2004 (PADI, 2003a). The Instructor Manual is divided into various sections. The first contains the PADI Seal Team Instructor Guide, a section designed for children to heighten and maintain their interest in diving before they can engage in the PADI Junior Scuba Diver or Junior Open Water Dive course at the age of 10. One of the 'AquaMissions' is to show children how to "analyse litter and pollutants to determine what they are and where they come from" (Seal Team section; PADI, 2003a, p. 33). The skills acquired through the exercise are described as being to: "Demonstrate a feet-high, head-low search position used in underwater cleanups. Perform a basic search pattern used in underwater cleanups" (PADI, 2003a, p. 34). Dive instructors are provided with information regarding the questions that children might be asked ("What's bad about pollution and litter going into the ocean, rivers or lakes?", "How do we stop pollution?") and pedagogic advice ("Hold up a litter piece. [Ask children what it is] Identify what the objects are and where you found them. Explain that scientists study pollution and litter to find out what it is and where it comes from"). Courses can be held by PADI Dive Masters without special training. Another issue of importance taken up in the Seal Team section is buoyancy, which is trained as part of the "Inner Space Specialist Goal" (PADI, 2003a, p. 37).

The theoretical section in the Instructor Manual's Open Water Diver course manual includes only one paragraph on environmental management (PADI, 2003a, pp. 3–21), advising instructors to:

- Emphasise the need for each student to be especially cautious when diving over bottoms inhabited by organisms, for personal safety and to protect the aquatic organisms. [...]
- Emphasise that nearly all aquatic animals are non-aggressive and harmless, and to not chase, tease or threaten underwater creatures.

Regarding environmental knowledge, dive instructors are to expect open water students to provide answers to the following questions: (1) Aquatic bottom compositions include what six types? (2) What are the two ways to avoid bottom contact? (3) What are the two basic classifications for interaction between divers and aquatic life? (4) Nine simple precautions minimise the likelihood of being injured by an aquatic animal — what are they? (5) Why should divers follow local fish and game laws? These five questions are the only ones addressing environmental issues out of a total of 240. Regarding practical skills, Open Water divers are supposed to show that they are able to achieve and maintain buoyancy. This, however, is confined to the skill of "hovering for at least 30 seconds [in] water too deep to stand up in" and "swim at least 10 metres/yards underwater while maintaining neutral buoyancy". However, where only poor buoyancy can be maintained, this is not likely to affect whether the candidate successfully passes the certification (see interviews with dive instructors below).

The Instructor's Manual's section, Adventures in Diving Program Instructor Guide (corresponding to the Advanced Open Water Diver certificate) provides information on course standards, general knowledge development of advanced divers and the knowledge required to pass the AWARE Fish Identification course. This course could be seen as one of the few speciality courses potentially enhancing the environmental knowledge of divers. However, to pass the course, divers have to answer 10 questions, out of which only few seem to deal with fish ecology, and even fewer to address such issues at a profound level. The questions include: "Approximately how many different fish species exist worldwide?", "The simple strategy for identifying fish is to focus on families, rather than trying to learn every fish species (true or false)", "List at least four common fish groupings used to identify fish in your local area" and "List some of the characteristics that assist in distinguishing between fish families". Other questions include "AWARE is an acronym for?" and "Project AWARE's mission includes teaching the world about the importance of preserving the aquatic environment (true/false)".

Other courses with environmental management relevance that can become part of the Advanced Open Water Diver certification are the Peak Performance Buoyancy course, and the Underwater Naturalist course. The Peak Performance Buoyancy course (5 h) has both practical training and theoretical elements, which will help divers to understand how buoyancy can be improved and also raise interest in buoyancy training. The link to environmental impacts of diving is indirect, however, as the course does not seem to make a connection between poor buoyancy performance and its potential consequences in marine environments.

The Underwater Naturalist course (12 h) provides information about (1) the planning, organisation, procedures, techniques, problems and hazards of diving in different aquatic environments; (2) a basic overview of major aquatic life groupings; (3) factual information that dispels myths of potentially dangerous aquatic life; (4) overview of basic aquatic life interactions and associations; (5) responsible human interactions with aquatic life and (6) diving techniques used to help preserve bottom-dwelling aquatic life and minimise aquatic life disturbance. The course contains some basic information on marine ecology, with examination being based on 10 questions including "List three physical/structural differences between aquatic and terrestrial ecosystems", "List four inaccurate ways people may perceive aquatic animals", "Explain how to responsibly feed fish and other aquatic life" and "Describe the dive techniques to use to preserve bottom-dwelling organisms and to minimise disturbing all aquatic life".

Two other speciality courses are of relevance in the context of environmental education, which are described in the Speciality Diver Courses section of the Dive Instructor's Manual. First, there is the AWARE Coral Reef Conservation course (2 h), which can be delivered by anyone with PADI Assistant Instructor status without approval by PADI or the need to obtain an instructor certification (PADI, 2003a, section 5–2). The Manual does not provide information on content, but recommends that the course should consider: (1) an introduction to Project AWARE, (2) information on the importance of coral reefs to marine ecosystems and coastal areas, (3) reef biology, (4) status of the world's reefs and (5) suggestions and information about actions that may help to protect reefs, including responsible diving and snorkelling practices. Students do not have to pass an exam to become certified. Second, the Project AWARE Speciality Program (4 h) includes goals such as to: (1) spread the AWARE philosophy about protecting worldwide aquatic ecosystems, (2) inform about the importance of worldwide aquatic ecosystems, (3) issues concerning the environmental status of worldwide ecosystems, (4) in particular critically degraded marine environments, and (5) inform about specific actions that may help to conserve aquatic ecosystems (PADI, 2003a, section 17–2). The AWARE Speciality course can be held by anyone with PADI Assistant Instructors status or higher. There is no need to attend instructor training or be certified as instructor for this course, so long as the Instructor Outline for the course as distributed by PADI is used. The outline (28 pages) contains fact-based material on environmental issues. In order to complete the course, participants have to answer 14 questions including "Why are coral reefs important to the aquatic environment"; "What are the main sources of pollution in the aquatic environment?" and "What are the three reasons that worldwide fisheries are facing collapse?".

In terms of practical training, the Peak Performance Buoyancy course (5 h) might also be of importance, providing additional theoretical knowledge on buoyancy (1 h) and improving buoyancy through two 2-h training dives. Neither the Rescue Diver nor the Dive Master course description in the Instructor's Manual contain aspects of environmental management.

Finally, it is worth noting that the Instructor's Manual gives information about a PADI initiative to reward environmental initiatives by dive centres. Dive centres can receive the environment award if they have, during the past 12 months (PADI, 2003a):

1. Displayed information supporting the Project AWARE philosophy.
2. Produced and distributed a quarterly communication piece (newsletter, flyer, postcard, email or other publication) that includes information regarding environmental awareness and/or conservation.
3. Conducted or sponsored one of the following:
   - A cleanup day at a local beach, lake, quarry, or waterway.
   - A mooring buoy installation and/or a monitoring project.
   - A research project that generated information about the aquatic environment.
   - An event that benefited an environmental organisation.
4. Sponsored or conducted at least one Peak Performance Buoyancy clinic or course,or an Underwater Naturalist, Project AWARE or AWARE Coral Reef Conservation Speciality course.

Open Water Diver Manual

The 2005 Open Water Diver Manual contains little information on environmental management or appropriate behaviour in marine environments. There is a one-page advertisement for Project AWARE; however no more detailed information is provided on what the project is about. Furthermore, the book (260 pages) contains roughly one page of text with some general comments on the fragility of marine life and general principles of behaviour, generally following the principles of 'do not touch, do not disturb, do not interact' (PADI, 2005, pp. 131–132, 165).

Adventures in Diving Manual (Advanced Open Water Diver Manual)

The Advanced Open Water Diver certificate can really be seen as a specialisation in comparison to the Open Water Diver. The certificate includes a deep dive and a navigation dive, plus three out of a selection of 15 other dives (see Figure 6.2). Depending on the dives made, students will have to pass specific examinations. In the context of environmental knowledge and appropriate behaviour in marine environments, three courses are of relevance, including AWARE fish identification, peak performance buoyancy and underwater nature study. The Adventures in Diving Manual (PADI, 2003b) contains chapters on these topics (see discussion of Instructor's Manual above). Regarding the dives chosen, students can theoretically pick all three — the fish identification, buoyancy and underwater nature-study dives — or indeed none of these. Consequently, the level of knowledge gained with regard to environmental issues will depend on individual choices.

Teaching Materials — Some Preliminary Conclusions

PADI puts great emphasis on environmental management in its promotional materials, as well as on its international and national websites. In particular, the AWARE campaign is widely marketed. However, the analysis of teaching materials has shown that environmental management aspects in diver education might be limited and characterised by a number of weaknesses:

1. Environmental education for divers is focused on raising awareness, even though it remains uncertain which level of diver awareness is actually achieved and how this awareness is characterised.
2. The knowledge of marine ecosystems, conservation and appropriate behaviour in marine environments is examined in a superficial way, and its acquisition depends on the personal interest of the diver (through choosing or not choosing specific courses).
3. There is no information at all on the interaction of climate change and dive tourism, i.e. more global perspectives on environmental change and tourism's contribution to and interaction with these changes.
4. The examination of key skills of divers such as to establish and maintain buoyancy is subject to the judgement of individual dive instructors. Even divers not achieving the required buoyancy skills seem regularly to pass such examinations.

Overall, it can be concluded that while environmental management is, according to PADI, a central goal of the dive organisation, this is hardly reflected in the wider integration of environmental issues in either instructors' or divers' curricula and training. Rather, diver education as currently practiced seems to raise awareness in a general sense and seems to be connected with PADI's desire to promote itself as a pro-environmentally active organisation. However, some of this environmental knowledge will only be acquired by divers actively choosing the relevant courses.

Perspectives on PADI Education

Interviews carried out with dive instructors add insights to the understanding of diver education, both with respect to environmental issues and the wider training process within which they are based. Participants have been anonymised using letters of the alphabet to distinguish them from one another in this section. Note that all of the quotes have been translated from the original Swedish by the authors.

Generally, the length of education and intensity of education in terms of the time needed to complete a course, as well as the ratio of students to teachers, seems to vary both between and within dive organisations. For instance, while the PADI Open Water course can be completed within three days in many tropical destinations, it takes a minimum of 30–40 h to complete the NAUI Scuba diver course.

Regarding identical dive courses within the PADI organisation, there might be a general difference between dive centres located in holiday destinations, particularly in tropical destinations, and those in, for instance, large cities in Europe, in the sense that the former will generally seek to reduce the number of days of a course (and thus the fee charged) to the minimum in order to attract more clients. This has implications for any diver's education, as novice divers will have to decide whether they prefer a more thorough education or a compressed course, the latter generally entailing lower fees. As novice divers seldom have a thorough understanding of the dive education market and the differences between, for instance, CMAS and PADI, their decision might often be based on presumption (i.e. in favour of PADI because it is the most widely known and largest organisation worldwide).

There are also differences in the teacher-to-student ratio between the various dive organisations when it comes to training in natural water bodies. The Instructor Manual (PADI, 2003a), for instance, gives a ratio for water training as 10 to 1 for Open Water Diver certificates and 8 to 1 for Advanced Open Water Diver certificates, while CMAS has, according to Dive Instructor A, a ratio of two students per instructor.

Overall, all of the instructors who were interviewed agreed that stretching courses over a longer period of time would be preferable. This raises the question of why PADI would want to maintain such a system. Ultimately, as pointed out by all three dive instructors, there might be economic reasons for this. As one PADI instructor (B) remarked

> [...] it is a permanent feature in PADI's instructor training that you are supposed to sell. Sell courses [...], present equipment, present courses, all the time: sell, sell, sell, sell ... You could say that you go through a salesman training, not a dive instructor training.

Any diver moving up in the PADI educational hierarchy is thus required to participate in a large number of courses and to buy PADI's specific educational materials, which could be seen as serving the ultimate goal of increasing turnover, a feature well known in the dive world. Indeed, Dive Instructor B suggested that: "PADI's nickname anywhere in the world is 'Put Another Dollar In'". Opportunities to sell a large number of courses, to have high student-to-teacher ratios, and short course periods might also explain the attractiveness of PADI for dive centres around the world. Dive Instructor A consequently reasoned that should he ever consider opening a dive centre, it would be with PADI, as this organisation guarantees a higher turnover.

The implications this has for diver education and diving in general are not clear. First of all, comparably low course fees and short course times will make it attractive to take an Open Water Diver certificate. From there, diver careers may move in different directions. One large group of divers — holiday divers — is likely never to move beyond this first certificate. Given the intense and general character of the Open Water Diver certificate, the knowledge of these divers might not be particularly profound, with predominant knowledge in some areas, such as safety. Over time, both the practical skills and theoretical knowledge of such holiday divers is likely to erode, depending on their individual careers (see discussion above). Another group of divers might go one step further and become certified as Advanced Open Water Divers. These divers might be more profoundly interested in diving, and more regularly update their knowledge and train their skills. Finally, a third group of divers might seek constantly to move upwards in the educational hierarchy and participate in a large number of courses. These are likely to be the most knowledgeable divers, both in terms of theoretical and practical skills.

As discussed earlier, PADI's educational system does not seem to address environmental issues in any particular depth. To improve their understanding of marine ecology and conservation, divers can participate in five speciality courses addressing the marine environment/training skills. These include AWARE Fish ID (Fish identification, 12 h), Coral Reef Conservation (reef biology and threats, 4 h), Project AWARE Specialist (coastal zone sustainability, 4 h), Underwater Naturalist (marine biology and responsible diver behaviour; 12 h), and Peak Performance Buoyancy (5 hours) (PADI, 2003a, 2006b; see also discussion above). The courses Project AWARE Coral Reef Conservation and Peak Performance Buoyancy can be taught by anyone with a rank of Assistant Instructor, while for other PADI Specialty Diver courses, instructors need to be certified, demanding both higher instructor levels and participation in special training for instructors (PADI, 2003a). It is not clear, however, how regularly dive centres actually offer the above speciality courses, and how many divers participate in these. As Dive Instructor B remarked: "I have never seen a dive school offering the Project AWARE specialist course. They [PADI] are great at marketing AWARE, with posters and t-shirts, but there is no interest for this".

It is unclear whether PADI's dive instructor training puts emphasis on knowledge of the environment, appropriate diver behaviour in marine environments, or sustainability in more general terms. For instance, Dive Instructor A reported that the only environmental aspect he remembers being taken up during his training was to follow Swedish fisheries law, and to not collect prawns and lobsters. While it might be argued that this particular dive instructor was trained more than 10 years ago, this does question the knowledge of dive directors, i.e. the people training dive instructors. Tending to be more experienced individuals, such dive directors may well have been trained at a time when environmental change was not as yet perceived as an issue of central importance. However, unless a dive director prioritises environmental management, this is not likely to become part of the training of dive instructors, with the consequence that neither will dive instructors see this as a high priority issue in the education of non-professional divers. Dive instructors might also expect dive organisations to take responsibility. As Dive Instructor C noted:

> [...] the only way to influence underwater behaviour is to include these issues in curricula, that this is made clear in curricula, and then that the pressure comes from outside [the dive organisation ...] For instructors there need to be exact descriptions about how education should be managed, and what the student is expected to know and do.

The education of dive instructors might be central in ensuring appropriate behaviour of divers in marine environments, however, because it is their behaviour, attitudes and values which influence divers, in particular novices. Respondent C suggested that divers might often simply imitate the behaviour of instructors: "*monkey sees: monkey does*". The factual, observable behaviour of dive instructors is thus of great importance, even in comparison to theoretical instructions. Pointing out irresponsible behaviour, for instance, by showing divers a dead coral broken by other divers, can reinforce the lesson (see Barker and Roberts, 2004).

In this context, it is also important to note that there might be substantial differences between dive centres, as these might range from lifestyle-based enterprises to serious, long-term committed companies. The role and importance of environmental management is likely to vary depending on the motives behind establishing and operating the dive centre, as well as the attitudes of its employees. Dive Instructor C, discussing personal experiences during a temporary employment in Portugal noted:

> [...] the first thing I see there in the morning is one of the instructors sniffing some cocaine. [...] Then they have 12 students who are supposed to go on a discovery dive, and they tell me, well, you can go with them [*by yourself*]. [...] I just said 'I am not going to do this' — 'well, then you can go home again' — 'OK, I will go home then' — 'but we have no one else', so I should stay. You have to be extremely tough and tell them that you want to stick to the rules [*eight students per instructor; up to 12 with two instructors*], it's your responsibility and [...] I don't want to see anyone dying because he got his certificate from me.

Environmental issues might in fact have gained a more central role in training recently, even though the focus tends to be on raising awareness. As the member of the Board of Directors (PADI Nordic) remarked during the interview, it is PADI's main task: "[...] to train competent and safe divers who want to continue diving and care about the environment". This is also expressed by the two Dive Master course students, who report that appropriate behaviour in marine environments is mentioned so frequently during their training that it almost becomes a running joke: "and please remember not to destroy anything" and "take only pictures and leave only bubbles". The quotes also reveal that appropriate behaviour is usually discussed in general and abstract terms. There is thus a diffuse understanding of threatened environments and the need for appropriate behaviour, in the sense that divers should have control over their buoyancy and not carry with them any items from the seafloor. As Dive Instructor C suggested: "PADI teaches that we should see ourselves as guests in the sea. It's their [the marine species] environment and not ours, and it's important that [...] we don't touch. We only should watch [...]." This points to a lack of a deeper understanding of why the environment changes, and which concrete factors contribute to ecosystem degradation. As Dive Instructor C pointed out:

> [...] what influences us, that's algae blooms for example. We get algae blooms because of environmental destruction, [...] and that's why we would need more information. Because we can only say 'now the situation is like this and you cannot do this and that', but we cannot explain the development of the phenomenon. I think that's a little sad. Because somewhere we could have influenced the situation, the whole cycle of things, if we could explain. But I don't know about these issues, I only know it's got to do with environmental destruction. [...] It's sad that we divers don't have more information, because we could influence these developments when it comes to the marine environment, I think.

Interviews also reveal an understanding of environmental problems lying outside the dive industry itself, as exemplified by the quote above. Respondents also frequently mentioned the overuse of resources by other actors (such as the shipping industry or the global fishing industry). In contrast, the dive industry itself is perceived as inherently benign and environmentally friendly. There is also a perception that PADI has sufficiently considered environmental issues, as expressed by the member of the board of directors (PADI Nordic):

> [...] we have connections to marine environmental issues in all our curricula, in our manuals and so on, which are meant to go out from PADI Project AWARE to our instructors, dive guides, who in turn, through presentations and lectures, [...] spread the message to the divers, the students. [...] And then we also have the speciality courses [...]. And then there is of course a lot of promotional material, protect our reefs, protect our sharks, protect our wrecks and so on, and on, and on...

However, as shown in the previous section on dive materials, a content analysis reveals that the quantity and quality of environmental information might not be as impressive as the quote suggests. Regarding the practical training of divers, environmental damage can be avoided through training on buoyancy and dive guide intervention. This, however, might be limited in reality by the short length of dive courses as well as examination standards. According to Dive Instructor B, the reality is that despite certain standards (maintain buoyancy for 30 s, etc.), virtually any student is certified, even those not achieving good buoyancy. Intervention of dive instructors in cases of inappropriate diver behaviour is not regularly the case. As PADI Instructor B remarked: "During all dives I have made [several hundred], I have just seen one or two dive guides who have intervened with people touching things." This, again, might be a result of poor awareness of these issues by dive instructors, or the virtual impossibility of controlling large diver groups.

Discussion

The previous sections have suggested that dive organisations and dive centres have a pivotal role in both theoretical and practical diver education. The results indicate that several aspects deserve further discussion, including course length, student-to-teacher ratios, and the integration of environmental management into the educational process.

Course Length

Findings indicate that PADI's educational system might have been created predominantly based on economic considerations. The course length of beginner courses can be (especially in holiday destinations) compressed to the absolute minimum, possibly to make courses attractive for as many tourists as possible. As 3-day periods might be considered hardly sufficient to teach students basic diving skills and the most essential aspects of safety, it is not surprising that environmental aspects are not addressed in any real depth. This is true even as the diver progresses up the dive hierarchy, a process which is based on participation in short courses based on the participant's free choice and not therefore necessarily focusing on environmental issues. Course length is also important in the context of teacher education. Progress in the PADI dive education hierarchy can be rapid, and is largely determined by the number of dives taken. In consequence, teachers might have no extended experience of marine environments, and their knowledge of what actually constitutes appropriate or inappropriate diving behaviour might be limited.

Student-to-Teacher Ratio

PADI has set maximum standards for student-to-teacher ratios (8:1), although dive centres might not necessarily comply with this. It seems that larger groups make it more difficult to address environmental issues, both in theory and practice, as safety has to be prioritised. The marine environment might suffer from larger groups, which are more likely to disturb marine species, e.g. through uncontrolled movements, and divers in large groups need to pay greater attention to each other in terms of available swimming space, uncontrolled movements affecting each other, and so on. Consequently, divers might focus on their individual safety, rather than on how they affect the marine environment. This might also be true for environmental learning through observation. As Cater (Chapter 3, this volume) points out, buddying up has the advantage that four eyes will see more than two, but there might be an inverse relationship if group sizes become too large. Individual divers in large groups might actually see less, as many species will hide when confronted with the first divers. Larger groups are also more difficult to control, making dive-guide intervention more difficult (Photo 6.1).

Environmental Management: Awareness, Knowledge, Behaviour and Practical Skills

It has been shown that environmental management in diver education should ideally create awareness of relevant problems and a sound knowledge base, including both local and global perspectives on the marine environment. This should in theory result in more appropriate behaviour, aided by practical skills. PADI's educational system might be

Photo 6.1: Large diver groups cause crowding and are difficult to control (Photgraph: Simon Hartley).

characterised by a number of weaknesses in this respect. First, the organisation focuses on raising awareness, probably also with a view on communicating its pro-environmental engagement. This is mainly achieved through project AWARE, an initiative that is widely communicated. However, for the sake of the fairness it should be noted that many divers might not have any idea about their impacts on the environment, and creating a basic level of awareness might actually be a crucial step towards environmental education. Second, environmental knowledge is only considered superficially in the general education of divers. Divers might mostly gain the idea of "do not touch, do not disturb, do not carry with you marine life or artefacts", but their education might not provide them with a more profound knowledge. While the simple rule of "do not touch, disturb or carry away" might in fact be generally sufficient to control diver behaviour, there are indications that higher levels of environmental knowledge result in more responsible behaviour and less damage (Cottrell & Meisel, 2004; Thapa, Graefe, & Meyer, 2006). The current content of diver's environmental education might also be questioned because environmental change is turned into abstract, global phenomena. For instance, global climate change and the contribution of the dive industry to this is not mentioned anywhere, even though for instance Wilkinson (2004) lists the need to reduce greenhouse gas emissions as one of the major management tasks to preserve coral reefs. Third, practical skills do not seem to be standardised, in the sense that each diver has confirmed buoyancy skills. Fourth, the speciality courses taking up environmental aspects in some depth are voluntary, and arguably chosen only by divers with an existing interest in this area. These divers are more likely to behave appropriately in marine environments anyway.

Conclusions

Impacts on marine environments can stem from inappropriate behaviour of divers. Both hard and soft management strategies have been suggested to improve this situation, including the limitation of diver numbers in heavily dived areas, better education of divers on environmental issues, and *in situ* intervention by dive instructors in case of observed inappropriate diver behaviour. Restriction of access to dive sites represents a hard management approach based on carrying-capacity concepts. While such management steps might be necessary in heavily dived areas, other dive sites might profit from soft management approaches focusing on improved diver education. This has been shown to require awareness raising and the acquisition of more substantial knowledge of marine ecosystems and practical diving skills. Likewise, dive guides could be advised to observe diver behaviour more carefully and to intervene as required. However, both approaches are dependent on the education of divers and dive instructors. Divers need to be aware of their potential to impact marine environments negatively, to know how this impact can be avoided, and to have the practical skills to control their behaviour. Likewise, dive instructors need to be aware of diver impacts and to communicate their knowledge to divers: they have to be able to control efficiently the number of divers they are guiding, and they need to be willing to intervene. If this is to be achieved, the structure of the dive industry needs to be reconsidered. First, as indicated in the findings of this study, lifestyle aspects might have great importance in the dive industry, as a share of dive instructors might be active in this tourism sector partially or primarily because they can adhere to leisurely, non-committed lifestyles. Corporate social responsibility and environmental management might not have the highest priority in the perception of these instructors. As both the theoretical and practical outcome of the training process will depend primarily on individual dive instructors and their commitment to environmental management, this is probably the most relevant aspect to focus on in attempting to improve the situation. Second, sustainability in tourism might only be achieved in cases where there is a long-term commitment to a location, something that might not usually be the case in the tourism industry (see Gössling, 2003). Within the dive industry, it might primarily be dive centres that have existed for a longer period in a given area, being run by the same people who have developed a sense of place and an understanding of the threats, leading to a greater interest in and engagement with environmental management.

The findings of this study indicate that structural changes in the dive industry could contribute to reduce environmental problems related to inappropriate diver behaviour, taking into consideration the obstacles identified in this chapter. Barker and Roberts (Chapter 9, this volume), for instance, indicate that divers are principally willing to participate in conservation programmes, and interested to learn more about the underwater environment. Likewise, studies by Cottrell and Meisel (2004) and Thapa et al. (2006) indicate that divers with a perceived good knowledge of the marine environment and a higher degree of specialisation in diving are more likely to engage in pro-environmental, responsible behaviour than other divers. The dive industry should build on these findings to provide more profound knowledge and training skills, even though this might mean extending courses and reducing group sizes.

References

Åkerman, J., & Höjer, M. (2006). How much transport can the climate stand? Sweden on a sustainable path in 2050. *Energy Policy, 34*, 1944–1957.

Ammenberg, J. (2004). *Miljömanagement*. Lund: Studentlitteratur.

Barker, N. H. L., & Roberts, C. M. (2004). Scuba diver behaviour and the management of diving impacts on coral reefs. *Biological Conservation, 120*, 481–489.

Bohdanowicz, P., & Martinac, I. (2006). Determinants and benchmarking of resource consumption in hotels. Case study of Hilton International and Scandic in Europe. *Energy and Buildings* (online first), *9*, 82–95.

Bows, A., Anderson, K., & Upham, P. (2006). *Contraction and convergence: UK carbon emissions and the implications for UK air traffic*. Technical Report, Tyndall Centre for Climate Change. http://www.tyndall.ac.uk/research/theme2/final_reports/t3_23.pdf (Accessed 9 May 2007).

Byrnes, T.A., & Warnken, J. (2006). Greenhouse gas emissions from marine tours: A case study of Australian tour boat operators. *Journal of Sustainable Tourism, 14*, 255–270.

Cottrell, S.P., & Meisel, C. (2004). Predictors of personal responsibility to protect the marine environment among divers. In: J. Murdy (Ed.), *Proceedings of the 2003 northeastern recreation research symposium* (pp. 252–261). Newtown Square: USDA Forest Service.

Cyber Diver. (2006). 2006 World top 10—Dive destinations. http://www.cyber-diver.com/best.html (Accessed 9 May 2007).

Dixon, J. A., Fallon Scura, L., & van't Hof, T. (1993). Meeting ecological and economic goals: Marine parks in the Caribbean. *Ambio, 22*, 117–125.

Garrabou, J., Sala, E., Arcas, A., & Zabala, M. (1998). The impact of diving on rocky sublittoral communities: A case study of a Bryozoan population. *Conservation Biology, 12*, 302–312.

Gössling, S. (2002). Global environmental consequences of tourism. *Global Environmental Change, 12*, 283–302.

Gössling, S. (2003). Tourism and development in tropical islands: Political ecology perspectives. In: S. Gössling (Ed.), *Tourism and development in tropical islands: Political ecology perspectives* (pp. 1–37). Cheltenham: Edward Elgar Publishing.

Gössling, S., Borgström-Hansson, C., Hörstmeier, O., & Saggel, S. (2002). Ecological footprint analysis as a tool to assess tourism sustainability. *Ecological Economics, 43*, 199–211.

Gössling, S., Kunkel, T., Schumacher, K., & Zilger, M. (2004). Use of molluscs, fish and other marine taxa by tourism in Zanzibar, Tanzania. *Biodiversity & Conservation, 13*, 2623–2639.

Hawkins, J. P., & Roberts C. M. (1993). Effects of recreational scuba diving on coral reefs: Trampling on reef-flat communities. *Journal of Applied Ecology, 13*, 25–30.

Hawkins, J. P., Roberts, C. M., van't Hof, T., De Meyer, K., Tratalos, J., & Aldam, C. (1999). Effects of recreational scuba diving on Caribbean coral and fish communities. *Conservation Biology, 13*, 888–897.

Lynes, J. K., & Drenge D. (2006). Going green: Motivations for environmental commitment in the airline industry. A case study of Scandinavian Airlines. *Journal of Sustainable Tourism, 14*, 116–138.

Medio, D., Ormond, R. F. G., Pearson, M. (1997). Effect of briefings on rates of damage to corals by scuba divers. *Biological Conservation, 79*, 91–95.

Muthiga, N. A., & McClanahan, T. R. (1997). The effect of visitor use on the hard coral communities of the Kisite Marine Park, Kenya. In: *Proceedings of the eighth international coral reef symposium*, Smithsonian Tropical Research Institute, Balboa, Panama (pp. 1879–1882).

PADI (Professional Association of Diving Instructors). (2003a). *Instructor manual*. PADI International (no publisher).

PADI. (2003b). *PADI adventures in diving*. Gothenburg: PADI Nordic AB.

PADI. (2005). *Open water diver manual.* Gothenburg: PADI Nordic AB.

PADI. (2006a). Statistics. http://www.padi.com/english/common/padi/statistics/1.asp (Accessed 30 March 2006).

PADI. (2006b). PADI courses. http://www.padi.com/padi/en/kd/padicourses.aspx (Accessed 9 May 2007).

Peeters, P., van Egmond, T., & Visser, N. (2004). *European tourism, transport and environment. Final version.* Breda: NHTV CSTT.

Roberts, L., & Harriott, V. J. (1994). Recreational scuba diving and its potential for environmental impact in a marine reserve. In: O. Bellwood, H. Choat, & N. Saxena (Eds), *Recent advances in marine science and technology 1994* (pp. 675–705). Townsville: James Cook University of North Queensland.

Rouphael, A. B., & Hanafy, M. (2007). An alternative management framework to limit the impact of SCUBA divers on coral assemblages. *Journal of Sustainable Tourism, 15,* 91–103.

Rouphael, A. B., & Inglis, G. J. (1997). Impacts of recreational scuba diving at sites with different reef topographies. *Biological Conservation, 82,* 329–336.

Rouphael, A. B., & Inglis, G. J. (2001). Take only photographs and leave only footprints? An experimental study of the impacts of underwater photographers on coral reef dive sites. *Biological Conservation, 100,* 281–287.

Rouphael, A. B., & Inglis, G. J. (2002). Increased spatial and temporal variability in coral damage caused by recreational scuba diving. *Ecological Applications, 12,* 427–440.

Rouphael, T., & Inglis, G. J. (1995). *The effects of qualified recreational SCUBA divers on coral reefs.* CRC Technical Report. James Cook University of North Queensland.

Scuba Travel. (2006a). Top ten dive sites. http://www.scubatravel.co.uk/topdives.html (Accessed 9 May 2007).

Scuba Travel. (2006b). 100 top dive sites of the world. http://www.scubatravel.co.uk/topdiveslong.html (Accessed 9 May 2007).

Shackley, M. (1998). 'Stingray City': Managing the impact of underwater tourism in the Cayman Islands. *Journal of Sustainable Tourism, 6,* 328–338.

Talge, H. (1992). Impact of recreational divers on scleratinian corals at Looe Key, Florida. In: *Proceedings of the 7th international coral reef symposium 2,* Guam (pp. 1077–1082).

Thapa, B., Graefe, A. R., Meyer, L. A. (2006). Specialization and marine based environmental behaviors among SCUBA divers. *Journal of Leisure Research, 38,* 601–615.

Tratalos, J. A., & Austin, T. J (2001). Impacts of recreational SCUBA diving on coral communities of the Caribbean island of Grand Cayman. *Biological Conservation, 102,* 67–75.

Walters, R. D. M., & Samways, M. J. (2001). Sustainable dive ecotourism on a South African coral reef. *Biodiversity and Conservation, 10,* 2167–2179.

White, A., & Rosales, R. (2003). Community-oriented marine tourism in the Philippines: Role in economic development and conservation. In: S. Gössling (Ed.), *Tourism and development in tropical islands: Political ecology perspectives* (pp. 237–262). Cheltenham: Edward Elgar Publishing.

Wilkinson, C. (Ed.) (2004). *Status of the coral reefs of the world: 2004.* Townsville, Queensland, Australia: Australian Institute of Marine Sciences. Available at: http://www.aims.gov.au/pages/research/coral-bleaching/scr2004/pdf/scr2004v1-all.pdf (Accessed 9 May 2007).

World Tourism Organization (WTO). (2001). *Tourism 2020 vision. Vol. 7. Global forecasts and profiles of market segments.* Madrid: WTO.

Zakai, D., & Chadwick-Furman, N. E. (2002). Impacts of intensive recreational diving on reef corals at Eilat, northern Red Sea. *Biological Conservation, 105,* 179–187.

SECTION IV: MANAGEMENT OF DIVING TOURISM

Chapter 7

Dive Tourism, Sustainable Tourism and Social Responsibility: A Growing Agenda

Claudia Townsend

Introduction

For a number of years, much of the diving industry has recognised its responsibility for and interest in environmental conservation. The Professional Association of Diving Instructors (PADI), as well as other diver-certification organisations and individual businesses, has put significant resources into conservation and developed public-awareness programmes. However, the corporate-responsibility agenda in business and in tourism has been expanding over recent years to include not only environmental but also social accountability. Dive businesses are beginning to catch up with this more holistic approach.

The diving industry has a strong and growing presence in developing countries. A glance at any dive travel brochure will reveal dive holidays being sold to the Middle East, Indian Ocean, Pacific and Caribbean islands. Many of the destinations in brochures and on websites are in developing countries. The need to protect fragile ecosystems in these countries is recognised by many dive operators and their clients, but what of the industry's potential contribution to local development and poverty reduction? This is not an area that has been widely discussed or explored, despite the growth of the corporate social responsibility movement in many sectors, including Tourism (see for example Kalisch, 2002; World Travel and Tourism Council, 2002.) Sustainable development and, by extension, sustainable tourism, rests on the 'three pillars' of sustainability: economic, environmental and social (Brundtland, 1987). While dive operations often call themselves sustainable, a detailed look can show this to mean that environmental concerns alone are addressed (Mendelovici, 2005; Tourism Concern, 2002).

This chapter will consider dive tourism's response to sustainability to date and look at measures it could take towards socially sustainable tourism that benefits local people as well as the environment in destinations.

New Frontiers in Marine Tourism: Diving Experiences, Sustainability, Management
Copyright © 2008 by Elsevier Ltd.
ISBN: 978-0-08-045357-6

The Dive Industry and the Natural Environment

Since Cousteau began scuba diving and brought images of the undersea world to millions in his documentaries in the 1960s, scuba diving and environmental protection have been linked. It is Cousteau who is credited, in popular environmental history, with opening the world's eyes both to the diversity of the underwater environment and to the threats facing it (Grajal, 1998; Hammond, 2005; National Wildlife Federation, 2006).

Many scuba divers are attracted to and remain involved in diving because of an interest in the underwater environment (Meisel & Cottrell, 2004). Both they and the dive businesses they patronise have an interest both in protecting and being seen to protect the marine and coastal environment.

There are a number of organisations, such as the PADI AWARE (Aquatic World Awareness, Responsibility and Education) Foundation and the REEF Environmental Education Foundation (REEF), that have been set up by the dive industry or by divers themselves, focusing specifically on marine conservation. These organisations have done a great deal to collect information on the marine environment globally, to raise awareness and support for marine conservation, and to provide funding for marine conservation projects. Some of these are outlined below.

There are also a number of organisations that harness the power of divers as volunteers for marine conservation. Organisations like Coral Cay Conservation, Blue Ventures and Earthwatch use paying volunteers on working holidays to undertake scientific work, most often surveying reefs or other ecosystems to provide an ecological baseline, monitor change and learn about the impacts of certain environmental conditions. These organisations are mainly founded and run by scientists who want to do research but who without using volunteers would have neither the manpower nor the funding to do so.

These organisations also have an important role to play in awareness-raising on marine conservation for the volunteers who work with them, and by extension their friends and families. These volunteers gain a solid understanding of marine ecology and issues in marine conservation, which is likely to stay with them throughout their diving careers and to be passed by word of mouth to family and friends at home.

A few organisations, such as the REEF environmental awareness organisation, use volunteers to collect information on any dive, at home or away, rather than organising and selling a trip to be a conservation volunteer. There are also industry-led environmental programmes: PADI's AWARE programme is probably the largest at least in its geographical coverage. It began in the US and now has programmes in the United Kingdom, Australia, Switzerland and Japan. It has developed training and educational materials for divers, encouraged environmental activities and provided funds to groups for conservation projects around the world.

There are, therefore, many positive examples of diving benefiting conservation. The conservation of natural resources will generally have benefits for local people, the most obvious being where fishing is restricted or banned in order to increase future fish stocks, which can then be fished by local people. However, there are few examples of initiatives where diving can be shown to be directly benefiting key needs of local communities, such as basic healthcare and education.

A Brief History of Sustainable Development and Sustainable Tourism

The term sustainable development was coined in 1987, when the World Commission on Environment and Development published 'Our Common Future'. This document defined sustainable development as:

> … development that meets the needs of the present without compromising the ability of future generations to meet their own needs (Brundtland, 1987, p. 43).

Traditionally, businesses and economies prioritise financial viability, often referred to as their 'bottom line'. Sustainable development is a concept that prioritises not just the economic bottom line but balances a 'triple bottom line' (Brundtland, 1987). This covers economic, environmental and social dimensions. These dimensions are also known as the three 'pillars' of sustainable development.

Sustainable development can be applied to all sectors and industries. As the world's largest industry (Roe & Urquhart, 2001), tourism has an important contribution to make to sustainable development. It also needs to ensure its own sustainability as an industry. Tourism can bring with it both positive and negative impacts that need to be managed to ensure that destinations remain attractive and authentic. The impacts of tourism are dealt with in depth in many other publications and are too numerous and complex to cover in detail here. They can include benefits such as increased income to local people or improved infrastructure, as well as costs such as damage to ecosystems or the breakdown of social systems.

The World Tourism Organization describes sustainable tourism as:

> **Sustainable tourism development guidelines and management practices are applicable to all forms of tourism in all types of destinations,** including mass tourism and the various niche tourism segments. Sustainability principles refer to the **environmental, economic and socio-cultural aspects of** tourism development, and a **suitable balance must be established** between these three dimensions to guarantee its long-term sustainability (World Tourism Organization, 2004, p. 1, emphasis in the original).

Since the 1970s, tourists, the industry and academics have been discussing ways to make tourism less damaging and more positive for destinations. Most of the early discussions focussed on the negative environmental and social impacts tourism could bring, such as disturbing animals or bringing unwanted cultural change. The term 'ecotourism' became widely used to refer to a new kind of tourism that focussed on nature and that respected and protected natural resources.

There are tens of definitions of ecotourism, and these differ quite widely. Recent analysis (Fennell, 2001) showed that nature and its conservation is considered key to the meaning of ecotourism (with 61.2% of definitions mentioning conservation and 45% stating that ecotourism takes place in natural areas). Many definitions also mention other aspects of sustainability, most commonly referring to local culture (57.6%) and mentioning benefits to local communities as inherent to ecotourism (48.2%). This focus on local people and culture has become more important in recent years.

Widespread confusion and misuse now means that terms like sustainable and eco are often used interchangeably and some claim, without much action to back up marketing claims (Mendelovici, 2005; Tourism Concern, 2002). New forms of tourism, such as fair-trade, responsible, ethical and pro-poor tourism, have all gained currency and customers. These focus on people in destinations, especially in developing countries, and how tourism might improve their lives.

It is, however, actions that are more important than definitions, and there are certainly some excellent and innovative examples to be found around the world of sustainable tourism in action. Many enterprises undertake to employ and train local people, buy goods locally and give advice and help with their production, assist with local health and education or enter into business partnerships with local communities. It is not only small, community-minded lodges that work this way; more and more large tour operators are also including social issues in their audits. The tour operators have been producing environmental reports for many years but are now starting to do the same for social issues. For example, First Choice — one of Europe's largest tour operators — has progressed from reporting purely on their environmental measures to social reporting (First Choice, 2005). Their 2005 'Environment and People' report includes issues such as creating local employment and training opportunities, working with suppliers, and eliminating workplace discrimination, as well as environmental impacts and activities.

Corporate Social Responsibility

Corporate social responsibility (CSR) has been adopted in different forms and to various levels by many companies, often in response to scandals like those that affected Nike about poor conditions for workers in sweatshops. A number of companies have been criticised by the media and non-governmental organisations (NGOs), who have called for consumer boycotts of their products because of the company's perceived exploitation of people or the environment.

Perusal of the websites of large corporations shows that many now produce a sustainability or CSR report that reports on their triple bottom line. Companies have been accused of using these reports as public-relations vehicles without actually implementing any serious changes or to do the minimum in order to avoid government regulation (Hamann & Kapelus, 2004; London School of Hygiene and Tropical Medicine, 2002; Tourism Concern, 2006). However, many companies are now responding, perhaps to an internal sense of responsibility as well as to outside pressure from NGOs, government (Department for Trade and Industry, 2003) and more and more consumers who want to buy ethically produced products, including holidays (Mintel, 2005).

Tourism has been slower than some industries to take on CSR principles and reporting. As the World Travel and Tourism Council wrote in 2002:

> The response of the Travel & Tourism industry is still piecemeal and change is relatively slow. One reason for this is the highly fragmented nature of the industry, the great majority of which consists of independent small and medium sized businesses scattered across the globe, often running on fragile

operating margins. The real challenge is to move beyond the current *ad hoc* approach, to evolve new patterns of Travel & Tourism business that integrate social, economic and environmental sustainability and to encourage a vast and fragmented industry to follow suit. In short, what is required is a greater leadership in corporate social responsibility within the Travel & Tourism industry (World Travel and Tourism Council, 2002, p. 5, emphasis in original).

Tourism is a more complex industry than many others in that it includes many sectors: transport, accommodation, food, products, sites of interest, and so on. It is very difficult, for example, for a tour operator selling a trip to track all of the suppliers and producers who supply their client on a two-week trip. Despite this, more and more tourism businesses, large and small, in both originating and destination countries are taking social issues on board. This is evidenced by the increase in reporting of social issues outlined above and by the proliferation of associations for community-based and responsible tourism enterprises in developing countries. Examples include Fair Trade and Tourism South Africa (FTTSA), the Uganda Community Tourism Association (UCOTA) and the Costa Rican Community-Based Rural Tourism Association (ACTUAR).

CSR is not the same as philanthropy. While there is a place and a use for companies giving money or goods to charity or good causes, it is not the same as engaging with communities in the places they work in order to bring long-term opportunities and improvements to people's lives (Ashley, 2006). This means looking at the way companies do business at all levels. For example, who do they buy products from? How many employees are local? Are wages fair in the local context? Are there workplace health and safety and discrimination policies? How can local people benefit from new tourism infrastructure?

Dive Tourism and Social Responsibility

Diving forms a niche within the tourism industry. It has not been singled out for criticism over social impacts in the same way that other industries, or even the tourism industry as a whole, have been. It has been blamed for some environmental damage (see, for example, Hawkins et al., 1999) and has responded to this with programmes such as those mentioned above. It has not had to respond to criticisms of negative social impacts on any grand scale; there may have been local protests where divers have been given resource-use rights while local people have been excluded. However, there has been no broad criticism of the industry as a whole on social grounds.

Furthermore, diving is not a cohesive industry. There are the large certification and training organisations such as PADI that have influence and can encourage certain business practices, but dive companies themselves are in the main individually owned small or medium-sized companies; some part of a resort or hotel and some offering diving as well as other watersports or excursions.

There are some excellent examples of individual companies investing in and working with local communities (some of which are outlined below), but no global, industry-wide move towards or understanding of social issues and dive tourism.

Dive tourism is not particularly different to tourism in general in the potential impacts it can have, positive and negative, on local communities. Like any form of tourism, it may bring with it cultural change, conflict over use of resources (for example when marine areas are closed to fishermen but open to divers), resentment of outsiders and envy of their spending power, and so on. Conversely, it can bring employment opportunities in a new and growing industry, genuine cultural exchange and income for local businesses.

Dive tourism is different in some respects, however. There are higher barriers to entry into the dive business for most people in developing countries than for some other tourism businesses, such as accommodation, restaurants or souvenir selling. Diving is an expensive business: costs are high for training to become qualified as a professional and to set up and run a business, and because of high costs of equipment and boats. To work in diving as a dive master or instructor also requires a good level of education, as well as competency in at least one language tourists speak and in which training materials are available.

Although in the author's experience it is often the case that foreigners or outsiders own and run tourism businesses in rural areas of developing countries, this is even more the case for dive businesses. This can certainly not change overnight: investment, experience and understanding of the market are necessary for any new tourism business and in many destinations can only come from outside. However, new businesses in this situation can choose to make a commitment to working with, training and employing local people as much as possible, or they can choose to continue to import ready-trained and experienced staff from outside the area.

It is, of course, not realistic to expect jobs that require foreign languages, customer-service skills, knowledge of computers and so on to be filled by local people in an area where educational standards are very low. Businesses who take a long-term view, however, can invest in education and training for the future. For example, a hotel owner in Madagascar chose to assist local schools financially in order to create a better-educated next generation of people among whom there will, they hope, be potential employees (Sonja Ranarivelo, Boogie Pilgrim, Madagascar, personal communication). Assisting a local school is not therefore an entirely altruistic measure because the aim may well be to create future employees who know and are committed to the area, which should reduce staff turnover in the future.

Dive businesses, like all tourism businesses, have a responsibility to ensure that their presence brings economic and social benefits to their place of work rather than negative change. They also have a business interest in developing good relations with local people. There are many ways that they can do this and there are good examples to follow from tourism businesses generally and from individual dive companies. Some good examples follow.

Wakatobi Dive Resort

Wakatobi Dive Resort in Southeast Sulawesi, Indonesia, is a resort that caters to divers looking to get off the beaten track. It is Swiss-owned and managed and aims to provide comfort and a certain level of luxury to divers and their friends and families.

The resort has an environmental protection programme, which it has developed in collaboration with the local community and which includes the development and management of a marine protected area. The owners of the resort have realised that environmental protection is not necessarily a priority for people who are struggling to meet their basic needs. The resort has a number of practices in place to increase benefits to local people from the presence of divers. According to the resort owners, these include:

- Direct employment of 100 local people as well as part-time employment on construction and maintenance. On the island where the resort is based (Onemobaa), this means one in every two families has a salary coming in from the resort. It can be assumed, therefore, that the direct economic impact of the resort on the small island itself is significant.
- Selling locally produced products through the resort to guests.
- Sponsoring electricity for the local village (of 500 people) including a 2 km power line to the village, transformers, electrical installations in every household and providing 24-h maintenance team in exchange for the villagers honouring a 3 km reef sanctuary on their traditional fishing grounds.
- Providing educational materials in schools.
- Sponsoring waste-management and other community projects in villages in the district.
- Focussing on providing livelihoods for the poorest, in this case widows, by providing work specifically for them producing natural roof tiles for the resort (made from sago palm leaves).
- Sponsoring a credit scheme for local small businesses.

While much of the focus of the resort's activities is on reef conservation and the environment (more information on environmental activities can be found on the resort website, see Wakatobi Beach Resort, 2006), this is done in collaboration with local people and the conservation activities are aimed at benefiting everyone, not just the resort and divers. The link between poverty, social development and conservation is recognised here and problems are addressed in collaboration between the resort and local people. The process is described thus:

> Recognizing the need for sustainable marine resource protection in the Wakatobi National Marine Park, the Collaborative Reef Conservation Program was developed by the founders of Wakatobi Dive Resort in consultation with local leaders and village elders. It is a program designed to motivate the people living within the marine park to realize the value of, and care for, the reefs in the area. It does so by providing an economic alternative to fishing and incentivizes those that help protect and manage the reefs. Cooperation between local fishermen and visiting divers are promoted by generating an income from tourism that is channelled directly into the community. It took many years of continuous and consistent efforts to build deep trust and understanding within the community to the level where all members of each village respect and honour the agreement. Based on the success of an initial pilot project 1998–2002 that turned 6 km of reef into an effective no-fishing sanctuary, the Collaborative Reef Conservation Program has being extended further. Currently it comprises all of the 17 communities around the resort with 20 km of some of the finest reefs of the world and several dozens of top dive sites being protected (Lorenz Mäder, Wakatobi Dive Resort, personal communication).

The resort director points out how difficult it is to train or employ local people as divers. Although boat captains, crew and those who fill tanks are all local people, efforts to train local people in diving have not been successful. This is for cultural reasons (beliefs about the sea and the dangers that swimming in it presents) as well as educational hurdles. Working as an instructor would require not only a good level of education, but also language skills, understanding of tourists' needs and culture, and customer-service skills. The director points out that the presence of one foreign dive instructor means 20 local jobs are created. In the case of Wakatobi, the remote location, local traditions, education and incomes make training people as divers more or less impossible at the moment (Lorenz Mäder, Wakatobi Dive Resort, personal communication).

There are more and more examples like this, of hotels and other tourism businesses that have close and mutually beneficial relationships with local people and are developing long-term partnerships that will benefit the destination.

There remain few dive companies that are addressing the barriers to local people benefiting from the dive industry mentioned above, by trying to help local people work as dive professionals. While it is useful and important that tourism values and uses local traditional skills, companies should help employees to develop their skills and so create opportunities for them. It is simpler for hotels to bring in outsiders for all skilled and customer service jobs because existing local skills do not match those jobs. Proactive tourism businesses that are committed to their local area make a genuine effort to change that status quo over time through training, education and contributing to community development.

The Ecotourism Training Centre

In most developing countries where educational standards are low, people do not commonly speak a language spoken by tourists and in which dive training materials are available. Therefore it requires a great deal of time and effort for someone to train as a dive master or instructor. The Ecotourism Training Centre (ETC) in Thailand is a rare example of that effort being made. It is not a profit-making enterprise and relies on contributions (including the support of PADI) in order to undertake its training activities. However, it does provide a useful example of what can be done to involve committed disadvantaged people in the dive industry (Reid Ridgway, ETC managing director, personal communication).

The ETC was set up in the aftermath of the Asian tsunami in 2004, with the aim of providing training in English-language skills, computer skills and scuba diving. It recognises that additional skills are necessary as a prerequisite to dive training and provides these for students. Students come from a variety of backgrounds, including a number with a very basic primary-level education and no English. Their commitment, harnessed through the Centre's resources, has led to the successful training of a number of disadvantaged young Thai men and women as dive masters. Many are planning to go on to become dive instructors.

The manager of this programme, Reid Ridgway, makes the point that the dive industry is a fragmented one, with no central body to oversee the business. PADI and other training organisations certainly have influence over businesses, and they have been instrumental in encouraging and recognising environmental good practice. They cannot, however, force individual dive businesses to do more to employ and train local people.

Most dive companies do not have the skills or resources to provide language training or basic education in mathematics and science required alongside or before dive training. Mr Ridgway feels that the responsibility for increasing local involvement in diving lies with many sectors, including governments wishing to regulate for greater local employment in tourism as well as dive businesses and organisations like his own. Improving local employment and participation in the dive industry is in the interests of government and the private sector and no one agency can do this alone. It is therefore the responsibility of multiple agencies in the public and private sectors, and can only happen if they work together and each takes some responsibility. Government, local people and non-profit organisations can help to identify necessary auxiliary skills and funding to provide training and education, while the industry can encourage more local involvement through links with local schools and training programmes, internships in business and working together with others to identify the skills that are lacking. An example of a company that has gone some way to doing this is outlined below.

Sandals Beach Resort, Montego Bay, Jamaica

Sandals is part of a Caribbean-wide, Jamaican-owned chain of all-inclusive beach resorts for couples. This type of tourism does not usually get much good press with regard to its sustainability because all-inclusive resorts are thought to cut their guests off from the local economy (Pattullo, 1996). They may provide employment but local businesses benefit little from guests who do not leave the resort's borders. Some all-inclusive resorts have also been accused of treating local people badly by denying them access to beaches and land (Pattullo, 1996).

Montego Bay, a major tourism destination in Jamaica, has attracted large numbers of people looking for work in tourism from across the island. This migration has resulted in large settlements on the edges of the resort area. Since many of the inward migrants do not find work, social conditions in some of these settlements are very poor, with insufficient infrastructure, education and health and high rates of unemployment and crime. Riots in 1999 affected Montego Bay and other tourist areas and acted as a spur for Sandals to improve their relations with local communities (Horace Peterkin, personal communication).

The Sandals management at Montego Bay responded to this social unrest with a programme to link the resort with the neighbouring settlement of Flankers. They have worked to develop good relations with this community through sponsoring an out-of-school education centre and with a programme to provide traineeships in the resort for young people from the settlement. Trainees are given recognised training in one of the hotel's departments. This includes the dive club where some trainees have reached dive master level. This training does not always result in employment at Sandals, but the training provided is recognised by other hotels as top quality, so that graduates of the programme are in demand elsewhere. Other hotels and resorts are beginning to copy this way of working.

In this case, it took a complete breakdown in relations between neighbouring communities and the tourism industry to bring about change: a breakdown that affected the tourism economy seriously. Some in the industry recognised that providing opportunities for disadvantaged local people would not only improve this situation but could also provide a pool of well-trained, local employees (Ashley, Goodwin, McNab, Scott, & Chaves, 2006; Horace Peterkin, General Manager, personal communication).

Student Scholarships and Social Responsibility: A Growing Agenda for PADI

In addition to grants like the one given to the ETC, mentioned above, PADI International (the UK arm of the organisation) has formalised a scholarship programme for students wishing to become dive professionals who do not have the means to pay for training and exams (Suzanne Pleydell, Group Manager for Education & Instructor Development at PADI, personal communication).

Currently, this programme offers 20 students a year a scholarship to train as an instructor. Students need to show an existing interest and basic capability by having an 'Open Water' diver qualification (the first, most basic level of dive certification offered by PADI). They also need the support of a dive centre to provide their training over time. PADI will then provide training materials and cover their course and exam fees, which are significant for professional-level qualifications and well beyond the reach of the majority of people in developing countries.

This scholarship programme, and ad hoc scholarships offered elsewhere have benefited students in North Africa, South Africa, Kenya and the Mediterranean region. The programme requires a joint commitment from PADI itself, a dive centre and the student. Such a partnership between sectors and individuals is a good example of the way that the various disparate parts of an industry, each with limited resources, can pool their efforts to help more people from developing countries to enter the diving profession.

Suzanne Pleydell recognises that ecotourism is not just about the environment but also about benefiting local communities. This has begun to be reflected in the PADI AWARE 'Go Eco' campaign that provides a code of conduct for responsible divers and dive operators (see Project Aware Foundation, 2006). While mostly concerned with the potential environmental impacts of tourism, the code also refers to actions such as buying from local businesses and respecting local cultures. Dive centres that agree to abide by the Go Eco code are recognised and rewarded by PADI with publicity.

As more and more dive centres are set up in developing countries, PADI recognises that good relations with and the involvement of local people is essential both to business development and to environmental protection. The scholarship scheme makes entry into the dive business more possible for some students who have the backing of their dive centre. It is to be hoped that these newly qualified dive professionals will provide role models for others in their countries and that diving becomes more accessible as a result.

Summary and Recommendations

Sustainable tourism is tourism that benefits the economy, society and the environment. Diving is growing all the time in developing countries where relations with poor local communities are important and where companies have the chance to benefit not only the marine environment but also to play their part in social development. The dive industry is highly competitive and disparate. It is also an expensive business to get into and to run, with high training and equipment costs. For many people in developing countries, educational and language barriers also make access to the dive industry more or less impossible. However, there is growing interest in fair-trade, pro-poor and socially sustainable tourism, from both providers and consumers. In response, there are some excellent and working examples of tourism businesses that have taken the time and provided the resources to develop long-term relationships with local communities. Working with neighbours to develop products and services that the tourism industry needs is a long-term project, but it ultimately means that staff turnover can be reduced, loyalty increased and that products can be bought locally.

For dive companies, the investment required is significant and help is required from governments (both local and donor), NGOs and dive-training bodies. Some of the aims of each of these sectors can be met by increasing local people's participation in and benefit from the diving industry. Each sector has its own resources and expertise to add to the pool. No one sector can achieve broad change alone. Experience shows that when government tries to do the work of the private sector it often fails and that the private sector cannot reasonably devote the time and resources necessary.

The following groups need to work together to identify needs and share resources:

- *National and local governments* who wish to see more local employment in tourism should work with the industry to identify the skills that are lacking. They can then look at the gaps in training in school and adult education curricula in order to develop education and training to fill those gaps.
- *Dive companies* who recognise the benefits of employing local people can take the time to work with local schools and training centres to raise awareness of careers in diving as well as encouraging local employees to further their dive education. While it is unrealistic for most small dive companies to take on full-time employees to train them to instructor level, forward-thinking companies can make an effort to develop the language and diving skills of local staff employed in non-diving roles. Barriers of language and education will remain, but where people see their peers getting involved in diving, those barriers may seem less difficult to overcome. Dive centres often employ people in jobs that do not require diving or language skills initially, such as boat crews, tank fillers and boat captains. Experience in these jobs can lead to a good understanding of tourists and new language skills. Where these employees are interested and encouraged to take up diving, and both the employer and employee is willing to give time and effort to training, issues such as education and language skills can be overcome in time.
- *Dive tourists* can ask questions about company policy, not only with regard to the environment but also about social issues. Consumer demand helps push companies towards social responsibility. Tourists can make it clear to companies that they are buying or not buying their product because of the way they work or do not work with local people. The growth in fair-trade products and ethical tourism over recent years is evidence that the industry responds to consumer demand.
- *Training and certification agencies* could be more proactive in looking at the barriers to local people's involvement in diving in many developing countries. Scholarships are a good way to do this, as are more local-language training materials. Increased recognition, through labels, certification and publicity, not only for environmental but also for social

development activities, might also encourage more dive centres to take action based on the example of others.

- *Equipment manufacturers* could offer prizes and scholarships to students on training courses in equipment repair and maintenance. To date, equipment manufacturers have not become involved, perhaps because they are not 'on the ground' so do not see these issues as affecting them. They are, however, an important part of the dive industry and their training is important for increased local involvement.
- *NGOs* that work on diving and environmental issues often already recognise the links between conservation and poverty reduction. By facilitating linkages between communities and the private sector they can improve understanding between the two of each other's needs and help to fill in gaps, for example, in levels of general education.
- *Sustainable tourism projects* (these may be NGOs, private sector, donor or government-led or indeed multi-sectoral) should ensure they consider the dive industry in areas where it is relevant and work actively to involve and assist dive companies in their projects, helping with practical solutions for partnership with local communities.

It is not possible or desirable to try and push people into diving and dive careers. Neither is it impossible for people who do not come from the usual background of dive professionals to get involved. While the barriers may be high it does not mean they are necessarily insurmountable. Realism is important — not everyone wants to or can become a dive instructor. However, as in the case of Wakatobi, communities where most people have no or very basic education and living conditions can still benefit actively from dive tourism. Elsewhere, an active, combined effort from dive centres, training agencies, NGOs and people who want a career in diving can most certainly overcome the barriers that have tended to imply that most dive professionals in developing countries are foreigners.

While it is not realistic to expect dive companies in developing countries to pour time and money into basic education that might eventually lead to dive training, it is certainly possible for diving to be a sustainable business, not only environmentally but also socially. This means strong and genuine partnerships with local people and businesses, being proactive in buying locally, assisting with education and infrastructure where possible, and making a long-term investment in good relations.

It also means a long-term investment on the part of all stakeholders: training agencies, private operators, governments, educators, NGOs and divers that works towards bringing down the barriers that keep many people in developing countries out of the scuba-diving industry. Sustainable tourism means working towards the long term, helping to provide good jobs with prospects and opportunities for development.

The examples described in this chapter demonstrate that this can be done by private operators (Sandals and Wakatobi), donors and NGOs (ETC) and dive-certification agencies (PADI). Whether the dive industry is based in a remote outpost or is an all-inclusive resort in a mass-tourism destination, local people can be actively involved in making decisions about tourism and how it affects them.

The diving industry is not easy to get into for poor people who have little education and few foreign language skills. Perhaps for this reason, the industry is often ignored by those working on community-based tourism. It is far more reasonable and realistic for people to use their existing skills and knowledge, such as handicraft production, to develop tourism products and businesses. Examples show, however, that when people want to get into the industry and have the support of private operators as well as organisations like PADI and the ETC, such development is clearly possible.

References

Ashley, C. (2006). *Facilitating pro-poor tourism with the private sector. Lessons learned from 'Pro-Poor Tourism Pilots in Southern Africa'*. London: Overseas Development Institute Working Paper Number 257.

Ashley, C., Goodwin, H., McNab, D., Scott, M., & Chaves, L. (2006). *Making tourism count for the local economy in the Caribbean: Guidelines for good practice*. London: Pro-Poor Tourism Partnership and the Travel Foundation.

Brundtland, G. (Ed.) (1987). *Our common future: The World Commission on Environment and Development*. Oxford: Oxford University Press.

Department of Trade and Industry. (2003). *Sustainability and business competitiveness: Executive summary. Measuring the benefit for business competitive advantage from social responsibility and sustainability*. London: DTI.

Fennell, D. (2001). A content analysis of ecotourism definitions. *Current Issues in Tourism, 4*, 403–421.

First Choice. (2005). Environment and people report. http://www.fcenvironmentandpeople.com/fcenviro/sitemap.html. (Accessed 15 November 2006.)

Grajal, A. (1998). Jacques Cousteau and his world's inspiring beauty. *Conservation Biology, 12*, 487.

Hamann, R., & Kapelus, P. (2004). Corporate social responsibility in mining in Southern Africa: Fair accountability or just greenwash? *Development, 47*, 85–92.

Hammond, L. (2005). Menfish and the great hydrosphere. In: A. Rome (Ed.), Anniversary forum: What books should be more widely read in environmental history? *Environmental History, 10*, 666–770.

Hawkins, J. P., Roberts, C. M., van't Hof, T., De Meyer, K., Tratalos, J., & Aldam, C. (1999). Effects of recreational scuba diving on Caribbean coral and fish communities. *Conservation Biology, 13*, 888–897.

Kalisch, A. (2002). *Corporate futures: Consultation on good practice. Social responsibility in the tourism industry*. London: Tourism Concern.

London School of Hygiene and Tropical Medicine. (2002). *Press release: Tobacco industry accused of corrupting ideals of corporate social responsibility*. London: London School of Hygiene and Tropical Medicine.

Meisel, C., & Cottrell, S. (2004). Differences in motivations and expectations of divers in the Florida Keys. In: J. Murdy (Ed.), *Proceedings of the 2003 northeastern recreation research symposium*. Gen. Tech. Rep. NE-317 (pp. 393–401). Newtown Square, PA: Department of Agriculture, Forest Service, Northeastern Research Station.

Mendelovici, T. (2005). Conference report. Venezuelan International Ecotourism Conference 2003 — Ecotourism and adventure travel: World innovations and new experiences. Puerto Ordaz — Bolivar State, October 29 to November 1, 2003. *Journal of Ecotourism, 4*, 65–69.

Mintel. (2005). *Ethical holidays — UK — October 2005*. London: Mintel Leisure Intelligence.

National Wildlife Federation. (2006). Conservation Hall of Fame: Jacques Cousteau. http://www.nationalwildlife.org/about/inductees_cousteau.cfm. (Accessed 15 November 2006.)

Pattullo, P. (1996). *Last resorts: The cost of tourism in the Caribbean*. London: Cassell.

Project Aware Foundation. (2006). Go ECO — Explore, conserve, observe. http://projectaware.org/uk/english/ecotourism.asp. (Accessed 15 November 2006.)

Roe, D., & Urquhart, P. (2001). *Pro-poor tourism: Harnessing the world's largest industry for the world's poor*. London: IIED.

Tourism Concern. (2002). *Press statement and briefing: Why tourism concern is cautious about the International Year of Ecotourism.* London: Tourism Concern.

Tourism Concern. (2006). *Press release: Global hotel chain's claims of responsible development are a 'greenwash', says pressure group.* London: Tourism Concern.

Wakatobi Beach Resort. (2006). http://www.wakatobi.com. (Accessed 15 November 2006.)

World Tourism Organization. (2004). Sustainable development of tourism conceptual definition. http://www.world-tourism.org/frameset/frame_sustainable.html. (Accessed 15 November 2006.)

World Travel and Tourism Council. (2002). *Corporate social leadership in travel and tourism.* London: World Travel and Tourism Council.

Chapter 8

Diverting Pressure from Coral Reefs: Artificial Underwater Parks as a Means of Integrating Development and Reef Conservation

Peter van Treeck and Michael Eisinger

Introduction

Despite many global and regional initiatives to conserve coral reefs, their worldwide status has changed for the worse in recent decades. During the Seventh International Coral Reef Symposium in Guam in 1992, coral reef scientist estimated that 10% of the world's reefs had already been lost, 30% were in a critical state and were predicted to be lost within the next 10–20 years without efficient management, while a further 30% were threatened with a potential destruction within the next 20–40 years. Five years later, the first two comprehensive reports on the overall status of coral reefs were released (Bryant, Burke, McManus, & Spalding, 1998; Wilkinson, 1998) indicating that aside from the reefs that had already been severely damaged or destroyed, a further 56–58% of reefs were at medium-to-high risk. At that time, predictions for the future of reefs were still cautiously optimistic, pointing out the capacity of coral reefs to recover if pressures were reduced or removed. In the 2000 report of the Global Coral Reef Monitoring Network (GCRMN) (Wilkinson, 2000), however, the picture was more than clear: the state of reefs had continued to decline, mainly as a result of the catastrophic bleaching events in 1998, where 16% of the reefs worldwide were destroyed in just 9 months. The most-damaged reefs, with an average of 46% of their area being in a damaged state, were in the Wider Indian Ocean. However, it was suggested that the chances of a slow recovery were the highest for these reefs because of the comparably low levels of anthropogenic stress they were facing.

In the two latest GCRMN reports, published in 2002 and 2004 (Wilkinson, 2002a, 2004), the prognoses for coral reefs were quite alarming: 40% of the reefs would be lost in 40 years and another 20% in the following 20 years if no urgent management action was implemented. These predictions, however, were still considered conservative in view of the severe anthropogenic stress caused by the growing population in the most-threatened Southeast and East Asian reefs. The 'Reef at Risk' analysis from this region (Burke, Selig, & Spalding, 2002) revealed that 88% of reefs were under moderate-to-very-high human pressure. As the overall values were only averages, including more-or-less unspoiled remoter areas, such high levels of pressure might reasonably be expected also to prevail in other locations and regions.

At the present time, conservation achievements on a regional scale are not yet significant enough to mitigate the overall decline in the status of world reefs. Wilkinson (2002b) states that while on the one hand there might be gains in the health status of coral reefs in some areas within the coming two decades, provided there is sufficient political and financial support, on the other hand many reefs lie in areas where it is difficult to expand small-scale achievements to the national scale because of missing political lobby and awareness, or where management and coral reef monitoring programmes are still totally absent. Furthermore, protected areas are not always the instant key to success. McClanahan's (1999) study noted that only 9% of the world's marine protected areas (MPAs) were efficiently managed and had achieved their original management objectives. A considerable number of MPAs that have been declared actually exist only on paper or on maps. Sometimes MPAs are not even recognised by the national governments that host them. In 1995, for example, 125 out of 160 MPAs in the Western Indian Ocean had not yet reached the implementation stage (McClanahan, 1999). Ten years later, there is no evidence that this picture has significantly changed.

Major Threats to Coral Reefs

At the present time, repeated bleaching events associated with global climate change represent the major threat to coral reefs, resulting in the loss of huge reef areas over a comparably short time. This significantly reduces the capacity of the reef to recover and to grow (Bellwood, Hughes, Folke, & Nyström, 2004; Wilkinson, 2002a). Other severe impacts are the result of the increasing human population and its economic activity: excess sediment and nutrient loads because of poor land-use practices and agriculture (e.g. terrigenous or 'land-derived' run-off by the clear-cutting of hinterland forests and mangroves), industrial and urban sewage discharges, coastal construction activities including the mining of coral rock, and destructive fishing methods such as those involving the use of dynamite and poison (see, for example, Brown, 1988; Hughes et al., 2003; Jackson et al., 2001; Wilkinson, 1993).

In addition to the above-mentioned anthropogenic stressors, coral reefs also suffer from natural disturbances such as tropical storms, coral diseases and predation by the crown-of-thorn starfish *Acanthaster planci*. Outbreaks of this coralivourous starfish have destroyed large reef areas in the Pacific and Indian Ocean (see, for example, Done, 1985) which, however, recover slowly if no further human-made stress is added. The increasing frequency of *Acanthaster* outbreaks and new devastating coral diseases give good reason for speculations that these forms of biological stresses might be triggered or aggravated by human activities (Brown, 1997; Pandolfi et al., 2003).

Coastlines and beaches have always been subject to extensive pressure by humans. Water sports are as popular as ever and the market is still growing. The dimensions have changed, however, over the last decade, with increasing concern directed at the boom in mass tourism. A particular concern has been diving tourism, which in some regions has grown to become a major threat to coral reefs (Carter, 1990; Harriott, Davies, & Banks, 1997; Hawkins & Roberts, 1993; Spalding, Ravilious, & Green, 2001). In Egypt, for example, the explosion of coastal tourism since the early 1980s, with a massive growth of poorly planned resort towns, has led to the degradation or loss of many near-shore fringing reefs (Spalding et al., 2001). In Hurghada, for example, traces of sediment input by construction activities, physical damage from anchoring and over-diving are still evident, although the situation is improving, for example through the installation of more than 250 off-shore mooring buoys. Strict planning measures have been adopted now for new construction activities, mainly through the establishment of a network of coastal protectorates managed by the Egyptian Environmental Affairs Agency (EEAA). However, it is questionable whether these actions alone can withstand the enormous rush of tourists. In older publications (Bryant et al., 1998; Cesar, 2003; Hassan, 2002) the number of hotel beds was expected to increase over one thousand percent by 2005. The actual situation, however, is even more dramatic. In Sharm El Sheikh, for example, the numbers increased from approximately 1000 in 1992 to over 44,000 hotel beds in 2005 (Mohammed Salim, Ras Mohammed National Park Authority, personal communication) and there are plans to increase this to 200,000 by the year 2017 (Hassan, 2002). This development will in turn lead to an increase in the number of divers and snorkellers invading the reefs. One assessment identifies 61% of the Egyptian reefs as being moderately-to-highly threatened by diving activities (Spalding et al., 2001).

Although the environmental education of recreational divers is improving and becoming an obligatory part of diving courses, while permanent buoys are increasingly being installed to reduce anchoring damage by diving boats, and although awareness programmes are flourishing, the reefs are declining in terms of living coral cover. The factor so far not successfully tackled (for economic reasons) is simply the high number of reef visitors such as divers and snorkellers (Cesar, 2003; Eisinger, 2005; Kay & Liddle, 1987; Neil, 1990) which invade the accessible reefs. Credit does nevertheless need to be given to the efforts of local authorities such as the EEAA in Egypt to control the huge number of snorkellers through the provision of walkways in order to minimise impacts on the reef flat and reef crest (personal observation).

In the following section, recreational diving will be considered as an important threat to reefs. The section will also analyse the traditional usage patterns by 'reef tourists' and the economic frameworks within which tropical countries with reef-lined coasts (Cesar, 2003; Sudara & Nateekarnchanalap, 1988) typically try to handle the problem.

Mass Diving Tourism: Facts and Limits

In general, the optimal way to conserve sensitive natural environments is to minimise the amount of anthropogenic impacts, a task which is feasible for many destructive activities such as dynamite and poison fishing and several forms of pollution. For most of these threats, substitutions or mitigation strategies are available. In the case of recreational diving, however, realistic alternatives are generally missing. The availability and accessibility of natural reefs are considered to be essential prerequisites for the activity, regardless of the certainty that many such reefs are being locally overused and show various signs of degradation.

The concept of imposing strict limits, for example on the number of diving tourists and boats for certain reefs, might slow down the 'consumption' of the reefs in a short-term but will neither sustain the reefs nor the economies depending on them. Up to now, the concept of 'ecological carrying capacity' has often been neglected or misinterpreted. The carrying capacity of a coral reef is defined as its ability of a reef to support a range of extractive and invasive uses without perceptible changes and degradation of its biological productivity and species diversity over a reasonable period of time (Harriott et al., 1997; Wafar, 1997). The concept of ecological limits is, however, open to debate and this is not just in the case of its application to coral reefs. Whereas some argue that the limits implied are fixed and inelastic, others argue that ecological carrying capacity is flexible and cannot simply be reduced to a single measure (Jameson, Ammar, Saadalla, Mostafa, & Riegl, 1999; Zakai & Chadwick-Furman, 2002). The latter especially holds true for coral reefs, where in many calculations (e.g. Jameson et al., 1999), no precise reference to the size of the reef area or other relevant parameters is provided. For example, one hectare might tolerate 10 dives of one hour per day by skilled divers, which accounts for approximately 3600 dives per year, but it does not tolerate one dive per day by an absolutely unskilled diver, which equals only one-tenth of the calculated pressure. Consequently, without such a size reference and without the definition of what counts as 'perceptible' changes to the ecosystem, the whole carrying capacity concept is rather subjective and hence entirely unworkable at the basis of a practical management approach.

The reefs off the Egyptian city of Sharm El Sheikh are a prime example of an unprecedented transgression of carrying capacities. As a case study of this immense diving pressure, this chapter will use the Gordon reef in the Straits of Tiran and will try to relate this pressure to the effectively used reef area. As no official data on the current diving situation are available, the presented calculations represent a first approximation. This is based on personal observations by the authors and on communications by rangers of the Ras Mohammed National Park.

Working on the assumption that Gordon Reef is an idealised round platform reef with a diameter of 250 m, the circumference amounts to approximately 785 m. Gordon Reef, along with the other platform reefs in the Strait of Tiran (Thomas Reef, Woodhouse, Jackson Reef), rises up from depths of over 100 m. The actually dived area on a classical platform reef with a relatively steep reef slope (often with drop-off conditions) is a belt of no more than 20 m wide because divers are not able to retain sight of the reef structure and inhabitants if they move further away. This corresponds to a hypothetically dived total area of 15,700 m² (around 1.6 ha) for the platform reef. Only a maximum of 50% of the calculated area can be accessed by divers, however, due to the one-hour time limit fixed by the dive operators and due to the limited air supply. Normally, dives start from the mooring point of the boat at the wave-protected southern part of the reef and normally also end there, implying that mostly the same reef sections are visited. With the exception of 'drift dives' (which are much rarer and for the purpose of our simplifying calculation are not included here) the northern parts of the reef largely remain undiscovered. Taking this into consideration, the effectively used reef area during one dive is reduced to approx. 0.8 ha. This still corresponds to more than 1.5 soccer fields and is therefore a quite large diving area.

The next step in assessing diving pressure on Gordon Reef is to calculate the number of dives. At the present, approximately 400 boats from over 100 diving centres operate daily in the southern Sinai area and/or provide live-aboard tours. The latter visit the reefs around Ras Mohammed and in the Straits of Tiran and offer diving tours of several days' duration. Assuming 20 divers on a medium-sized boat at normal occupancy rates, this amounts to a total of 8000 divers or 16,000 dives (generally, divers make two dives per day, personal observation). Projecting this to one entire year with 320 diving days, this adds up to 5,120,000 dives at reefs off Sharm El Sheikh. Cesar (2003), meanwhile, suggests an average of one dive per diver and day for Sharm El Sheikh. Even so, Cesar still calculates a total of 1,305,985 dives for the year 2000. Considering the number of hotel beds in Sharm El Sheikh has almost doubled since then (Jeudi de Grissac, 2002), the total of approximately 5 million dives calculated above on the basis of two dives per day does not seem unreasonable. Currently there are 26 official dive sites, but a more realistic assumption given the increasing rush of tourists to the reef would be that there will soon be at least 50 dive sites. This gives an average of 102,400 dives per dive site and year, a value which is beyond all questions far in excess of the carrying capacities of the local reefs. Similar quantities were calculated by Abou Zaid (2002) for the most-visited reefs off Hurghada, the other major tourist centre in Egypt located approximately 150 km south of Sharm El Sheikh on the African mainland.

A 0.8 ha reef area with 102,400 dives per year, implies a pressure of 128,000 dives per hectare per year (or 12.8 dives per m^2 per year). This means that every year, each square metre of reef is exposed 12.8 times to a dive of approximately one hour.

This example shows that the carrying capacity is a very complex function based on a diverse range of variables (Jameson et al., 1999; Wafar, 1997), all of which have to be assessed in order to define meaningful limits. Indeed, in addition to physical size, a range of other factors play a crucial role, including location and natural physical condition of the reef (topography, depths, currents); the composition and biodiversity of the coral community (type and fragility of corals); the productivity of the reef; onshore developmental activities; the susceptibility of the reef to natural disasters; interactions with other ecosystems; the current level of tourism and future prospects (such as additional means of accessing the water, for example by boat or from the shore, the level of skills possessed by divers, types of activity and so on) and applied management strategies. Even for the same reef, the carrying capacity might vary over time as these key factors change. The whole concept requires continuous and extensive monitoring and a very sophisticated typology of reefs. Until such as system is established there is only one obliging principle: the fewer divers on a reef the better.

This sobering conclusion brings us back to the core of the problem: the dilemma of conflicting interests between nature conservation and economic demands. If only the national economy would allow it, the complete banishment of every anthropogenic activity from every reef would clearly be the best option to allow reefs in poor condition to recover or to allow an undamaged reef to remain in its pristine state. Unfortunately, this is rarely feasible, as most coral reefs are located in developing countries which cannot afford to close access to reefs for the sake of nature conservation. In this respect, strict limitations cannot be in the interest of planners and investors, as local and even national economies can depend very heavily on 'scuba dollars'.

Aside from tourism as source of revenue, we have to bear in mind that more than 500 million people are more-or-less dependent on reefs for their livelihood or as a significant source of income (Burke et al., 2002; Spurgeon, 2004). Even in countries such as Egypt, where 20 years ago only a few people lived along the coastline (mainly in artisanal fishing communities), today new resort towns provide jobs for thousands of people. Furthermore, it has to be remembered that the number of accessible reefs is limited in most cases. This means that reducing the number of reef tourists on one reef, or completely closing a reef in order to protect it, might merely result in the problem being shifted to another reef. In addition, it would appear to be somewhat contradictory for a resort to increase the number of tourist beds by several fold while simultaneously discussing a reduction in the number of divers from current levels.

This dilemma is forcing all parties to elaborate new concepts which can incorporate both ecological and economic interests and reduce diving pressure on the reef concerned by offering alternatives (van Treeck & Schuhmacher, 1999). Up to now, management has often sought to apply restrictions rather than practical solutions such as alternative underwater attractions (van Treeck & Schuhmacher, 1999). In the following section, a concept is presented which offers attractive substitutes to natural coral reefs for recreational divers, including options to experience the 'original' natural system. By separating the conventional linkage between divers and natural reefs, the dilemma between economic and ecological interests might be mitigated. At the same time, pressure on the sensitive reef system may be significantly reduced.

SCORE (Save COral REefs): A Concept to Combine Sustainable Development and Nature Conservation

During the First Egyptian Conference on Protected Areas and Sustainable Development in 2002, Klaus Töpfer, at that time executive director of the United National Environment Programme (UNEP), stated that nature conservation is an indispensable objective but that it should not be achieved at the expense of development. This is really just a generalisation of the dilemma discussed in the previous section of this paper. The concept presented in this section reflects this viewpoint by proposing the creation of alternative underwater attractions. These are intended to provide relief for natural reefs without imposing significant restrictions to overall diving opportunities in the local area. The concept might best be implemented in ecologically less fragile areas such as sand flats or already degraded reef areas with a certain proximity to a healthy reef community.

It can be argued that artificial underwater scenery is quite capable of meeting the essential demands of scuba divers. One of these demands is the desire to escape gravity and to move freely in three dimensions. Indeed, it is astonishing how much fascination emanates from any kind of wreck (sunk either accidentally or intentionally to serve as dive site) or large artificial structure on the seabed, structures which would be simply considered as scrap if found on land. If they are also overgrown by colourful reef organisms such as soft corals and inhabited by large numbers of fish, divers are usually more than satisfied (personal observation).

Furthermore, such installations could serve as facilities for other purposes, such as environmental education, reef rehabilitation, dive training or as a 'stepping stone' in a system of new substrate islands. Such stepping stones are healthy reef communities (either on natural or artificial substrates) which are intended to act as source of larvae for the recovery of neighbouring degraded areas. Ironically, dive education itself (specifically basic training) still tends to take place on genuine reefs, with adverse consequences resulting in many cases. Artificial alternatives could offer a location for divers to practice routine exercises for improving their buoyancy and other skills, while simultaneously providing some biological interest to the trainee divers.

ERCON (Electrochemical Reef CONstruction): The Key Technology

By far the greater proportion of so-called 'artificial reefs' are made of industrial construction materials such as concrete, steel, plastic or scrap material dumped on the sea floor (see, for example Schuhmacher, 2002). In contrast, as Figure 8.1 and Photo 8.1 show, that the technology discussed in this section uses hard substrates that are formed *in situ* from compounds

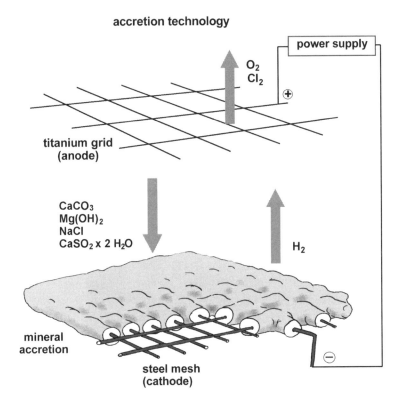

Figure 8.1: Scheme of electrochemical accretion technology (for technical details see van Treeck, 2002).

A: 2001

B: 2004

C: 2006

Photo 8.1: Development of the protoreef community on a crane-like extension of a tetrahedron structure (Photograph: Michael Eisinger).

that are already present in seawater through the simple principle of electrolysis. The technique therefore minimises the amount of alien material introduced into the marine environment. When connecting to a direct-current power supply, magnesium and calcium minerals precipitate on a steel matrix which functions as the cathode, whereas low concentrations of chlorine and oxygen evolve around the anode (titanium mesh spanned over the cathode). The accreted material consists mainly of calcium carbonate which, having similar features to reef limestone, is suitable to be colonised by a wide variety of reef organisms. For details on the accretion technology, see Hilberts, Wilson, and Fallis (1995), Meyer and Schuhmacher (1993), van Treeck (2002) and Heesen (2002). Furthermore, the substrate is suitable for the transplantation of coral fragments, a method which significantly advances coral recovery by shortening the time needed for natural colonisation, a process that usually takes several decades (Schuhmacher, van Treeck, Eisinger, & Paster, 2000; van Treeck & Schuhmacher, 1997).

Aims of SCORE

The SCORE concept follows a simple philosophy: every dive inside an artificial underwater park is a dive outside natural reefs. The main goals of SCORE are to:

- Divert diving activities from sensitive natural reefs to artificial theme parks
- Apply an ecologically compatible method to build park structures
- Enhance reef recovery by providing suitable substrata
- Accelerate colonisation through the transplantation of corals
- Integrate the park into a holistic network of nature preservation, environmental education and coastal management.

Setting up the SCORE Park

In order to illustrate the SCORE concept, imagine a hypothetical bay along a fringing reef where the installation is to be set up. A flexible system of modules is used in order to address the various requirements of ecology, functionality, security and aesthetics. This is made up of special modules, each with a different purpose such as dive training, environmental education and coral rehabilitation. These modules can be shaped and combined with each other according to the specific objectives set for the park. The framework for the various modules is made of a steel mesh or other suitable steel components which are coated with calcium carbonate by applying the above-mentioned accretion technology. The resulting material is suitable as a substrate for colonisation by corals and other reef organisms. The concept allows a stepwise integration of additional elements in an existing park. The following different modules are feasible, depending on the objectives of the park:

Recreation Module

This module is a spacious structure allowing the exploration from the inside and outside, providing a range of demands for divers with different coordination skill levels. The creation of different reef-like habitats provides a framework for spontaneous settlement by characteristic organisms. Aesthetically, this module should represent the main attraction of the entire park.

Training Module

This module is the most abstract and provides for the education and advanced training of scuba divers under complex but artificial conditions. It comprises a platform for testing and improving various diving skills, with the option to perform orientation, rescue and other exercises. The training module is intended to form the entrance to the proposed park, and is the central unit providing anchoring sites for dive boats. Dives carried out by absolute beginners could take place here.

Rehabilitation Module

The rehabilitation module is intended to provide a natural integration of the artificial elements into the genuine setting of the 'natural' coral reef. It offers the opportunity for underwater photography and education in the marine sciences. In contrast to the recreation module, access to this unit would be restricted in order to ensure that the reef remains properly protected.

Environmental Education Module

The possibilities here are manifold. Such a module could take the form of an underwater trail for presenting interesting ecological and ethological phenomena such as fish cleaning stations (where fishes get rid of parasites or particles by small cleaner fishes or shrimp that feed on this diet) and other symbioses. It would familiarise the diver with the most important floral and faunal elements of a coral reef. Architecturally, it might function as a link between the other components of the installation.

In terms of shape and endowment with corals and other organisms, the design of individual modules can take into account both their intended function within the park and their proximity to the natural reef community. Those units which face severe pressure by divers are primarily designed to fulfil sporting features and requirements. As soon as the emphasis is shifted towards environmental education and coral rehabilitation, detrimental use must be limited. The main objective is to create attractive and functional conditions for the different tasks and needs of scuba diving, concentrated in a relatively small area. The scuba diver is asked to adapt his or her activities to the prevailing conditions and not the opposite way around.

The infrastructure required for the installation and the ERCON technology such as power supply, anodes, cables and so on is relatively limited and could be re-used in the long term, thus minimising the associated costs.

Mode of Functioning of the SCORE Park

Figure 8.2(a) represents a map of the hypothetical bay before implementation of the SCORE park. Diving activities mainly focus on the near-shore reefs with access from the shore and from boats (two anchoring sites). The sandy bottomed areas in the middle

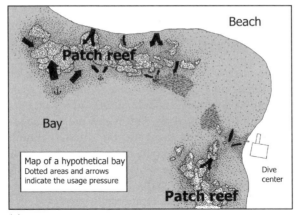

(a)

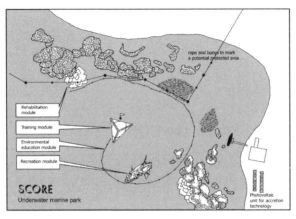

(b)

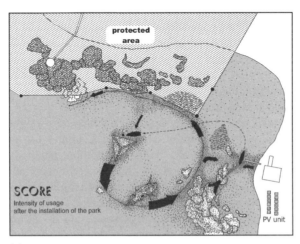

(c)

Figure 8.2: Maps of a hypothetical SCORE park.

of the bay are rather unattractive for divers and not used for any recreational activities. In order to illustrate the effect of the SCORE concept, the intensity of usage before and after installation of the park are described and indicated in the maps by arrows and dotted areas.

In Figure 8.2(b), the underwater theme park has been installed comprising various attractive modules: a training module for improving diving skills; an underwater trail for environmental education; a 'discovery' module in form of a wreck; and two rehabilitation modules. The resulting shift of usage intensities are indicated in Figure 8.2(c). Activities now mainly focus on the artificial structures in the centre of the bay (known as diver-aggregation devices, or 'DADs') which are approached from the seaward side by boat. This avoids mechanical breakage of corals due to divers entering the site from the shore or as a result of poor buoyancy skills. Although approximately 50% of the bay is excluded from a direct utilisation and represents a protected area, divers still can approach this part of the reef from the margins if they can prove that they have good buoyancy skills. In general, the greater the skills divers are able to demonstrate, the further they are allowed to progress onto the genuine reef. It has to be underlined that the SCORE concept does not impose any limitation to the overall diving activities. The measures implied simply imply a shift towards the more sustainable use of existing resources.

From Vision to a Pre-Study: The CONTRAST Project

All of the methods needed to realise a SCORE park have already been tested, particularly during CONTRAST (*Co*ral *N*ubbin *Tra*nsplantation *St*udy), a research project jointly run by the University of Essen and the EEAA Ras Mohammed National Park Authority. The main focus of the project was the application and further development of ERCON for reef rehabilitation, including trials to select suitable coral species for transplantation (Schuhmacher et al., 2000).

The findings of this study suggested that the net independent power supply for ERCON could be significantly improved by using photo-electric panels as renewable energy resources. Coral fragments ('nubbins') for the transplantation studies were derived from ship groundings or other sites with enhanced mechanical breakage of corals such as reef edges (where there is trampling by reef walkers and snorkellers) and successfully transplanted onto the artificial reef structures.

Following the survival and growth of the coral nubbins over a three-year period, the researchers identified a wide spectrum of coral species suitable for the proposed transplantation method (Schuhmacher et al., 2000). In addition, hundreds of natural coral recruits were found on the ERCON structures which is all the more noteworthy as spontaneous settlement by larvae is essential to make the structures a living part of the reef community (Eisinger, 2005). One big tetrahedron structure, for example, exhibited more than 450 new coral colonies after a period of four years, thus by far exceeding the number of transplanted corals. Photo 8.2 is a sequence of photographs showing the succession of an ERCON structure.

Photo 8.2: Tetrahedron structure 5.5 years after installation (Photograph: Michael Eisinger).

The formation of bigger structures out of smaller modules was also successfully tested. Photo 8.3 shows a 3-metre-high pyramidal structure made up of four units additionally equipped with crane-like extensions and populated with coral fragments. This impressive and complex installation offers a large number of openings and crevices for a wide variety of reef dwellers and could function as 'discovery module' within a SCORE park. A variety of fish species immediately accepted the new structure either as an aggregation point or as their permanent habitat.

As well as providing an attraction for recreational divers, such structures could also serve as 'stepping stones', thus supporting spontaneous re-colonisation of degraded reef areas by stony corals and other organisms.

Photo 8.3: Sample of an EAT grid which was originally containing two *Millepora dichotoma* fragments 5 years after transplantation (Photograph: Michael Eisinger).

Conclusion

Against the background of the latest reports on the worldwide degradation of coral reefs, there is no doubt that the state of reefs is serious. If we want to conserve at least some of the remaining reefs for our children, we have to take immediate action. This action should focus on realistic approaches and consider nature conservation efforts in the context of human welfare and the sustainable use of natural resources. The SCORE concept could be such an approach by ensuring a coexistence of development – as exemplified by diving tourism – and nature conservation.

While it is important to look at reefs not only from the environmental perspective but also as a means of production and a source of income for growing populations, their conservation should be given highest priority on the agenda. The clarification of responsibilities for near-shore waters, including reefs, and their integration into management concepts might stimulate private investors to take an active part. This might transform former 'pure consumers' into 'sustainable users'. Arguably, what we are currently witnessing in many reef areas displays remarkable analogies to what is known as 'the tragedy of the commons' (Hardin, 1968). The idea behind is briefly illustrated by an example from the Swiss Alps. Traditionally, each rural village has a pasture for common use. These common-use pastures are generally heavily overgrazed because nobody takes responsibility for the commons. At the same time, the same farmers keep their own land in good condition avoiding any kind of abuse. It is amazing how rapidly such badly treated pastures change their appearance to the better if sold to an exclusive user. As long as the surrender of overuse is not economically compensated or even enables potential competitors to maximise their benefits (if I leave some grass, my neighbour will take it), no self-induced sustainable usage practice will be established.

The lesson to be learnt from this example for reef environments sounds simple: hand over the responsibilities for defined reef areas to a defined entity and make sure that there is no way for the leaseholder to shrug off these responsibilities if the reef is ruined. Responsibility is the only way of installing sustainability. In other words: nobody burns a tree if they depend on its fruits and shade. Under such conditions, the economy will provide the strongest argument for nature protection. Any investment (as long as it is done in a meaningful way) will pay off. In principle, the same holds true for the creation of underwater attractions in ecologically less sensitive areas, thus diverting pressure from fragile ecosystems.

Looking back at more than a decade of proposals for the implementation of artificial underwater parks being made at conferences, workshops and symposia, and in spite of almost unanimous approval for the concept, no such park has yet been implemented. Investment will only take place if revenue is guaranteed. Nor would an investor construct an artificial structure on land they do not own and control. Hence, should we not accept that the sea is simply a means of production and treat it as such? If the product to be offered to the customers (divers, visitors, tourists) is a flourishing reef, why not hand it over to responsible investors? The alternative (well-protected sanctuaries and protected areas) is only feasible for economically independent countries but these represent the minority of states with coral reefs. It would seem that the destiny of coral reefs as a tropical ecosystem will be determined elsewhere.

References

Abou Zaid, M. (2002). *Impact of diving activities on the coral reefs along the Red Sea coast of Hurghada.* Report. Marine Biology and Fish Science Section, Zoology Department, Al-Azhar University.

Bellwood, D. R., Hughes, T. P., Folke, C., & Nyström, M. (2004). Confronting the coral reef crisis. *Nature, 429*, 827–833.

Brown, B. E. (1988). World-wide death of corals: Natural cyclic events or man made pollution? *Marine Pollution Bulletin, 18*, 9–13.

Brown, B. E. (1997). Disturbance to reefs in recent times. In: C. Birkeland (Ed.), *Life and death of coral reefs* (pp. 354–379). New York: Chapman and Hall.

Bryant, D., Burke, L., McManus, J., & Spalding, M. (1998). *Reefs at risk: A map-based indicator of potential threats to the world's coral reefs.* Washington, DC: World Resources Institute.

Burke, L., Selig, L., & Spalding, M. (2002). *Reef at risk in southeast Asia.* World Washington, DC: Resources Institute.

Carter, R.W. (1990). The recreational use and abuse of coastline of Florida. In: F. Fabbri (Ed.), *Recreational use of coastal areas* (pp. 3–17). Amsterdam: Kluwer Academic.

Cesar, H. S. J. (2003). *Economic valuation of the coral reefs of Egypt.* Report prepared for the MVE-unit of EEPP, funded by USAID.

Done, T. J. (1985). Effects of two *Acanthaster* outbreaks on coral reef community structure: The meaning of devastation. *Proceedings of the 5th International Coral Reef Congress, 5*, 315–320.

Eisinger, M. (2005). *Beiträge zu ökologischen und ökonomischen Aspekten der Korallentransplantation auf elektrochemisch erzeugte Substrate als Methode zur Rehabilitation degradierter Korallenriffe*. Dissertationsschrift, PhD thesis, Universität Duisburg-Essen.

Hardin, G. (1968). The tragedy of the commons. *Science, 162*, 1243–1248.

Harriott, V. J., Davies, D., & Banks, S. A. (1997). Recreational diving and its impacts in marine protected areas in eastern Australia. *Ambio, 26*, 173–179.

Hassan, A. H. (2002). environmental impact assessment (EIA) as tool for sustainable tourism. Abstract from the first Egyptian international conference on protected areas and sustainable development, 2002, Sharm El Sheikh, Egypt.

Hawkins, J. P., & Roberts, M. R. (1993). Can Egypt's coral reefs support ambitious plans for diving tourism? *Proceedings of the 7th international coral reef symposium 2*, Guam, pp. 1007–1013.

Heesen, K. (2002). Zusammensetzung und Bioerosion elektrochemisch erzeugter Hartsubstrate im Meer. Staatexamensarbeit für die Sekundarstufe I/II, Universität Duisburg-Essen.

Hilberts, W., Wilson, B., & Fallis, N. (1995). Autopia ampere-building with sun and sea. *Intelligent Bauen, 41*, 202–211.

Hughes, T. P., Baird, A. H., Bellwood, D. R., Card, M., Connolly, S. R., Folke, C., Grosberg, R., Hoegh-Guldberg, O., Jackson, J. B. C., Kleypas, J., Lough, J. M., Marshall, P., Nyström, M., Palumbi, S. R., Pandolfi, J. M., Rosen, B., Roughgarden, J. (2003). Climate change, human impacts, and the resilience of coral reefs. *Science, 301*, 929–933.

Jackson, J. B. C., Kirby, M. X., Berger, W. H., Bjorndal, K. A., Botsford, L. W., Bourque, B. J., Bradbury, R. H., Cooke, R., Erlandson, J., Estes, J. A., Hughes, T. P., Kidwell, S., Lange, C. B., Lenihan, H. S., Pandolfi, J. M., Peterson, C. H., Steneck, R. S., Tegner, M. J., & Warner, R. R. (2001). Historical overfishing and the recent collapse of coastal ecosystems. *Science, 293*, 629–638.

Jameson, S. C., Ammar, M. S. A., Saadalla, E., Mostafa, H., & Riegl, B. (1999). A coral damage index and its application to diving sites in the Egyptian Red Sea. *Coral Reefs, 18*, 333–339.

Jeudi de Grissac, A. (2002). The Gulf of Aqaba Protected Areas Network, South Sinai, Egypt. Abstract from the first Egyptian international conference on protected areas and sustainable development, 2002, Sharm El Sheikh, Egypt.

Kay, A. M., & Liddle, M. G. (1987). Resistance, survival and recovery of trampled corals on the Great Barrier Reef. *Biological Conservation, 42*, 1–18.

McClanahan, T. R. (1999). Is there a future for coral reef parks in poor tropical countries? *Coral Reefs, 18*, 321–325.

Meyer, D., & Schuhmacher, H. (1993). Ökologisch verträgliche Baupozesse im Meerwasser. *Geowissenschaften, 12*, 408–412.

Neil, D. (1990). Potential for coral stress due to sediment resuspension and deposition by reef walkers. *Biological Conservation, 52*, 221–227.

Pandolfi, J. M., Bradbury, R. H., Sala, E., Hughes, T. P., Bjorndal, K. A., Cooke, R. G., McArdle, D., McClenachan, L., Newman, M. J. H., Paredes, G., Warner, R. R., & Jackson, J. B. C. (2003). Global trajectories of the long-term decline of coral reef ecosystems. *Science, 301*, 955–958.

Schuhmacher, H. (2002). Use of artificial reefs with special reference to the rehabilitation of coral reefs. *Bonner Zoological Monograph, 50*, 81–108.

Schuhmacher, H., van Treeck, P., Eisinger, M., & Paster, M. (2000). Transplantation of coral fragments from ship groundings on electrochemically formed reef structures. *Proceedings 9th International Coral Reef Symposium Bali 2000, 2*, 983–990.

Spalding, M. D., Ravilious, C., & Green, E. P. (2001). *World atlas of coral reefs*. Berkeley: University of California Press.

Spurgeon, J. (2004). Valuation of coral reefs: The next 10 years. In: M. Ahmed, C. K. Chong, & H. Cesar (Eds), *Economic valuation and policy priorities for sustainable management of coral reefs*. Penang, Malaysia: WorldFish Center.

Sudara, S., & Nateekarnchanalap, S. (1988). Impact of tourism development on the reef in Thailand. *Proceedings of the sixth International Coral reef Symposium, Townsville*, *2*, 273–278.

van Treeck, P. (2002). *Beiträge zur Wiederbesiedlung natürlicher, semi-natürlicher und künslicher Riffsubstarte durch Steinkorallen und andere marine Invertebraten*. Dissertationsschrift, PhD thesis, Universität Essen.

van Treeck, P., & Schuhmacher, H. (1997). Initial survival of coral nubbins transplanted by a new coral transplantation technology: Options for reef rehabilitation. *Marine Ecology Progress Series*, *150*, 287–292.

van Treeck, P., & Schuhmacher, K. (1999). Mass diving tourism – a new dimension calls for new management approaches. *Marine Pollution Bulletin*, *37*, 499–504.

Wafar, M. (1997). Carrying capacity of coral reefs. In: V. Hoon (Ed.), *Proceedings of the regional workshop on the conservation and sustainable management of coral reefs. Proceedings* 22, CRSARD, Madras.

Wilkinson, C. R. (1993). Coral reefs of the world are facing widespread devastation: Can we prevent this through sustainable management practice? *Proceedings of the 7th International Coral Reef Symposium*, *1*, 11–21.

Wilkinson, C. R. (1998). *Status of coral reefs of the world: 1998*. Townsville: Australian Institute of Marine Science.

Wilkinson, C. R. (2000). *Status of coral reefs of the world: 2000*. Townsville: Australian Institute of Marine Science.

Wilkinson, C. (Ed.) (2002a). *Status of coral reefs of the world: 2002*. Townsville: Australian Institute of Marine Science.

Wilkinson, C. R. (2002b). Coral reefs at the crossroad. http://www.aims.gov.au/pages/research/coral-reefs/at-the-crossroad.html (Accessed 19 January 2007).

Wilkinson, C. R. (2004). *Status of coral reefs of the world: 2002*. Townsville: Australian Institute of Marine Science.

Zakai, D., & Chadwick-Furman, N. E. (2002). Impacts of intensive recreational diving on reef corals at Eilat, northern Red Sea. *Biological Conservation*, *105*, 179–187.

Chapter 9

Attitudes to and Preferences of Divers toward Regulation

Nola Barker and Callum Roberts

Introduction

Marine environments, especially those with coral reefs, are increasingly being used as a setting for tourism activities, particularly scuba diving and snorkelling (Orams, 1999). For various countries across the world, coral reefs make valuable contributions to their economies. In Sri Lanka, where coastal tourism is the mainstay of its economy, their reefs are estimated to be worth a net annual tourist value of US$214,000 (€193,000) per km^2 (Berg, Őhman, Troëng, & Lindén, 1998). In the Caribbean, the island of Bonaire generated an estimated total gross revenue of US$23.2 million (€19.7 million) in 1991 through dive-based tourism (Dixon, Fallon Scura, & van't Hof, 1993), while another island in the Caribbean, Saba, was estimated to generate US$2 million (€1.5 million) per year (Fernandes, 1995). Riopelle (1995) found the net present value of benefit from divers and snorkellers using West Lombok's reefs to be US$23.5 million (€18 million). In Australia, tourism in the Great Barrier Reef area generated an estimated US$682 million (€511 million) for the year 1991–1992 (Driml, 1994).

Despite their value, over half of the world's reefs are potentially threatened by human activity ranging from coastal development, destructive fishing practices, over-exploitation of resources, pollution and tourism, including direct impacts from swimmers, divers and snorkellers (Bryant, Burke, McManus, & Spalding, 1998; Hawkins et al., 1999; Muthiga & McClanahan, 1997; Tratalos & Austin, 2001; Zakai & Chadwick-Furman, 2002). Management strategies must encompass these anthropogenic threats if they are to protect reef and other marine resources effectively, and managing diver behaviour through regulation is an important aspect of that.

Divers are subject to regulation from the time they begin training for their various dive qualifications through to regulations imposed by dive companies, clubs, regional,

New Frontiers in Marine Tourism: Diving Experiences, Sustainability, Management
Copyright © 2008 by Elsevier Ltd.
ISBN: 978-0-08-045357-6

national and international laws. The internationally recognised dive clubs and certification organisations rely on members fulfilling strict training requirements and abiding
by their regulations. Once divers are qualified, their diving activities are managed by
those who work for dive businesses and clubs. After initial training, some of the most
common forms of diver regulation include education and the use of briefings, in-water
supervision, controlling the use of sites by limiting the number of divers allowed at sites
and the use of zoning and protected areas. The use of entrance or user fees can also assist
in regulating the use of reefs and, importantly, can help fund their management and conservation. The growing concern about damage to the environment by divers has led to
scrutiny of the effect of those regulations and whether they are effective in controlling
diving activities. This chapter discusses the effects of management measures on diver
behaviour and draws on research conducted on coral reefs throughout the world, but in
particular to that undertaken in a marine park in St. Lucia, a popular diving destination
in the Caribbean.

By understanding divers' attitudes to and preferences for particular regulations, managers can find the most effective ways to control diver impacts and promote the sustainability of reef use. The various management methods used to control divers are discussed
in this chapter. The chapter also illustrates some of the tools available to optimise the use
of aquatic environments while simultaneously preserving their integrity.

Education and Supervision of Divers

One way to reduce diver damage is through education. The point at which most divers
begin to learn to minimise their impact on marine life is during their initial training. One
aspect included in training by organisations such as the Professional Association of Diving
Instructors (PADI) and The National Association of Underwater Instructors (NAUI
Worldwide) is buoyancy control. The aim is to teach divers to maintain and use their equipment to allow them to dive safely and efficiently. They therefore learn to be streamlined,
swim in a horizontal position and positioned well above the reef or other structures. This
equips divers with the skills to prevent them from coming into contact with marine life and
harming both it and themselves (Photo 9.1). While these skills are taught in some detail to
divers taking courses for qualification, there are increasing numbers of tourists who undertake 'resort dives'. Such dives give tourists a diving experience for a day without the need
for comprehensive study of diving theory and practice. They are given minimal training
and gain only limited practical skills, which means that damage levels to reefs by resort
divers could be much higher than from trained divers.

Although further training beyond an initial certification and accruing hours spent
diving may increase a diver's awareness of their impacts and improve their diving
skills, it does not always appear to do so. Roberts and Harriott (1994) found that divers
with further training had less than half the number of uncontrolled contacts with the
benthos compared to divers with basic training, although the total sample size for that
study was small ($n = 30$). Conversely, research by Barker (2003) found that diver experience in terms of diver qualification and number of dives logged in total dive history did

Photo 9.1: Divers banging into the reef (Photograph: Bernita Jn Baptiste, Scuba St. Lucia).

Photo 9.2: Camera users cause more damage than other divers (Photograph: Bernita Jn Baptiste, Scuba St. Lucia).

not appear to be linked to contact rate ($n = 353$). That supports findings by Harriott, Davies, and Banks (1997) ($n = 136$) who found no significant difference between total number of contacts and diving experience (measured as less than or more than 100 dives) or dive qualification.

Typical advanced training courses available through PADI, for example, include titles such as rescue, navigation, deep diving, search and recovery, underwater photography (Photo 9.2), night diving, enriched air (Nitrox), dry suit and peak performance. Some will necessarily include training that will lead to improved diver awareness and control while underwater, but as some of the research has shown, even if divers are educated about good practice in looking after the underwater environment, it may not be something they automatically adopt in the long term. Irrespective of whether divers take further courses, once qualified, divers need only prove to dive companies that they have completed their initial qualification. They can then rent equipment or join a dive trip. Certain companies require divers to carry out a 'checkout dive', which may or may not involve having to demonstrate proficiency in particular tasks such as mask clearing and regulator recovery, but it is the authors' experience that this form of control is not typical.

For reasons of safety, it is universally recommended that divers do not dive alone, and although a few do, most dive in pairs. Not only can buddies look after each other, but this generally accepted practice may increase the likelihood of one or the other buddy reminding their partner of good practice. This may therefore also serve as a method of self-supervision and regulation. However, no published research has been done in that area.

Often, diving activities are part supervised from shore, such as through the monitoring of staff, boats and tourists coming in and out, and on the dive itself through the delivery of briefings and assistance given by dive leaders. There may be national laws on how dives should be undertaken in any given country or what should, or should not, be included in a pre-dive briefing. However, the usual intent of a briefing is that divers are given the information they need to ensure their enjoyment and safety. A briefing typically includes information on the underwater topography and the marine life divers are likely to encounter, as well as safety information. In some cases, a briefing may consist only of scant details such as a rough map of the area and otherwise divers are left to themselves. In many cases therefore, briefings may not even mention, let alone cover, how to minimise ones impacts while diving.

Research has shown that education in the form of briefings and in-water demonstrations can reduce impacts of divers on the marine environment (Medio, Ormond, & Pearson, 1997; Townsend, 2000). Medio tested the effect of giving a briefing that covered aspects of coral biology, impacts caused by divers and the concept of a protected area, supported by photographs, sketches and diagrams. Following this, an in-water demonstration showed divers the different forms of live reef cover and non-living substrate that could be touched without causing apparent damage. Medio found that this 45-minute educative session changed divers' behaviour by reducing the rate of diver contact with reef substrates from 1.4 to 0.4 contacts per diver per 7-min observation. Simultaneously, the rates of contact with living corals, as opposed to non-living substrate, decreased from 0.9 to 0.15 instances per diver per 7-min observation. This method clearly resulted in a statistically significant reduction in diver contact rates. If it could be adapted to a typical diving establishment which would not have specialist staff or time to give such long briefings, it could modify diver behaviour for the good of the environment. Townsend (2000) did just that. She tested the effect of in-house staff giving a modified briefing that included three short messages: (i) the fragility of the coral, (ii) the necessity of keeping at least one metre off the bottom to avoid kicking coral or kicking up sediment (Photo 9.3) and (iii) horizontal body positioning to avoid kicking the bottom. Those messages were further reinforced with posters positioned on the dive boats. Townsend found that divers given the modified briefing had fewer contacts (1.95 per 10-min observation) with substrate than divers not given the briefing (6.56 per 10-min observation). Statistical analyses of the likely influence of other variables such as age, gender and experience were inconclusive.

An important caveat made by Townsend is that existing levels of education, as well as staff commitment to conservation, were higher in her study in relation to other companies in the British Virgin Islands and compared with other countries she had visited. Such issues must undoubtedly be taken into account when designing programmes to manage diver behaviour and their impacts.

In St. Lucia, Barker and Roberts (2004) found that briefings had little effect on diver behaviour if given by dive shop staff, and only when divers were alerted to their actions while underwater was there any reduction in impact attained (see Table 9.1).

By signalling to divers that they were too close to the reef, were hitting it or kicking up sediment, dive guides reduced contacts and damage to the reef. Divers whose damaging behaviour was brought to their attention by dive-leaders had five times fewer contacts with the reef per dive than divers who were not notified (see Figure 9.1).

Photo 9.3: Divers kicking up sediment (Photograph: Bernita Jn Baptiste, Scuba St. Lucia).

For a 40-min dive with dive-leader intervention, mean and median number of times divers contacted the reef were 2.4 and 1. Without intervention, divers contacted the reef a mean of 11.6 times with a median of 6 times. Visitors interviewed in St. Lucia also commented that better control of divers' behaviour would have improved their diving experience. When the author (Barker) interviewed divers that had been reprimanded during their dive by their dive leader (without implying that the author had seen them being reprimanded), they indicated that they accepted that their behaviour needed to be modified. As most of the contacts made by divers with the reef appeared unintentional, that result is not a surprise. People often preferred to be told if they were damaging the environment rather than be left to carry on doing so.

Table 9.1: Results of a Scheirer–Ray–Hare test on the effect of briefing and intervention measures by dive leaders on the contact rate of divers.

	SS/MS$_{total}$	df	*P*-value
Intervention	6.199	1	0.01
Briefing	1.386	1	0.24
Intervention briefing	0.104	1	0.75

Note: SS = sum of squares, MS = mean square, df = degrees of freedom. The Scheirer–Ray–Hare test is a non-parametric equivalent to a two-way analysis of variance (Dytham, 1999). Only underwater intervention by dive leaders had a significant impact in reducing diver contacts with the reef. The non-significance of the briefing term shows that briefings were ineffective on their own. The non-significant interaction term suggests that intervention was not enhanced by a prior briefing.

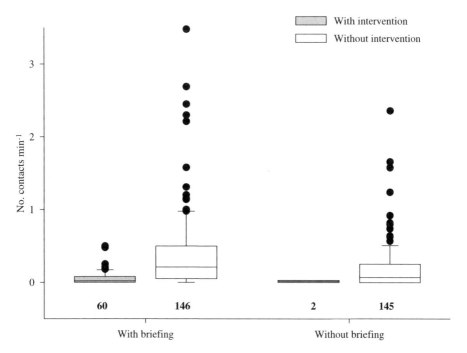

Figure 9.1: The effect of briefing and intervention by dive leaders on diver contact rate. Boxes represent the inter-quartile range which contains 50% of values. A line across the box indicates the median. The whiskers extend to the 5th and 95th percentiles and filled circles are the outliers. Numbers directly below the boxes represent sample size. Only two instances occurred where divers were not given a briefing but where the divemaster intervened. Both divers had low contact rates and the sample size was not large enough to draw confidence intervals.

Limiting the Number of Divers Allowed to Use a Site

Another regulatory measure used to reduce damage to aquatic life includes restricting visitor numbers to sites so as to spread visitor load over sites more equally and/or to exclude them from particularly sensitive sites. Although not widely adopted, site limits have been used to address problems of crowding and environmental degradation. As this chapter has already mentioned, the impact of divers and snorkellers can be significant, especially when there is a concentration of activity resulting in popular areas receiving more visitors than it can cope with. The term 'carrying capacity' is often used to refer to the number of people and animals that can use a resource without causing 'unacceptable impacts' to a particular environment (Resource Assessment Commission (RAC), 1993), a variant of this approach is known as the 'limits of acceptable change' (LAC). Of course, carrying capacity for tourism varies from reef to reef. It is also dependent on factors other than just numbers of people. Such factors include the amount of management and education, as well as the location of the reef in relation to other human activities and development, the type of activity the reef is being used for, and reef structure and composition (Clark, 1991; Harriott et al., 1997; Salm, 1986; Schleyer & Tomalin, 2000; Zakai & Chadwick-Furman, 2002).

Examples of where limits on the number of people are allowed to use a resource include the island of Sipadan (16.4 ha), where Malaysian authorities enforce a limit of 100 divers on the island's reefs per day (Musa, 2002). In Spain's Medes Islands (21.5 ha), managers have set a limit of 450 dives per day (Mundet & Ribera, 2001). Where diver use is spread over larger areas, a tradeable permit system may be a more appropriate and effective means to control visitor numbers (Cumberbatch, 2000). Access to the most attractive sites would be priced more highly in terms of the cost of the permit required to dive them, while access to lower-quality sites would have lower permit prices. To implement such a scheme, dive carrying capacity for each site would need to be determined. The corresponding number of tradeable permits would then be issued to dive operators through a bidding process, which would in total allow exactly the decided dive levels at each site during the period for which the permits are valid. In this way, such a system could improve efficiency and potentially generate more income for an area than a flat-fee permit system would be able to. As permits are in limited supply they obtain a scarcity value and any holders can sell their excess permits to another business.

Estimates of sustainable diver carrying capacities for reefs range from 4000–7000 dives per site per year (see Table 9.2). These numbers are specific to those sites studied and may

Table 9.2: Estimates of carrying capacities for coral reefs.

No. dives per site per year	Location	Reference
4000–6000	Bonaire, Netherland Antilles	Dixon et al. (1993, 1994)
Up to 5,000	Eastern Australia	Harriott et al. (1997)
5000–6000	Egypt, Bonaire and Saba	Hawkins and Roberts (1997), Hawkins et al. (1999)
5000–6000	Eilat, Israel	Zakai and Chadwick-Furman (2002)
Maximum of 7000	Sodwana Bay, South Africa	Schleyer and Tomalin (2000)

not be automatically applicable to other dive sites, but they help to illustrate the link between levels of acceptable change to an ecosystem and the corresponding numbers of users within it. The estimates were based on the premise that above those intensities of use, the reefs would suffer significant coral-cover loss and high frequencies of colony damage (Prior, Ormond, Hitchen, & Wormald, 1995; Riegl & Velimirov, 1991; Zakai & Chadwick-Furman, 2002). However, the figures may be conservative as the reefs on which those carrying-capacity estimates were based had little or no management of in-water impacts by divers and snorkellers. Hawkins, Roberts, Kooistra, Buchan, and White (2005) found that diving at levels up to around 2,000 dives per site per year had no detectable long-term impact on reefs of the Caribbean island of Saba. Where the total area of reef available for diving is limited, such as at Eilat in the Northern Red Sea, it may be very difficult for managers to keep diver numbers below these limits (Zakai & Chadwick-Furman, 2002).

As mentioned earlier in this chapter, carrying capacity will be influenced by factors beyond just the number of users, including the level of other damaging activities and impacts present. Sites close to human settlement are often subjected to extractive activities including fishing and mining, and pollution from household, industrial and agricultural activities (Hawkins & Roberts, 1997). A site being used to teach people how to dive is likely to receive more damage than if it is used by qualified divers (Harriott et al., 1997), and if a site is being used by both divers and snorkellers, then total impacts are likely to be greater.

Dive groups can also be limited in size. Visitors to St. Lucia said that smaller dive groups would have improved their diving experience (Barker, 2003). Group size thus appeared to be a management measure that would be readily accepted. Visitors surveyed elsewhere in the Caribbean, Spain and Malaysia were also concerned by overcrowding (Mundet & Ribera, 2001; Musa, 2002; Rudd & Tupper, 2002). The Caribbean study found that willingness to pay for dives was greater if diving could be done in small groups (Rudd & Tupper, 2002). Thus, not only are divers willing to pay more for less-crowded diving, but as suggested earlier in this chapter, smaller groups would allow for greater supervision of divers. It is reported in the following section of this chapter that divers are often willing to pay more to visit well-managed sites, so the potential of smaller groups to result in reduced revenue for tour operators may not be a problem. Together, the measures discussed result in greater satisfaction as far as the customer is concerned and help reduce the negative impacts of divers because they can be assisted more effectively.

The continued popularity of sites and diving activity throughout the world, even at sites with restrictions placed on the total number of divers allowed to the visit the site or the maximum numbers of divers allowed in dive groups, suggests that people accept such measures and, in some cases, are willing to pay more for the privilege. Whether or not such limits are enough in themselves to protect environments and to keep impacts within an acceptable level is debatable. As tourism increases, so does demand for dive sites and managers can use this as an opportunity to maximise revenues.

Regulation by Zoning Specific Areas for Divers and Setting up MPAs

Marine protected areas (MPAs) provide a focus for conservation management and this usually includes the management of visitors. Most of the best examples of visitor management come from places with MPAs such as Saba and Bonaire in the Caribbean. Current typical visitor management of MPAs includes the establishment of mooring buoys to prevent the use of anchors that would otherwise damage the reef. Limitations may also be put on the number of boats allowed to tie up to a mooring. For example, in the Saba marine park, only one boat is allowed per mooring at any one time. MPAs provide regulatory oversight of visitor activities that is welcome from the perspective of environmental management. However, such protected areas are still the rare exception. Only 0.6% of the area of the world's oceans is covered by MPAs. The figures for coral reef habitats are barely any better. While 19% of the global area of coral reefs is encompassed by MPAs, very little of that area, perhaps only 2% of reefs, is effectively protected (Mora et al., 2006). Even where MPAs exist and implement basic measures to limit visitor damage, few have yet faced up to the scale of visitor pressure. In many cases, reefs in MPAs are degrading badly. For example, The Ras Mohammed National Park in the Red Sea has installed moorings, pontoons and visitor walkways in order to manage impacts, but thousands of tourists clamber across the reefs every day, trampling on corals and other organisms. Similarly, reefs of the Virgin Islands National Park and Biosphere Reserve at St. John in the US Virgin Islands have been 'protected' since 1962, but they have degraded just as badly as those in the same area that have not been similarly designated (Rogers & Beets, 2001).

Few MPAs have yet attempted in-water management of tourist impacts, other than basic management of boating activities. Instead, their protection efforts largely centre on the control of fishing and pollution. But control of divers and snorkellers is critical for the protection of reefs and other marine habitats, particularly if they are to accommodate a growth in tourism. Visitor surveys in St. Lucia showed that when choosing a holiday destination, MPAs were preferred by many tourists over destinations without protected areas (Barker, 2003). Having an MPA therefore gives a destination a competitive edge. Yet unless MPAs exert sufficient control over visitor activities, their popularity may undermine their efforts to protect natural resources. The same study found that tourists also wanted to see more active policing of the marine park (Barker, 2003). Tourists evidently wish to see more than just 'paper parks'.

The best MPAs usually include zoning to separate or limit damaging activities. The Bonaire Marine Park, like many others, has anchoring zones outside of which anchoring is forbidden. Many protected areas have no-take zones where fishing is not permitted, and these are often the focus of scuba-diving and snorkelling activity. However, few protected areas have yet used zoning to protect resources from presumed non-consumptive uses such as diving. If protected areas are to avoid habitat degradation, they will need to take a more imaginative and proactive stance on managing visitor impacts in the water, including the use of zoning. Such zones may well include areas that are taken off limits to diving and snorkelling, as well as limited access zones.

Fees and Divers' Willingness to Pay Them

MPAs help to manage and protect reefs, and attract tourists, but to do this they do need financial support. A recent global assessment of MPAs found that only 2% of the world's coral reefs are to be found within MPAs that effectively conserve resources (Mora et al., 2006). Attributes possessed by those MPAs included regulations on extraction, poaching, external risks, MPA size and MPA isolation. One way for MPAs to harness more of the potential income from tourists is to charge fees. If they managed to do so, a greater proportion of management costs and other attributes that contribute to effective conservation could be paid for. Revenues from fees could help MPAs categorised as inefficient or 'paper parks' to become fully functioning.

The Hol Chan Marine Reserve and Half Moon Caye in Belize charge between US$2.50 and US$5.00 (€1.9 and €3.8) per visitor per day; the Fernando de Noronha Marine Park in Brazil charges US$4.25 (€3.25) per visitor per day; the British Virgin Islands charges divers US$1 (€0.77) per day; Bonaire Marine Park charges US$10 (€7.7) per diver per year and Saba Marine Park charges US$3.00 per dive and US$3.00 (€2.2 and €2.2) per week for snorkellers (Lindberg & Halpenny, 2001). In the Medes Islands protected area of Spain, divers are charged a fee of US$2.2 (€2.6) per dive (Mundet & Ribera, 2001). In 2006, the Ras Mohammed Marine Park charged US$6.4 (€5) per day for diving, while the Soufriere Marine Management Area in St. Lucia charges around US$4 (just over €3) per day. However, for most marine parks the financial support from tourist user fees is not enough to pay for their management (Balmford, Gravestock, Hockley, McClean, & Roberts, 2004; Lee & Han, 2002). Saba and Bonaire marine parks are among the few which have become self-financing through user fees (Dixon et al., 1993; D. Kooistra pers. comm.). By way of contrast, in Costa Rica, less than 1% of the national parks 1992 budget came from entrance fees (Dixon & van't Hof, 1997). It is unlikely that MPAs are capturing the full potential for tourist funding (Green & Donnelly, 2003).

Studies suggest that tourists would be willing to pay higher fees to experience protected areas (Dixon, Fallon Scura, & van't Hof, 1994; Lee & Han, 2002; Walpole, Goodwin, & Ward, 2001). In 1992, a survey in Bonaire showed that 80% would be willing to pay at least US$20 (€15.7), double the fee then being charged (Dixon et al., 1994). Similarly, recreational use values of five National Parks in South Korea showed that tourists were willing to pay between six and seventeen times the fee of US$0.83 (€0.89) (Lee & Han, 2002).

A potential argument against implementing and increasing fees is that they may lead to a decrease in visitation; however research has shown that this is not always the case. A study of visitors to Komodo National Park in Indonesia suggested that a five-fold increase in fees from US$0.87 to US$4 (from €1 to €4.7) would result in only a 20% decline in visitation (Walpole et al., 2001). Research by Walpole et al. (2001) and others indicated that demand was relatively insensitive to price (Mundet & Ribera, 2001), although their studies had low starting fees of between US$0.87 and US$2.2 (€1 and €2.6). In Costa Rica, an increase in tourist fees from US$1.25 to US$15.00 (€1.06 to €12.8) in 1994 for visiting national parks may have contributed to the 47% decrease in visitation by non-residents (Laarman & Gregersen, 1996) but resulted in a five-fold increase in revenues (Dixon & van't Hof, 1997). However, on the positive side, for MPAs suffering from excessive use, raising visitor fees may be an effective way of reducing tourist pressure while maintaining revenue.

In St. Lucia, research undertaken in 2000 (Barker, 2003) showed that tourists spent approximately US$7.3 million (€7.8 million) on diving and snorkelling tours, nearly half of which (US$3.5 million, or €3.7 million) was attributable to tours taken within its marine protected area. Forty four percent of those sampled in St. Lucia stated that their decision to visit was positively influenced by the existence of the MPA. Not only were visitors to St. Lucia willing to pay the fee to use the MPA but over 90% were willing to pay more than the stated fees; then US$4 (€4.3) for a diver's daily fee, US$12 (€12.8) for a diver's annual fee and US$1 (€1.1) for a snorkeller's daily fee. That study found that using the maximum amount that 75% or 50% of visitors were willing to pay would increase annual revenue by 128% or 62%, respectively. That would bring park revenue from user fees to US$41,550 and US$58,475 (€44,336 and €60,261) respectively, representing 52% and 73% of the total management budget. Such increases in revenue could pay for higher management standards and support the park's conservation efforts (See Box 9.1).

Box 9.1: Maximising tourist support for management of marine protected areas: A case study of the Soufrière Marine Management Area, St. Lucia.

St. Lucia's travel and tourism economy accounts for over 50% of its GDP (WTTC, 2007). With the expansion of coastal tourism and an increase in diver numbers, pressure on the environment has increased. In 1995, the Soufrière Marine Management Area (SMMA), covering 11 km of the western coast, was established to manage some of the island's most popular coral reefs. To help cover management costs, visitor fees were implemented. By 2001, 33% of the SMMA's management costs were estimated to be financed by diver fees. Other contributors were yacht fees (62%), snorkeller fees (3%) and donations (2%) (SMMA, 2007). However, in order to finance the desired level of management, additional economic support was necessary (Kai Wulf, manager of the SMMA, pers. comm.) and so it was decided to investigate whether or not user fees could be increased.

In 2000, a contingent valuation method survey of divers and snorkellers (n = 786) to St. Lucia was undertaken to examine their maximum willingness to pay for marine park fees and the effect this would have on revenue generation. Open-ended questions were used to ask them whether they would pay more than the fees being charged at the time, and if so, by how much. The current fees were US$4 (€4.3) per day or US$12 (€12.8) per year for divers, and US$1 (€1.1) per day for snorkellers.

Tourists to St. Lucia spent approximately US$7.3 million (€7.8 million) on diving and snorkelling in 2000, nearly half of which (US$3.5 million, or €3.7 million) was spent on tours within the SMMA. Over 90% of divers and snorkellers were willing to pay more than the stated daily and annual fees (see Figure 9.2). Seventy-five percent of divers were willing to pay at least US$6 (€6.4) per day, and 50% were willing to pay US$7 (€7.5) per day. Seventy-five percent of divers were willing to pay at least US$20 (€21.3) for an annual fee and 50% were willing to pay US$30 (€32). Seventy-five percent of snorkellers (and up to 91.5%) were willing to pay at least US$2 (€2.1) per day, double the current fee, and 50% were willing to pay US$4 (€4.3). Although an annual fee is currently not available to snorkellers due to a perceived lack of demand and uneconomical returns (Kai Wulf, pers. comm.), 40.5% of respondents said they would like such an option. Seventy-five percent were willing to pay at least US$10 (€10.7) for it, and 50% were willing to pay US$20 (€21.3).

Using the maximum amount that 75% or 50% of visitors were willing to pay would increase annual revenue by 128% or 62%, respectively. This would bring park revenue from user fees to US$41,550 and US$58,475, respectively (€44,336 and €60,261), representing 52% and 73% of the total management budget. Such increases in revenue could pay for higher management standards and support the park's conservation efforts.

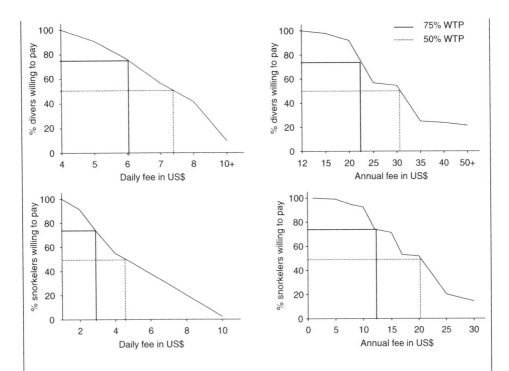

Figure 9.2: Maximum amount visitors surveyed were willing to pay for use of reefs in the Soufrière Marine Management Area in St. Lucia.

Multiple regression analyses did not find any of eleven measured independent variables (visitor gender; rating for fish, coral, visibility and overall satisfaction; total dives made in whole dive history; dive qualification; experience of St. Lucia's marine park; exposure to environmental issues; income; weather, measured on a gradient from sun to rain) to influence divers' willingness to pay significantly.

Revenue from diver fees in 2001 was US$71,675 (€84,766) and from snorkelling was US$5,400 (€6,368). Adding revenue from yacht-mooring fees and donations brought total income to US$80,139 (€94,776). This was below the US$98,016 (€115,918) which the MPA manager felt was required to cover minimum park management standards (Kai Wulf, pers. comm). An additional US$17,877 (€21,142) was therefore needed. This could come from increasing user fees to levels that 75% of visitors interviewed in this study were willing to pay. If fees in St. Lucia's marine park were set at what 50% of visitors were willing to pay, i.e. US$7 (€7.5) per diver per day, US$30 (€32) per diver per year and US$4 (€4.3) per snorkeller per day, the increase in the region would be US$32,800 (€38,791) per year. This would bring the total park revenue close to the US$140,000 (€165,570) estimated by the manager would pay for ideal management standards (Kai Wulf, pers. comm.). These calculations do not include the

(Continued)

potential revenue that could be gained from an annual snorkelling fee, which was an option 41% of visitors to the park would have liked and for which a third were willing to pay US$20 (€21.3).

Anecdotal evidence from this work in St. Lucia, and work by others elsewhere, suggests that visitors are willing to pay higher fees, so long as they can see where the money is going (Davis & Tisdell, 1998; Lindberg, 2001; Spash, 2000).

Often, a key factor in successful implementation of, and changes to, fees is the dissemination of information about proposed changes, and inclusion of users in the development of such systems. Tourists and residents alike need to understand the reasons for fee systems being in place and the rationale for any proposed increase in such fees. In many cases, fees are lower (and sometimes waived completely) for nationals and residents of a country in comparison to those charged to tourists. Information on fees can be distributed in many ways including by use of leaflets, printing pieces in local newspapers and conducting radio broadcasts. The St. Lucia research (Barker & Roberts, 2004) showed how interviews with tourists, combined with collaboration with marine park staff, assisted managers to increase the fees to a level that raised much-needed additional revenue while remaining within the range that most visitors were willing to pay.

Conclusions

The number of people learning to dive and visiting dive sites continues to grow year on year. Tourists generally accept the regulations that are imposed on them, whether through their initial training or at the destinations they visit once qualified.

The studies described in this chapter show that divers and snorkellers usually respond positively to environmental information and are receptive to education in the form of briefings resulting in increased self-awareness and a reduction in their damage to the underwater environment. However, the evidence suggests that briefings must be reinforced underwater in order to reduce harmful contacts with reefs. In-water supervision may be a more practical method to regulate divers for dive centres who do not have time, or the capacity, to conduct thorough environmental briefings. What is clear is that divers are keen to learn about the sites they visit and look to their guides for assistance. This offers the perfect opportunity for guides to help reduce negative impacts underwater. Guides can demonstrate appropriate behaviour such as staying well above the reef and not touching any organisms. They can also make clear in their briefings what hand signals they will use. Townsend (2000) and Barker (2003) found that divers often copied the behaviour of their guides. They are therefore in a strong position to influence the impact of their group and can also determine which sites can be used for particular activities. Training dives could, for example, only be performed in sandy areas away from susceptible life forms, or possibly be concentrated only at one or two sites so that the damage is confined. However, as we have seen, it is not only those divers who are learning how to dive that cause damage to the underwater environment. Guides and training instructors alike therefore must monitor divers' activities, regardless of the level they are at.

In addition to education and supervision, divers are sometimes subjected to controls on when and where they can dive. Limiting access is a regulatory method used in many areas to keep damage by divers within acceptable limits. However, few MPAs attempt to control diver or snorkeller behaviour underwater, aside from basic restrictions on collecting marine life. To avoid resource degradation, parks will have to take a much more proactive approach in the future. Divers are attracted to sites that have marine protected areas since these are perceived to harbour better marine life, and divers are usually willing to accept limits on their behaviour to protect the environment. The research conducted by Barker (2003) showed that divers chose destinations that had protected areas over those that did not and, in the case of St. Lucia, wanted to see more active policing of the marine park. This indicated that divers wanted to see evidence of management and regulation. Authorities and managers of resorts and dive destinations should therefore see this as a selling point and openly implement and enforce regulations.

Divers' impacts are not all negative and on the positive side divers represent a considerable source of income that can be injected into natural resource management. Fees and permits are regulatory methods used to control and, more importantly, help finance the management of resources. Research has shown that implementing a fee structure for entry to marine parks and other protected areas does not necessarily deter visitation and in many cases divers are not only prepared to pay them, but are prepared to pay considerably more. If parks maximised their visitor revenues they could afford to implement more and better management systems.

The measures described above are all options that managers can use singly or in combination, depending on the requirements of their particular region. Such measures can also be used in conjunction with non-regulatory measures such as the use of moorings, walkways and pontoons. By understanding divers' attitudes to and preferences for particular regulations, managers can apply the most effective ways to control diver impacts and ensure the sustainability of the environments to which they are attracted. This chapter has highlighted some specific examples of regulatory measures that work well to modify divers' behaviour. Education, assistance during dives, the numbers of divers allowed at sites or to dive in a group, restricted access to sites and zoning, and user fees are all forms of regulation accepted by divers. Small dive groups, paying user fees and evidence of active management are in some cases the factors that specifically attract a diver to a destination and increase their satisfaction of it. Managers should therefore work with their customers and visitors to provide a service that not only includes information, expertise and assistance to make diving a safe and fun activity, but also makes use of a combination of regulatory measures that are both accepted and, in some cases, actively preferred by divers.

References

Balmford, A., Gravestock, P., Hockley, N., McClean, C., & Roberts, C. (2004). The worldwide costs of marine protected areas. *Proceedings of the National Academy of Sciences USA, 101*, 9694–9697.

Barker, N. H. L. (2003). *Ecological and socio-economic impacts of dive and snorkel tourism in St Lucia, West Indies*. Unpublished doctoral dissertation, University of York, UK.

Barker, N. H. L., & Roberts, C. M. (2004). Scuba diver behaviour and the management of diving impacts on coral reefs. *Biological Conservation, 120*, 481–489.

Berg, H., Őhman, M. C., Troëng, S., & Lindén, O. (1998). Environmental economics of coral reef destruction in Sri Lanka. *Ambio, 27*, 627–634.

Bryant, D., Burke, L., McManus, J., & Spalding, M. (1998). *Reefs at risk: A map-based indicator of potential threats to the world's coral reefs*. Washington, DC: World Resources Institute.

Clark, J. R. (Ed.) (1991). *Carrying capacity: A status report on marine and coastal parks and reserves*. Report prepared by the participants of the third international seminar on coastal and marine parks and protected areas, Miami, Florida and Costa Rica, 11 May–5 June.

Cumberbatch, C. A. N. (2000). *Using economic instruments to manage the impacts of recreational scuba diving in marine protected areas: An authentic 'eco-eco' approach*. Unpublished masters dissertation, University of York, UK.

Davis, D., & Tisdell, C. A. (1998). Tourist levies and willingness to pay for a whale shark experience. *Tourism Economics, 5*, 161–174.

Dixon, J. A., Fallon Scura, L., & van't Hof, T. (1993). Meeting ecological and economic goals: Marine parks in the Caribbean. *Ambio, 22,* 117–125.

Dixon, J. A., Fallon Scura, L., & van't Hof, T. (1994). Ecology and microeconomics as 'joint products': The Bonaire Marine Park in the Caribbean. In: C. A. Perrings, K.-G. Mäler, C. Folke, C. S. Holling, & B.-O. Jansson (Eds), *Biodiversity conservation: Problems and policies* (pp. 120–138). Dordrecht, NL: Kluwer.

Dixon, J. A., & van't Hof, T. (1997). Conservation pays big dividends in Caribbean. *Forum for Applied Research and Public Policy, 12*, 43–48.

Driml, S. (1994). *Protection for profit. Economic and financial values of the Great Barrier Reef World Heritage Area and other protected areas*. Research Publication No.35. Townsville: Great Barrier Reef Marine Park Authority.

Dytham, C. (1999). *Choosing and using statistics: A biologist's guide*. Oxford: Blackwell Science Ltd.

Fernandes, L. (1995). *Integrating economic, environmental and social issues in an evaluation of Saba Marine Park, N.A., Caribbean Sea*. Report to Saba Marine Park and Saba Conservation Foundation, East West Center, Honolulu, USA.

Green, E., & Donnelly, R. (2003). Recreational scuba diving in Caribbean marine protected areas: Do the users pay? *Ambio, 32*, 140–144.

Harriott, V. J., Davies, D., & Banks, S. A. (1997). Recreational diving and its impacts in marine protected areas in eastern Australia. *Ambio, 26*, 173–179.

Hawkins, J. P., & Roberts, C. M. (1997). Estimating the carrying capacity of coral reefs for scuba diving. In: *Proceedings of the eighth international coral reef symposium*, Smithsonian Tropical Research Institute, Balboa, Panama (pp. 1923–1926).

Hawkins, J. P., Roberts, C. M, Kooistra, D., Buchan, K., & White, S. (2005). Sustainability of scuba diving tourism on coral reefs of Saba. *Coastal Management, 33*, 373–387.

Hawkins, J. P., Roberts, C. M., van't Hof, T., De Meyer, K., Tratalos, J., & Aldam, C. (1999). Effects of recreational scuba diving on Caribbean coral and fish communities. *Conservation Biology, 13*, 888–897.

Laarman, J. G., & Gregersen, H. M. (1996). Pricing policy in nature-based tourism. *Tourism Management, 17*, 247–254.

Lee, C., & Han, S. (2002). Estimating the use and preservation values of national parks' tourism resources using a contingent valuation method. *Tourism Management, 23*, 531–540.

Lindberg, K., & Halpenny, E. (2001). Protected area visitor fees: Overview. http://www.ecotourism.org/WebModules/WebMember/MemberApplication/onlineLib/MemberApplication/onlineLib/Uploaded/Protected%20Area%20Visitor%20Fee%20(Country).pdf (Accessed 10 May 2007).

Medio, D., Ormond, R. F. G., & Pearson, M. (1997). Effect of briefings on rates of damage to corals by scuba divers. *Biological Conservation, 79*, 91–95.

Mora, C., Andréfouët, S., Costello, M. J., Kranenburg, C., Rollo, A., Veron, J., Gaston, K. J., & Myers, R.A. (2006). Coral reefs and the global network of marine protected areas. *Science, 312,* 1750–1751.

Mundet, L., & Ribera, L. (2001). Characteristics of divers at a Spanish resort. *Tourism Management, 22,* 501–510.

Musa, G. (2002). Sipadan: A SCUBA-diving paradise: An analysis of tourism impact, diver satisfaction and tourism management. *Tourism Geographies, 4,* 195–209.

Muthiga, N. A., & McClanahan, T. R. (1997). The effect of visitor use on the hard coral communities of the Kisite Marine Park, Kenya. In: *Proceedings of the eighth international coral reef symposium,* Smithsonian Tropical Research Institute, Balboa, Panama (pp. 1879–1882).

Orams, M. (1999). *Marine tourism: Development, impacts and management.* London: Routledge.

Prior, M., Ormond, R., Hitchen, R., & Wormald, C. (1995). The impact of natural resources of activity tourism: A case study of diving in Egypt. *International Journal of Environmental Studies, 48,* 201–209.

Resource Assessment Commission (RAC). (1993). *The carrying capacity concept and its application to the management of coastal zone resources.* Information paper No.8. Canberra Coastal Zone Inquiry, Australian Government Publishing House.

Riegl, B., & Velimirov, B. (1991). How many damaged corals in Red Sea reef systems? A quantitative survey. *Hydrobiologia, 216/217,* 249–256.

Riopelle, J. M. (1995). *The economic valuation of coral reefs: A case study of West Lombok, Indonesia.* Unpublished dissertation, Dalhousie University, Halifax.

Roberts, L., & Harriott, V. J. (1994). Recreational scuba diving and its potential for environmental impact in a marine reserve. In: O. Bellwood, H. Choat, & N. Saxena (Eds), *Recent advances in marine science and technology 1994* (pp. 675–705). Townsville: James Cook University of North Queensland.

Rogers, C. S., & Beets, J. (2001). Degradation of marine ecosystems and decline of fishery resources in marine protected areas in the US Virgin Islands. *Environmental Conservation, 28,* 312–322.

Rudd, M. A., & Tupper, M. H. (2002). The impact of Nassau grouper size and abundance on scuba diver site selection and MPA economics. *Coastal Management, 30,* 133–151.

Salm, R.V. (1986). Coral reefs and tourist carrying capacity: The Indian Ocean experience. *UNEP Industry and Environment, Jan–Mar,* 11–14.

Schleyer, M. H., & Tomalin, B. J. (2000). Damage on South African coral reefs and an assessment of their sustainable diving capacity using a fisheries approach. *Bulletin of Marine Science, 67,* 1025–1042.

SMMA. (2007). SMMA Saint Lucia. http://www.smma.org.lc/ (Accessed 10 May 2007).

Spash, C. L. (2000). Assessing the benefits of improving coral reef biodiversity: The contingent valuation method. In: H. S. J. Cesar (Ed.), *Collected essays on the economics of coral reefs* (pp. 40–54). Kalmar, Sweden: CORDIO.

Townsend, C. (2000). *The effects of environmental education on the behaviour of scuba divers: A case study from the British Virgin Island.* Unpublished masters dissertation, University of Greenwich, UK.

Tratalos, J. A., & Austin, T. J. (2001). Impacts of recreational SCUBA diving on coral communities of the Caribbean island of Grand Cayman. *Biological Conservation, 102,* 67–75.

Walpole, M. J., Goodwin, H. J., & Ward, K. G. R. (2001). Pricing policy for tourism in protected areas: Lessons from Komodo National Park, Indonesia. *Conservation Biology, 15,* 218–227.

WTTC. (2007). http://www.wttc.org/framesetsitemap.htm (Accessed 14 February 2007).

Zakai, D., & Chadwick-Furman, N. E. (2002). Impacts of intensive recreational diving on reef corals at Eilat, northern Red Sea. *Biological Conservation, 105,* 179–187.

Chapter 10

Interpretation and Environmental Education as Conservation Tools

Claudia Townsend

Introduction

Dive tourism is potentially important for the environmental, economic and social sustainability of many marine and coastal areas. In order to be a positive force it must be managed to avoid negative impacts and maximise benefits. Damage to marine ecosystems by divers can be managed using education, which can also increase support for marine conservation. Education, however, needs to be carefully designed in order to be effective. Diver-preference studies have variously found that divers want to see underwater life (Meisel & Cottrell, 2004), rare and large fish species, a wide variety of fish and coral (Mundet & Ribera, 2001; Williams & Polunin, 2000), a healthy marine environment (Pendleton, 1994) and are attracted to marine protected areas (MPAs) (Barker & Roberts, Chapter 9, this volume; Green & Donnelly, 2003). Areas preferred by divers are therefore often areas that are important for biodiversity. Many of the clear, warm waters of tropical coral reefs that attract dive tourists are found in developing countries (Spalding, Ravilious, & Green, 2001), so the economies that rely on marine resources are also often fragile.

Ecologically sensitive areas attract divers and other marine tourists, who are often encouraged by the authorities responsible for protecting them because visitors bring income. Tourism is also often assumed to have less environmental impact than alternative extractive industries such as fishing or mining. Tourism is therefore sometimes seen as a potential alternative to other economic activities, which may even be banned. For example, there are a number of MPAs where fishing is restricted in part of the reserve or where certain species cannot be fished during defined periods to allow for the regeneration of depleted stocks (Ward, Heinemann, & Evans, 2001). This can cause resentment, especially when outsiders are allowed into areas local people are prohibited from using (Oracion, Millen, & Christie, 2005). Resentment can only increase if the outsiders, in this case the divers, are then seen to damage the marine resources closed to local people for conservation reasons.

Both the public and private sectors have an interest in protecting marine environments and resources. It is the job of MPAs and other environmental protection agencies to protect fragile areas and they need public cooperation and support in order to do so. In order to sell their products, dive and diving-tourism operators also depend on the presence of good environmental conditions for the varied coral and fish species divers prefer. Consequently, operators have an interest in sustaining environmental health. A number of techniques are available to manage divers on dive sites for the benefit of all. Various types of regulations can be employed, including zoning for restricted use in certain areas, limiting the number of divers on a site, insisting on the use of moorings, and banning certain activities or equipment like spear fishing or gloves for divers.

Education and interpretation are used both to inform divers of relevant regulations they must abide by and also to encourage divers to take actions to reduce their impact. Education can be carried out by conservation authorities and by dive operators. Dive operators can improve their clients' experience by providing good information about the site, the environment and dive skills. This chapter focuses on diver education and its potential benefits, not only in reducing direct diver impact on the environment during a dive but also in bringing broader benefits to the environment, local economies and societies. It also outlines some of the debates and research about the types of education and messages that are most effective in achieving those aims.

Environmental Education and Interpretation

While environmental education and interpretation are separate disciplines, they are both used to describe the process of providing environmentally relevant information to tourists. Both also aim to enhance visitors' experience at a site and reduce their damage to it.

Interpretation is defined as:

> ... the work of revealing, to such visitors as desire the service, something of the beauty and wonder, the inspiration and spiritual meaning that lie behind what the visitor can with his senses perceive (Tilden, 1977, p. 4).

By interpreting a site through guiding, information panels, leaflets and so on, the visitor's understanding and appreciation increases and their experience may be improved. Interpretation aims to make visits enjoyable and to encourage empathy with the site. That empathy may mean that visitors are less likely to behave in a damaging way and be more likely to do things like donate money or volunteer time towards the site's protection. However, the primary aim of interpretation is, as Tilden says, not necessarily to control or to change the behaviour of visitors with regard to their environmental impact. Indeed, "the chief aim of interpretation is not instruction but provocation" (Tilden, 1977, p. 32).

The term 'environmental education' tends to be used for more formal information provision, which is aimed at changing behaviour. This could be reducing energy use in the home or refraining from touching corals on a dive. The word 'education', with its connotations of school, implies a relatively formal process of providing information to people who lack it. Perhaps for this reason, some environmental education programmes and materials tend simply to provide information and expect that alone to change people's behaviour. However, many years of research into education and behaviour change show that providing information alone makes very little difference to people's behaviour (Bell, Greene, Fisher, & Baum, 1996). Relevant information is a necessary part of communication aimed at prompting behaviour change but it needs to coincide with an emotional experience and an opportunity to put new understanding and skills quickly into practice. Giving someone abstract information about environmental impacts and their role in minimising them may create good intentions but these may be quickly forgotten if an opportunity to put them into practice is not provided (Brylske, 2000; Manfredo & Bright, 1991; Orams, 1994, 1997; Veitch & Arkheim, 1995).

Interpretation and environmental education can help environmental managers and dive businesses to achieve a number of aims:

- To minimise divers' direct impact on the dive site through touching or kicking coral, feeding animals, collecting shells, kicking up sediment, etc.
- To increase divers' enjoyment of their dives through better understanding of the marine environment and improved comfort underwater when skills such as buoyancy are improved.
- To minimise other impacts divers may have on the marine environment during their trip when not diving (such as the fish they eat, the souvenirs they buy, etc.).
- To increase divers' commitment to marine conservation and their support both now and in the future.

This chapter uses the term 'education' for the sake of simplicity as a catch-all for research and disciplines that include environmental psychology, environmental education and interpretation.

The Ecological Impacts of Divers

Studies of damage to sites by divers are varied in both their approaches and their results. Although studies of diver impact are not always in agreement either about the significance of diver damage or which types of divers tend to cause the most damage, most of the studies that have compared damage to reefs on dive sites and areas not visited by divers have noted an increase in degradation of the dived areas (Garrabou, Sala, Arcas, & Zabala, 1998; Hawkins & Roberts, 1992, 1993; Hawkins et al., 1999). Although not all researchers agree on the biological significance of this damage, the study by Hawkins et al. (1999) suggests that it may indeed have long-term repercussions for the health of the reefs that are dived. Other researchers have anonymously followed divers to see how much damage they cause, by counting how often they make contact with corals or other marine species (see, for example, Harriott, Davies, & Banks, 1997; Talge, 1992). Further studies have discussed and researched the best ways to stop such impacts occurring, using environmental education and other management techniques such as mooring buoys or restricted access for divers to certain areas (Barker & Roberts, 2004 and Chapter 9, this volume; Medio, Ormond, & Pearson, 1997; Townsend, 2000).

Limiting diver numbers on a site is one way to manage this issue. However, deciding a site's carrying capacity is a complicated and inexact task (Davis & Tisdell, 1995; Dixon, Fallon Scura, & van't Hof, 1993). The impact that a certain number of divers are likely to have depends on any number of variables, such as diver qualifications, whether they have a camera (photographers have been found by some to be more careless about touching corals), whether a dive master is accompanying them, whether they dive at night or during the day, the topography of the site, and so on (Harriott et al., 1997). This means that setting very specific limits on the numbers of divers who can go to a site will not necessarily reduce the environmental impact of those divers. It may nevertheless reduce the income that the excluded divers would have brought to the local economy. In certain cases, managers have to set limits or use options such as increasing user fees for heavily visited sites. Education, however, is potentially the best and most popular way of ensuring that the maximum possible number of people can enjoy a dive site without overly damaging it (Davis & Tisdell, 1995; Medio et al., 1997; Townsend, 2000). If educating divers reduces their impact, then more divers can visit a site, effectively increasing its carrying capacity.

Most of the research done on diving and environmental education has looked at direct diver impact and ways to minimise it using education: pre-dive briefings, skills training or intervening on a dive when a diver's behaviour is damaging (Barker & Roberts, 2004; Medio et al., 1997; Townsend, 2000). The diver impact and education research has largely looked at the impact of pre-dive briefings on damage caused by divers, measured by counting the number of times a diver makes contact with living organisms or kicks up sediment, which can smother coral polyps. The limited research done shows that it is not in itself the fact of giving a briefing about environmental protection and the diver's role in that process that makes any difference to the damage they cause: it is the type of briefing or action taken by the dive master that has an impact (Barker & Roberts, 2004; Medio et al., 1997; Townsend, 2000).

Research undertaken by psychologists into behaviour change and the kind of messages needed to bring such changes about shows that it is not enough simply to provide information to people. Messages should not contain too many facts or overload on information but they do need to be interesting. Messages work best when they challenge people's existing beliefs enough to make them think but not so radically that they immediately reject what they are being told (Bell et al., 1996; Veitch & Arkheim, 1995).

Another key part of communication with the aim of prompting behaviour change is giving people an opportunity to act on the information they have been given. Advertisements will often tell you to 'call now' to get an offer or buy a product because they know that their message will soon be forgotten and they need to hook you immediately. If a person reinforces new knowledge with action quickly after they have received a message, the message is more likely to stick (Manfredo & Bright, 1991, Orams, 1994, 1997; Veitch & Arkheim, 1995). This means that diving has an inherent advantage over many settings where environmental messages are communicated with the aim of changing behaviour. For example, a radio broadcast that asks people to recycle more or use less energy usually requires people to remember and act on the message at another time and possibly in a different place. However, in a diving setting, a briefing is usually given immediately before divers enter the water, so that they have an immediate opportunity to act on what they have heard. Additionally, divers are usually captive audiences. In most cases they are on a boat, have to and want to listen to a briefing for safety and other reasons, and usually dive as part of a group with a dive master who keeps an eye on them. Furthermore, most divers in fragile areas such as coral reefs are interested in marine life and therefore in all probability more prone than a random sample of the general public to be interested in its protection.

As discussed in Chapter 9 of this volume by Barker and Roberts, and shown in other research on briefings and diver behaviour (Medio et al., 1997; Townsend, 2000), some briefings and dive-master interventions do make a difference. In research carried out with divers in the British Virgin Islands (BVI), briefings were designed to provide divers with an immediate opportunity to act (Townsend, 2000). Dive masters were asked to add three simple messages to their usual briefing, which may or may not have included other environmental information. These three messages were chosen on the basis of observation of divers, questionnaires for divers and consultation with dive professionals on the main causes of diver damage, which were found to be ignorance about the marine environment, poor buoyancy and poor body positioning. They are short and simple, and can be included in any briefing, even where time is limited. One of these messages was to inform or remind divers that coral is a living and fragile animal, and the other two were practical instructions to avoid causing damage, namely:

• Tucking in all gauges and dangling pieces of equipment so they do not trail on the bottom.
• Staying in a horizontal position so that fins do not kick the bottom or stir up sediment.

This experiment with improved diver briefings showed a marked decrease in the number of contacts divers made with coral and other marine organisms, from an average of 6.56 contacts made in a 10-min period to 1.95 contacts in 10 min. This, added to the research described in Chapter 9 by Barker and Roberts, suggests that briefings or interventions by dive masters can impact on diver damage but they need to point out how and when damage most often occurs and to remind divers of the simple and practical ways they can use their existing skills to avoid it. Briefings in the BVI, before the experiment outlined above, focussed on environmental facts. These do add interest and enjoyment to the dive and may increase divers' empathy with the marine world. However, they do not give divers the tools they need to reduce their impact. In the experience of the author, this is common in dive briefings for tourists in many destinations.

It is also common for briefings to tell people not to kick the coral or damage the reef without telling them how to avoid these outcomes. Divers are taught about buoyancy and finning positions in their basic training. However, this is not always linked to environmental protection and the link may not be obvious until pointed out, especially to novice divers. Warning divers not to damage the reef without helping them with practical tips may induce guilt and fear but will not necessarily stop them making physical contact with the reef or the sea floor.

Increasing Enjoyment and Broader Commitment to Conservation

Small group sizes and help with skills also add value to a dive and increase diver satisfaction. Increasing clients' enjoyment of a dive is important for the success of both dive companies and conservationists. If they enjoy visiting a site, divers are more likely to be willing to take action towards its protection. Such action might include paying more to visit a site, donating money for its protection, giving time as a volunteer for activities such as surveys or beach cleanups, and responding positively to other environment-related messages both while on holiday and when they go home.

Direct diver impact on reefs may be minor in terms of its ecological impact when compared with the other impacts of tourism in an area (Birkeland, 1997; Hawkins & Roberts, 1994; van't Hof, 2001; Ormond, Hassan, Medio, Pearson, & Salem, 1997). For the marine environment, particular concerns include increased run off onto reefs as a result of construction for tourist accommodation, increased fishing to feed tourists, a souvenir industry that may include collection of endangered species such as certain shells or corals, sewage from hotels, increased litter on beaches which enters the sea, and tourists frequenting sensitive areas such as bird or turtle nesting sites (Birkeland, 1997; Hawkins & Roberts, 1994; Ormond et al., 1997). The list goes on and depends on the particular sensitivities of an area as well as the existence and enforcement of planning regulations.

As is the case with many products, however, consumer choices can make an important difference to these impacts. Tourists can make an important difference with their choices of what to buy, for example they may refuse to buy endangered species, not eat lobster out of season or below a certain size, and use litter bins. They can also make a point of asking their tour operators and hotels about their environmental policies and practices. Beyond this, longer-term commitment to environmental protection and actions such as joining marine conservation organisations and using environmentally friendly household products once they have returned home may also result from an increased understanding and empathy with the marine environment on the part of diving tourists.

The question is whether educating divers on a dive boat or in the water can create any of these longer-term impacts. It can be argued that these impacts have greater ecological importance than any direct damage caused to a dive site. Less research has been done into these longer-term positive impacts than on immediate and direct negative impacts. However, the research that has been done shows that if people have an immediate 'opportunity to act' on the message they have heard, they are more likely to retain and act on that message in the longer term. Visitors to a dolphin-feeding programme who were given such an opportunity to act were also shown to be more likely to undertake positive environmental behaviour such as joining a conservation organisation or picking up litter on beaches (Orams, 1994, 1997).

Research also shows that environmental education needs to appeal not just to the intellectual but also, in psychological terms, to the 'affective domain'. That is to say that messages need to appeal to a person's emotional side as opposed to their intellectual or logical side (Manfredo & Bright, 1991; Veitch & Arkheim, 1995). Learning by experience is therefore potentially very effective and, again, diving has an advantage here. Whether someone is a novice or experienced and committed diver, a dive is usually an experience that appeals to the senses and emotions. The fact of being on a reef and seeing the ways that marine animals interact means that divers who are told about a process such as symbiosis are more likely to understand and retain the information than someone in a classroom would be. The same goes for learning about and practicing skills such as underwater buoyancy. In a swimming pool this can seem a little abstract. When a diver finds he or she can avoid banging into a coral structure using their breath, the importance of the skill has more resonance.

These psychological processes and ways of learning would suggest that if immediate diver impact can be reduced, divers are also more likely to take a message about the importance of conserving the marine environment away with them and act on it in other ways beyond the dive boat. Once divers are committed, through understanding and action, to making their actions benefit rather than damage, they are likely to be more open to further messages. Tourism can bring many benefits: economic, social and environmental. By giving divers an easy and enjoyable way to do good on their dive, we are more likely to be successful when asking them to think about what and how they buy souvenirs, where to stay or how to be culturally sensitive.

There are, then, some excellent opportunities for environmental education and building support for marine conservation inherent in most dive trips:

- The dive boat or the supervised dive group underwater provides dive masters or others giving briefings with a captive audience of people who have some level of existing interest in and knowledge of the underwater world.
- Divers must, whether on their first or thousandth dive, have undergone and been tested on skills and knowledge. This provides an opportunity to teach the skills necessary to avoid damaging marine life and to explain the environmental implications of having and using those skills.
- Divers in the most fragile environments are usually tourists diving with a dive master in a group, so they are supervised (to a greater or lesser extent depending on the operator and group size) and there is an opportunity for dive guides to help divers avoid damaging behaviour.
- All environmentally relevant messages given above or below water, before or during a dive, are reinforced by the immediate experience of diving. Divers have an opportunity to act on any good intentions that environmental education activities may have created. In turn, this immediate action on their part is likely to mean that they retain the message and their commitment to act on it in future, thereby helping to reduce other potentially negative impacts of tourism and increase the benefits that tourists can bring to an area.

Difficult Divers: Novices, Experts, Photographers...

There are, of course, also a number of difficulties in developing and delivering environmentally relevant education for divers. Its success relies on the audience being receptive and on the delivery being effective. As is the case for most communications activities, there is a fine line between keeping messages simple and clear, and turning people off by presenting messages that seem too simple and therefore patronising. On most dive boats there are a variety of people who have different levels of experience and knowledge on diving and environmental matters. Diving, like many other hobbies, has a culture attached to it. This can be seen in its vocabulary, in divers' equipment choices and in the signs divers might choose to give to other divers, such as t-shirts or marine park tags, that show where they have been on their dive travels (Lindberg & Halpenny, 2001a). This is no different to any other activity: surfers, walkers, birdwatchers and many more enthusiasts all have their own sub-culture and many people enjoy being a part of this. Along with this sometimes comes a certain 'snobbery' in the attitude of more experienced enthusiasts towards the 'newbies'. In the author's experience, divers with some experience often like to be recognised by other divers and dive masters as part of the gang and accorded a certain respect because of it. They may therefore resent being treated in the same way as novice divers because this does not recognise their status.

Research into diver impact by type of diver suggests that novices, male divers and photographers tend to cause more damage than others, although there are clearly many variables at play (Barker & Roberts, 2004). However, there is not enough research specifically targeting differences between divers by experience, demographics or equipment to provide consistent evidence on whether some groups are more damaging than others. Even if such research were available, it would be difficult and undesirable to regulate access to sites according to factors like gender or age. The positive impacts of effective education for divers apply across the board to all divers.

In interpretation, one of the methods used to get round the different information wants and needs of a mixed audience is to 'layer' information (Ballantyne, Hughes, & Moscardo, 2006). An information board in a national park might include a headline message of a few words but also have one or two different layers of increasing detail and complexity for those with greater interest or time to stop and read. The same may apply to information aimed at children and adults. This formalised layering of information is hard to achieve on a dive boat or underwater. It can be done in leaflets or information boards placed where divers are likely to see them. However, there is no guarantee that the core message will be communicated. Dive masters therefore need to give information that is interesting and enjoyable to all levels within the group. This should contain key safety information that is simple enough to be ingested by everyone but not so simple as to alienate those who consider themselves experts. It is hard to expect a dive master's pre-dive briefing to cater perfectly to all divers, so dive boats can have further information available in the form of species-identification books or charts. Meanwhile staff can talk individually to those with more interest or expertise. The aim of the briefing is usually to go over safety and practical issues, and to describe the dive site, rather than to give detailed environmental information.

There is a limit to the amount of information most people can take in at once. Safety is clearly a priority, so adding a lot of environmental information to the existing dive briefing is unlikely to have much effect, as most of the information will not be retained. If factors like a choppy sea, people's keenness to get in the water, hot sun and so on are added to the equation, it is clear that expecting dive masters to include a lengthy environmental briefing is unrealistic and ineffective. However, as Barker and Roberts conclude, one way around this is for dive group leaders to point out and rectify damaging behaviour while on the dive. Another way is to focus on simple and practical instructions in the briefing, which are included with the general reminders relating to safety, such as those related to the diver's position in the water as mentioned above. This sort of information can be given quickly and without any value judgement implied about a diver's existing knowledge or skills. For novices it may be new information, while for those with more experience it can be a reminder of environmentally relevant behaviour. Focussing on simple, practical messages and measures is also more realistic in that any dive master can do it. Giving more detailed environmental briefings depends on the environmental knowledge and interest of the person doing the briefing, as well as the other factors mentioned above (level of diver interest, weather conditions, time available, etc.). As Barker and Roberts (2004) have shown, leaving the briefing up to the dive master does not guarantee that good, environmentally relevant information will be given. Training for dive professionals that teaches them about effective ways to reduce diver impact and increase commitment to conservation could be added to training courses without a great deal of additional time and resources. Individual dive companies and MPA authorities could also provide such training and make inclusion of effective messages and measures mandatory on all dives.

Public or Private: Whose Responsibility?

In MPAs, where many people prefer to dive, the public authority responsible for management clearly has an interest in and responsibility for minimising diver damage while maximising income and other benefits from visitors. MPAs and other public agencies that protect the marine environment outside protected areas therefore have a role to play in developing and implementing education activities and materials. In terrestrial protected areas such authorities and agencies tend to be almost wholly responsible for education and interpretation. They create interpretation centres, trail boards and leaflets, as well as training and licensing guides to lead visitors in the protected area.

In marine areas, the authorities may have less direct input into interpretation, because private operators run most trips using their own vessels, so have direct access to tourists. There is not usually a traditional park entrance, like those at terrestrial parks, where authorities can provide information and regulate the information visitors receive through their own staff. This leaves authorities with no obvious space to put physical interpretation infrastructure, no park entrance and no on-land trail. Many MPAs collect any fees either by levying a charge on private operators for their use of the MPA or, when visitors are charged directly, it is often private operators who collect the fees on the MPA's behalf (Lindberg & Halpenny, 2001b).

Some areas have developed interesting solutions such as snorkel trails, which lead snorkellers from one underwater information plaque to another (Bill Gleason, personal communication). However, this is neither practicable nor desirable for most dive sites. Public authorities can produce materials such as leaflets, booklets, posters, and underwater species-identification cards, and then rely on dive shops and boats to display and distribute them. This can be a good option where MPAs and the private sector have a good relationship. However, MPAs do need to understand the needs and limitations of the private sector and work with them to develop materials and systems that will fit in with their business practices and will add value to the experience they are selling.

Private operators also have an interest in and, it could be argued, a responsibility towards providing interpretation and education to their customers. As Barker and Roberts (2004) note, divers appreciate such efforts, so information provision forms part of good customer service and generates satisfaction. The private sector is limited by profit imperatives, time available, space in a dive shop or on a boat, and by variability in staff willingness and ability to educate their customers. Private operators can, however, create a company culture that supports environmental protection, provide training for staff and make certain practices obligatory for all staff.

In MPAs, therefore, there is an excellent opportunity for the public and private sectors to work together, to the benefit of both, in the provision of environmentally relevant information and training, as well as for the enforcement of regulations. If they can develop systems and materials that suit the aims of both, MPA authorities will gain private-sector assistance in management (far more so than in most terrestrial protected areas), while dive companies will improve diver satisfaction as well as protect the resources on which their business depend.

Summary and Recommendations

Environmental education and interpretation for divers is one tool among many that can be used to manage diver impact on sites and to increase support for marine conservation. It has the advantage of being a 'soft' tool, in that it tends to increase diver enjoyment, unlike other 'harder' regulations that impose restrictions or fees on visitors and companies. Neither does it necessarily require huge resources from either MPA authorities or dive companies.

Research into which divers do the most damage, and on how ecologically significant that damage might be, does not provide clear conclusions. There are so many variables that affect impact. It does seem clear, however, that divers can damage sites both aesthetically and ecologically and that it is in the interests of everyone to minimise that damage.

The little research that has considered the effect of education on diver impact would suggest that when divers are given practical tools immediately before or during a dive to help them avoid causing damage, impact can be significantly reduced. This is supported by psychological theories of learning and behaviour change which say that giving information alone makes little difference. Rather, people need to be made to think about their actions and to act on the information or instructions they have been given as soon as possible if the lesson is to stay with them.

Beyond diver impact, environmental education is important because the world's many divers can provide an important body of support for marine conservation globally. Additionally, while they are on holiday divers can make responsible choices that benefit the local economy and environment. Giving divers the practical information and help they need to avoid damaging marine life can therefore have important benefits in the short, medium and even long term.

Dive operators, individual dive leaders and agencies responsible for managing marine environments visited by divers should work together to develop practical ways to ensure that effective messages are communicated to divers. Training for dive professionals about how to create and communicate effective messages and on emphasising the environmental relevance of skills such as buoyancy in training would also be effective.

References

Ballantyne, R., Hughes, K., & Moscardo, G. (2006). *Interpretive signage: Principles and practice.* http://www.talm.uq.edu.au/signage/index.html. (Accessed 15 November 2006).

Barker, N. H. L., & Roberts, C. M. (2004). Scuba diver behaviour and the management of diving impacts on coral reefs. *Biological Conservation, 120,* 481–489.

Bell, P. A., Greene, T. C., Fisher, J. D., & Baum, A. (1996). *Environmental psychology* (4th ed.). Fort Worth: Harcourt Brace Publishers.

Birkeland, C. (Ed.) (1997). *Life and death of coral reefs.* New York: Chapman and Hall.

Brylske, A. F. (2000). *A model for training tourism professionals in tropical marine resource management.* Florida: Instructional Technologies, Inc.

Davis, D., & Tisdell, C. (1995). Recreational scuba-diving and carrying capacity in MPAs. *Ocean and Coastal Management, 26,* 19–40.

Dixon, J. A., Fallon Scura, L., & van't Hof, T. (1993). Meeting ecological and economic goals: Marine parks in the Caribbean. *Ambio, 22,* 117–125.

Garrabou, J., Sala, E, Arcas, A., & Zabala, M. (1998). The impact of diving on rocky sublittoral communities: A case study of a bryozoan population. *Conservation Biology, 12,* 302–312.

Green, E., & Donnelly, R. (2003). Recreational scuba diving in Caribbean marine protected areas: Do the users pay? *Ambio, 32,* 140–144.

Harriott, V. J., Davies, D., & Banks, S. A. (1997). Recreational diving and its impacts in marine protected areas in eastern Australia. *Ambio, 26,* 173–179.

Hawkins, J., & Roberts, C. M. (1992). Effects of recreational scuba diving on fore-reef slope communities of coral reefs. *Biological Conservation, 62,* 171–178.

Hawkins, J., & Roberts, C. M. (1993). Effects of recreational scuba diving on coral reefs: Trampling on reef-flat communities. *Journal of Applied Ecology, 30,* 25–30.

Hawkins, J., & Roberts, C. M. (1994). The growth of coastal tourism in the Red Sea: Present and possible future effects on coral reefs. *Ambio, 23,* 503–508.

Hawkins, J. P., Roberts, C. M., van't Hof, T., De Meyer, K., Tratalos, J., & Aldam, C. (1999). Effects of recreational scuba diving on Caribbean coral and fish communities. *Conservation Biology, 13,* 888–897.

Lindberg, K., & Halpenny, E. (2001a). *Protected area visitor fees. Country review.* http://206.161.82.194/WebModules/WebMember/MemberApplication/onlineLib/MemberApplication/onlineLib/Uploaded/Protected%20Area%20Visitor%20Fee%20(Country).pdf. (Accessed 15 November 2006).

Lindberg, K., & Halpenny, E. (2001b). *Protected area visitor fees: Summary.* http://206.161.82.194/WebModules/WebMember/MemberApplication/onlineLib/MemberApplication/onlineLib/Uploaded/Ecotourism%20Factsheet%20-%202000.pdf. (Accessed 15 November 2006).

Manfredo, M. J., & Bright, A. D. (1991). A model for assessing the effects of communication on recreationists. *Journal of Leisure Research, 23,* 1–20.

Medio, D., Ormond, R. F. G., & Pearson, M. (1997). Effect of briefings on rates of damage to corals by scuba divers. *Biological Conservation, 79,* 91–95.

Meisel, C., & Cottrell, S. (2004). Differences of motivations and expectations of divers in the Florida Keys. In: J. Murdy (Ed.). *Proceedings of the 2003 northeastern recreation research symposium.* Gen. Tech. Rep. NE-317 (pp. 393–401). Newtown Square, PA: U.S. Department of Agriculture, Forest Service, Northeastern Research Station.

Mundet, L., & Ribera, L. (2001). Characteristics of divers at a Spanish resort. *Tourism Management, 22,* 501–510.

Oracion, E. G., Millen, M. L., & Christie, P. (2005). Marine protected areas for whom? Fisheries, tourism, and solidarity in a Philippine community. *Ocean and Coastal Management, 48,* 393–410.

Orams, M. B. (1994). Creating effective interpretation for managing interaction between tourists and wildlife. *Australian Journal of Environmental Education, 10,* 21–34.

Orams, M. B. (1997). The effectiveness of environmental education: Can we turn tourists into 'greenies'? *Progress in Tourism and Hospitality Research, 3,* 295–306.

Ormond, R., Hassan, O., Medio, D., Pearson, M., & Salem, M. (1997). Effectiveness of coral protection programmes in the Ras Mohamed National Park, Egyptian Red Sea. *Proceedings of the eighth international coral reef symposium* (pp. 1931–1936). Balboa, Panama: Smithsonian Tropical Research Institute.

Pendleton, L. H. (1994). Environmental quality and recreation demand in a Caribbean coral reef. *Coastal Management, 22*, 399–404.

Spalding, M. D., Ravilious, C., & Green E. P. (2001). *World atlas of coral reefs.* Prepared at the UNEP World Conservation Monitoring Centre. Berkeley, CA: University of California Press.

Talge, H. (1992). Impact of recreational divers on scleratinian corals at Looe Key, Florida. *Proceedings of the seventh international coral reef symposium 2* (pp. 1077–1082). Guam.

Tilden, J. (1977). *Interpreting our heritage.* Chapel Hill: University of North Carolina Press.

Townsend, C. (2000). *The effects of environmental education on the behaviour of scuba divers: A case study from the British Virgin Islands.* Unpublished masters thesis, University of Greenwich, London.

van't Hof, T. (2001). *Tourism impacts on corals reefs: Increasing awareness in the tourism sector.* Paris: UNEP.

Veitch, R., & Arkheim, P. (1995). *Environmental psychology.* New Jersey: Prentice Hall.

Ward, T. J., Heinemann, D., & Evans, N. (2001). *The role of marine reserves as fisheries management tools: A review of concepts, evidence and international experience.* Canberra: Bureau of Rural Sciences.

Williams, I. D., & Polunin, N. V. C. (2000). Differences between protected and unprotected reefs of the Western Caribbean in attributes preferred by dive tourists. *Environmental Conservation, 27,* 382–391.

Chapter 11

Managing Risk in Tourist Diving: A Safety-Management Approach

Christopher Coxon, Kay Dimmock and Jeff Wilks

Introduction

Tourist adventure and recreational activities such as scuba diving have a high potential for accidents and injuries. Minimising this potential requires a proactive and robust approach to risk management. This chapter takes both a theoretical and practitioner perspective to discuss the process of adopting a proactive approach to managing risk with diving tourists. By way of real-life tourist-diving examples, the intention is to outline how a safety-first perspective, which includes risk assessment, a safety-management system and adopting a safety culture, can assist recreational dive operators to manage diving tourists in a proactive way.

Scuba diving is an activity that has been recognised as one of the fastest growing sports in the world (Orams, 1999). Modern recreational diving is, in every sense, diving tourism (Ecott, 2001). Scuba is pursued by many participants across several categories of divers (Coxon, 2006). The main distinction is between commercial or professional divers and recreational divers. Recreational divers are non-professional divers who pursue the activity as a sport or hobby. Within this group are those who scuba dive occasionally and usually while taking a holiday, as compared to those who dive regularly and often locally. Tourist divers typically visit new, often tropical locations for a brief period with the intention of enjoying the marine life and underwater environment at the destination. Many are exotic locations hosting coral reef habitats and can be found 30° north or south of the equator (Ecott, 2001). Tourist divers are the divers at the centre of discussions within this chapter.

There are an estimated 5–7 million active divers worldwide (Tourism Queensland, 2004). Major centres of tourist divers include

- 34,600 scuba divers in Australia.
- Approximately 2.5 million divers in the USA.
- Approximately 100,000 divers in the UK.

New Frontiers in Marine Tourism: Diving Experiences, Sustainability, Management
Copyright © 2008 by Elsevier Ltd.
All rights of reproduction in any form reserved.
ISBN: 978-0-08-045357-6

Access to underwater sites is often utilised through the services of commercial scuba-diving operators. Such organisations are typically a source of expertise and equipment needed by diving tourists who are on a temporary visit to a destination and seek an underwater nature-based tourism experience.

As they carry out their responsibilities, a commercial diving tourism operator confronts a range of challenges in attempting to satisfy business targets and improve market share while seeking to provide a satisfying diving experience. For example, prevailing ocean conditions have the potential to hamper a scuba-diving experience, particularly if diver skills and capabilities are considered to be elementary for the conditions that present. Dimmock (2003) found that the level of diver ability was a change noted by commercial operators in recent years. In such circumstances, if the scuba dive proceeds, the commercial operator will want to employ a streamlined and proactive approach to the management of risk and safety. The information presented in this chapter is intended as support for such an approach.

Australia and Queensland in particular provide an example of a diving tourism hotspot. The Australian recreational diving market has been estimated to be worth AUS$1 billion (€598 million) from international visitors and AUS$547 million (€327 million) from Australian divers (Tourism Queensland, 2004). Around 5% of international visitors dive during their stay in Australia and about 0.5% of Australian domestic travellers dive while on holiday. Queensland is a stopover for 93% of international divers visiting Australia and around 40% of domestic diving holidays in Australia. The Great Barrier Reef Marine Park (GBRMP), Queensland's most popular diving destination, attracted more than 1.8 million visitors in 2002 and generates approximately AUS$1 billion (€598 million) from reef-based tourism each year. Approximately 740,000 dives are taken in the GBRMP each year. There are currently 684 tourism operators that are scuba-diving permit holders in the GBRMP (Tourism Queensland, 2004).

An industry of this scale, which is mirrored in many other diving tourism destinations worldwide, has a great need to ensure that its ongoing development is not marred by incidents involving its customers. This chapter discusses three broad but essential steps that can assist diving tourism operators to manage the safety risks of their customers. The steps involve developing

1. Tools — risk assessments
2. Frameworks — safety-management systems
3. Attitudes — safety cultures

The Risk-Assessment Process

Most tourist destinations have occupational and safety legislation requirements that are underpinned by a risk-assessment approach (Department of Industrial Relations, Queensland, 2000). Because it is included in many legislative frameworks the risk-assessment process has statutory legal significance that can severely impact on the business future of a dive operator should an incident occur.

Classic risk-assessment processes seek to identify hazards that exist for adventurers, and in this case the tourist diver, the potential risk involved and likely control measures to employ (Morgan & Dimmock, 2006). Such a model has the goal of seeking to eliminate

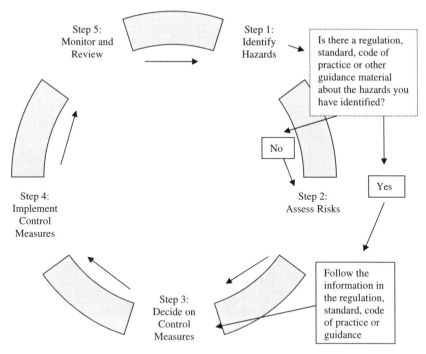

Figure 11.1: The risk-assessment process.
Source: Department of Industrial Relations, Queensland (2000).

risk. Figure 11.1 illustrates the major steps of the risk-assessment process. It also high-lights the role of external standards in determining the necessary controls. These standards may include legislative requirements and training agency or operator requirements.

The dive operator firstly identifies all hazards associated with their operation. These may range from very broad issues, for example, drowning following a vessel sinking, to very specific, for example, the ear or eye injuries caused by explosive gas releases during cylinder filling. Following this, the operator needs to determine whether there are stan-dards that exist, which may be applied to the operator that aim to control the hazard. These may include regulations, training industry or other standards, codes of practice or other guidance material. Where relevant standards do exist, they should be followed. Where there is no prescribed standard, the operator should undertake a risk assessment to rate the severity of the risk. This will give guidance in determining a suitable control measure to then minimise or eliminate the risk. All selected control measures should then be implanted. Finally by monitoring and reviewing the operating system, the dive operator may determine whether the control measures are controlling the risks adequately or whether hazards still exist. Each step in this process is described in more detail below.

Dive operators that follow this process will likely perceive risk to safety as a solely neg-ative factor that should be eliminated at all costs. This is the intended outcome for 'real' risks. Unfortunately, this process may inadvertently remove aspects of the experience, the 'perceived' risks, sought by diving tourists. Cater (2006) is of the view that it is the thrill of an adventure that tourists seek because of positive risk connotations experienced with

Photo 11.1: Some divers might purposefully engage with species that can be harmful to
human beings (Photograph: Roger Horrocks).

elements of residual risk (Photo 11.1). This can especially be the case for novice participants whether the risk is real or perceived (Holyfield, 1999).

Therefore the risk-assessment process for tourist diving should be tempered so that
the risks desired and perceived by the customers are maintained, whilst any real risks are
controlled. Achieving this balance is difficult and is further complicated by the variable
nature of the hazards found in tourist-diving operations. From the diving-tourist operator's perspective, undertaking the risk-assessment process requires a discriminating
understanding of the hazards facing tourist divers and the implications of any selected
control measures.

For example, a deeper dive to 30 m may have an increased hazard of drowning following an out-of-air situation. The risk is both real and should be perceived by the diver. The
risk may be controlled by limiting the bottom time or by increasing the air available to
the diver with higher-capacity cylinders. The former control is more likely to have a negative impact on the diver's experience than the latter. Therefore the higher-capacity cylinders are able to reduce the real risk but maintain the perceived risk.

Identifying Hazards

Most dive operators are aware of the numerous hazards that face recreational-diving
participants. To assist in recognising the types of situations that can occur and have
real potential for their operation, dive managers are able to source current material on

Table 11.1: Causes of death of breath-hold and scuba divers.

Cause of death	Breath-hold divers % (n = 75)	Scuba divers % (n = 178)
Drowning	48	56.1
Trauma	16	6.2
Hyperventilation	14.7	–
Cardiac	10.7	14.0
Cerebrovascular	2.7	1.2
Acute illness	1.3	–
Cerebral arterial gas embolism	1.3	15.7
Uncertain	5.3	3.8
Aspiration of vomit	–	1.2
Dissecting aneurysm	–	0.6

Source: Walker (1998).

diving maladies and incidents that describe the hazards of the marine environment, coupled with the peculiar physical and physiological attributes associated with breathing
compressed gases underwater. Table 11.1 shows a comparison of the causes of death
between breath-hold divers and scuba divers, highlighting in particular the greater risks
to scuba divers from cerebral arterial gas embolism related to diving at greater depths
than breath-hold divers.

This ongoing study of all Australian diving and breath-hold diving deaths since 1972
relies on reporting through the state coronial systems. Each death is reported in some
detail with periodic reviews of the accumulated data. Edmonds and Walker (1989), in an
earlier study of incident trends, suggested that the real tragedy was that the past lessons
had not been sufficiently appreciated. Despite some emerging trends such as the increasing numbers of technical diving incidents and incidents involving medical conditions
associated with an aging population, it seems that by and large the same comment could
be made today.

To move beyond recognition of these general diving hazards, diving tourism operators
must identify those hazards with direct application to their business. There is a need to
access and digest the best information from available sources that identify existing trends
or instances of tourist-diving incidents. Sources of valuable information for all diving
tourist operators and staff include print-based journals and the Internet. A list of sources is
presented in Box 11.1.

Individual operators need to discriminate in identifying the hazards relevant to their particular operation. Certain trends are common across the wider tourism industry. For example, an aging population in most Western countries is mirrored in an increase in the number
of diving deaths related to medical conditions associated with aging, especially cardiac
conditions (Leggat, 2006).

Discrimination may be used to differentiate between the hazards that are most common
between certain recreational dive industry sectors. In certain areas such as temperate
zones, where diving tourism is a small sector of all recreational diving being undertaken,

Box 11.1 Selected literature on diving hazards.

Ongoing empirical studies of dive incidents

For example:
- Australia: The ongoing reports of project "Stickybeak" published periodically in the South Pacific Underwater Medical Society Journal, http://www.spums.org.au/, and collated for publication by J.L Publication Ltd, Melbourne.
- USA: The Diver's Alert Network annual reviews of recreational scuba diving injuries and fatalities, http://www.diversalertnetwork.org/.
- UK: The British Sub-Aqua Club National Diving Committee annual diving incident reports, http://www.bsac.com/.

Periodical articles
Harder to track down and not always subject to review, for example:
- Articles in academic medical, diving or related journals, for example the Medical Journal of Australia, http://www.mja.com.au/.

Articles in academic tourism journals or publications
- For example: Wilks and Davis (2000).

Articles in the popular diving press
- The British "Diver" magazine is an example of one of the few popular diving journals with the courage to discuss dive incidents in its columns, http://divermag.com/availfrom.html.

Coronial reports
Countries with coronial systems typically publish highly detailed reports and recommendations for some diving incidents. For example:
- Coronial Report into the death of Thomas Creegan, http://www.justice.qld.gov.au/courts/coroner/findings.htm#3.
- Coronial report into the death of Jennifer Lee Berrington http://www.courts.sa.gov.au/courts/coroner/.

The Worldwide Web
Increasingly there are websites, discussion groups and blogs that provide forthright, and sometimes subjective, comment. For example: http://scuba-doc.com/tenfootstop/.

published data may reflect issues of less relevance to tourist-diving operations. For example, significant numbers of incidents in southern Australia and New Zealand are associated with private harvesting or spear fishermen (Walker, 1998).

In contrast, in Queensland dive operators have a particular interest in resort or introductory dives. The international appeal of the Great Barrier Reef means that many visitors use the location as the opportunity to take a 'resort dive' and visit the underwater world for the first time (Tourism Queensland, 2004; Wilks, 1992). This type of diving-tourist activity allows uncertificated divers to partake in restricted but supervised diving activities after minimal levels of instruction.

Following two resort-diving deaths in 2003, coroners' inquests were held in Queensland. The proceedings identified a number of hazards relevant to tourist diving in general and resort diving in particular. They included specific concerns about diver panic, supervision in water and instructor-to-student ratio (Department of Justice, Queensland, 2005a, 2005b). All diving tourism operators engaged in similar activities should have particular interest in conducting analyses of the hazards that created such a situation.

However, reviewing the misfortune of others is only one way to identify hazards. Consultation with all relevant stakeholder groups will identify and give different perspectives on the relevant hazards. One of the best sources is also closest to home. Staff members are invaluable in identifying hazards at all stages of the risk-assessment process. Other sources of assistance are industry associations, websites, journals, insurers and diver training agencies.

To focus a hazard analysis for tourist diving, the following headings are useful:

- Environmental conditions, e.g. currents, visibility, depths, temperature, isolation
- Activity factors, e.g. training, fish feeding
- Gas under pressure, e.g. decompression illness, multi-day diving, profiles, gas contamination
- Customers, e.g. experience, fitness, language ability, attitude
- Workers, e.g. skills, experience
- Equipment, e.g. suitability, maintenance
- Associated activities, e.g. boat handling, access and egress
- Emergency response factors, e.g. availability of rescue and first-aid equipment, communications, evacuations
- Other hazards, e.g. shipping, dangerous animals

Risk Analysis and Input Variables

When the hazards applicable to the particular operation are listed, the risk caused by each hazard can then be analysed. Classic risk-management models reduce this process to a simple exercise that combines the probability (likelihood of event) and outcome of event (level of injury) to achieve a risk rating. Many diving hazards are serious or life threatening and their probability exists whenever diving occurs. The resulting risk ratings, therefore, are likely to be high or extreme in most cases and will require immediate action to implement control measures. Figure 11.2 presents the resulting matrix of likelihood and consequences.

When the hazards have been assessed as risks they can then be graded according to their priority. The dive operator is able to move on to the most challenging part of the risk-management process, which involves selecting appropriate control measures that

Risk Priority Chart

LIKELIHOOD How likely could it happen?	CONSEQUENCES : How severely could it affect health and safety?			
	EXTREME - death or permanent disablement	MAJOR - serious bodily injury or serious work caused illness	MODERATE - injury or illness requiring casualty treatment	MINOR - injury or illness requiring first aid only, no lost time
VERY LIKELY - could happen frequently	1	2	3	4
LIKELY - could happen occasionally	2	3	4	5
UNLIKELY - could happen, but rare	3	4	5	6
VERY UNLIKELY - could happen, probably never will	4	5	6	7

Score	Action
1, 2 or 3	do something about these risks immediately
4 or 5	do something about these risks as soon as possible
6 or 7	these risks may not need immediate attention

Figure 11.2: Risk priority chart.
Source: Department of Industrial Relations, Queensland (2000).

will minimise the prioritised risks while maintaining the perceived risks desired by the participants.

Selecting Control Measures with Input Variables

Classic risk-assessment models use a 'hierarchy of controls' to guide the selection of the appropriate control. This is outlined above (see Figure 11.3). However, following such a model usually emphasises the elimination of risk and application of technical control measures.

Unfortunately, despite being useful in industrial contexts, this model has limited application for the diving tourism industry. For example, eliminating the hazard could have the effect of removing an element of adventure from the activity that has been an attraction for participants. Instead, the diving tourism industry relies primarily on the use of administrative controls that include:

• Provision of information, e.g. dive briefings or instruction (Photo 11.2)
• Systems of work, e.g. head-counting procedures, dive planning
• Emergency procedures, e.g. rescue or missing persons

Administrative controls are ranked close to the bottom of the hierarchy of controls (see Figure 11.3). The implication is that they are much less effective control measures when compared with controls further up the hierarchy. To ensure their effectiveness, they are best applied in multiple layers. Sliced Swiss cheese is a useful metaphor. If a risk is a beam of light, each layer of Swiss cheese is a control measure blocking some, but not all, of the

Control Priorities
Start at the top of the list and work your way down. Firstly, try to **eliminate the hazard** If this is not possible, **prevent or minimise exposure to the risk** by one or a combination of: • *Substituting* a less hazardous material, process or equipment • *Redesigning* equipment or work processes • *Isolating* the hazard (Note: These measures may include engineering methods.) As a last resort, **when exposure to the risk is not (or can not be) minimised by other means**: • Introduce *administrative controls* • Use appropriate *personal protective equipment*

Figure 11.3: Hierarchy of controls.
Source: Department of Industrial Relations, Queensland (2000).

Photo 11.2: Dive tourism operators are wise to reiterate advice and instructions at the dive site (Photograph: Simon Hartley).

light from the risk. To achieve adequate control of the risk several layers are necessary, with success achieved only when the layers work together to block all of the light.

The selection of control measures is mandated by legislative or agency bodies in many jurisdictions. The standards published by these agencies form a minimum but enforceable list of control measures. Normal business practices anticipate that the dive operator is aware of and familiar with all types of standards and their application as control measures. All relevant standards should be known, understood and applied. However, as minimum standards alone may not be sufficiently effective for a situation they are best considered as a starting point in risk management. In the event of a diving incident, failure to comply with a standard leaves any operator vulnerable. To assist with compliance, organisations like Workplace Health and Safety in Queensland provide simple self-audit checklists (Department of Industrial Relations, Queensland, 2005a).

Diving tourism operators are usually affiliated with at least one of the international dive-training agencies such as the Professional Association of Dive Instructors (PADI) or Scuba Schools International (SSI). Their published standards mandate many control measures. However, typically these are restricted to training activities that are carried out under the auspices of the training agency, for example, the skills required to be performed by trainee divers prior to certification. Each training agency has quality-assurance procedures that include the investigation of incidents and complaints. Failure to comply with any training-agency standards may render association memberships and insurance policies as void.

Some countries, including Australia and members of the European Union, have independent standard authorities with published standards covering certain aspects of recreational scuba-diving operations. For example, the 'Australian and New Zealand Standard 2299 Occupational Diving Operations: Part 3 Recreational Industry Diving and Snorkelling Operations' is a comprehensive document covering scuba on air, nitrox, mixed gases, rebreathers and snorkelling (Standards Australia, 2003). These standards are published to provide guidance as to best available practice. They have no direct legislative value unless called up in legislation (see below). However, even without this type of recognition, published standards can be used in civil proceedings as a measure of what might be considered 'reasonable' regarding a breach of duty of care.

Particular jurisdictions have statutory authorities with the power to enact and enforce health and safety provisions. Examples include the Health and Safety Executive in the United Kingdom (Health and Safety Executive, 2006) and Workplace Health and Safety in Queensland, Australia. (Department of Industrial Relations, Queensland, 2006). These agencies have extensive powers to apply heavy sanctions on an organisation that is not compliant. For example in 2000, a Queensland diving tourism operator was fined AUS$27,000 (€15,800) after failures in properly completing a dive-safety log resulted in two divers being left at sea.

The Queensland Code of Practice for Recreational Diving and Recreational Snorkelling at a Workplace 2005 (Department of Industrial Relations, Queensland, 2005b) contains sections dealing with:

- Ensuring no persons are left behind
- Medical fitness to dive
- Supervision of divers in open water

- Appropriate skills and knowledge of workers and divers
- Instruction and advice to non-English-speaking divers
- Equipment for diving
- Air quality in air cylinders
- Dive tables
- Diving depths
- Ascent diving
- Emergency plans
- Rescue of a diver
- First aid and oxygen
- Dive-safety log
- Diver's log
- Flying after diving
- Diving and moving vessels
- Divers and marine jellyfish stings

This code of practice is made under the Workplace Health and Safety Act 1995 (Queensland) and may be called as evidence to show that a diving tourism operator has breached their obligation to ensure health and safety (duty of care).

Even where standards have no jurisdiction, they form useful guides as to appropriate types of control measures. Legislative standards may also call up other standards, effectively giving them the power of law. For example, regarding the medical assessment of entry-level trainee divers, the 'Queensland Code of Practice for Recreational Diving and Recreational Snorkelling at a Workplace 2005' called up Appendices A and B of 'Australian Standard 4005 (1992) Training and Certification of Recreational Divers: Part 1: Minimum Entry Level Scuba Diving' (Standards Australia, 2000a).

Beyond simple compliance with existing standards, selecting control measures should be tailored to fit the diving environment being managed by the dive operator. Returning to the Swiss cheese example, the light enters at different intensities and angles when the hazard is variable. As such, one set of control measures may not always be appropriate. Understanding these 'input variables' means a dive operator will adopt flexible control measures appropriate to their own range of operational variables. For easy consideration, each input variable can be organised into one of three operational states; these are normal, stressed and unmanageable.

The hazards associated with the diving environment and customers will contain much variation. For example, the language abilities of dive customers to communicate with dive staff may vary from none through to complete fluency. Assessment of the risks associated with typical customer and environmental variables will allow the dive operator to select several control measures. These will cover most situations and are the normal controls. If, however, a situation presents where the hazards vary beyond this normal range, the operator faces two choices: the risk is considered unmanageable, and diving is postponed, or else a stressed situation exists where diving can only continue with modified and/or additional layers of control.

By way of a further example, resort divers are typically novice divers. Any lack of participant competence is in part controlled by close in-water supervision of a dive instructor (Wilks and Davis, 2000). Part of this supervision is achieved by limiting the ratio of participants to the dive instructor. The maximum ratio allowed in training-agency standards is four participants to one instructor. This can be considered a normal control measure. The dive operator should be prepared to reduce this ratio (3:1, 2:1, 1:1) where the normal hazards are stressed, such as during limited underwater visibility or poor participant fitness. As the hazard stress level is raised, a point where the diving should be cancelled should be identified and acted on if needed.

The dive operator will now have a list of control measures to be implemented. At its worst, this will reflect relevant standards. At its best, by applying layers of control that work in unison but are adaptive to changing input variables, the dive operator will move from a simple compliance approach to a safety-management system.

Reviewing the Risk-Assessment Process

When control measures have been selected and implemented, the ongoing task is to maintain their efficacy through a process of monitoring and supervision while critically reviewing the risk-assessment process to identify new or changing hazards. The process is ultimately a means of refining and aligning the implementation of control measures with various diving circumstances and situations.

Diving tourism operators familiar with quality-management systems will recognise that ongoing monitoring and review of their risk-assessment process is akin to the process of continuous quality improvement. Tourist-diving organisations are likely to vary in their approach to managing risk. The most successful will identify safety-risk management with business-risk management.

Successful implementation of a risk-assessment process builds a management system into an organisation. The monitoring-and-review process means that there is ongoing improvement and innovation. Accepting risk as a positive feature of the operation's management typically requires a shift in attitude. Acknowledging or seeking out risk and confronting the challenges posed creates a mechanism for a dive operator to flourish.

With apologies to the marine species involved, the risk management and attitude grid presented in Figure 11.4 offer a summary of the variety of approaches to risk management that are typically found in tourist-diving organisations.

Grunion

The management of risk is poor. Organisations in this quadrant are unthinkingly following a course of action with little understanding of the risk implications they confront. For example, this dive operator likely visits the same sites regardless of prevailing conditions. Like the grunion, this dive operator will end up stranded on a beach.

Stellar's sea cow

Management of risk is poor allowing incidents to happen. Attitude to risk is averse and passive. Operators in this quadrant avoid controlling risk and any opportunities for growth and innovation. This operator does not identify safe practices or growth areas in the diving market. In the corporate world, this operator is ripe for takeover or fades away as market changes or competition chips away at their business. Like Stellar's sea cow, they are likely to become extinct a few years after discovery.

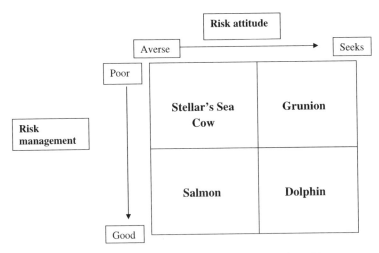

Figure 11.4: Risk management and attitude grid.
Source: Adapted from Holmes (2004).

Salmon
Management of risk is good. Attitude to risk taking is averse. The operator can identify possible problems thus negating the need to take action considered to be remotely risky. This dive operator develops procedural requirements that cover all conceivable risks to the extent that procedure impacts on the customer's experience. Like a Pacific salmon, this operator achieves his safety goal but dies on the return trip.

Dolphin
Management of risk is good. Attitude is one that seeks out the opportunities that present some risks, which use a combination of educated risk taking together with well-defined risk-assessment process. Like the dolphin, this organisation uses its intelligence to mitigate risk but constantly explores and seeks challenges in new directions. Ideally, we all want to be dolphins!

A review of the risk-assessment process enables a dive operator to consider the approach that has been taken towards risk within the organisation. Doing this will allow the operator to consider the general attitude towards risk and safety and the location of the organisation with respect to the risk attitude and management grid. From this point, decisions can be made about shifting perspective and position on the grid and moving towards establishing a system that encourages safety within the tourist-diving organisation.

Safety-Management Systems

Following the risk-assessment process, the second step involved in establishing a proactive approach to safety within a tourist-diving organisation is to build a safety-management system into the day-to-day operations. A safety-management system is required to provide an operational framework that supports the risk-assessment process. Establishing a safety-management system will involve the ongoing implementation and improvement of the risk-assessment process as an integral part of day-to-day operations.

A useful outline of a safety-management system can be found in the 'Australian and New Zealand Standard AS/NZS 4804: 2001 Occupational Health and Safety Management Systems – General Guidelines on Principles, Systems and Supporting Techniques' (Standards Australia, 2001). This approach integrates well with other commonly applied management systems such as the quality-systems management outlined in 'AS/NZS ISO 9001: 2000' (Standards Australia, 2000b) and the environmental management systems approach in 'AS/NZS ISO 14001: 2004' (Standards Australia, 2004). Since quality and environmental systems are already widely used, this is a means for the dive operator to align the safety-management systems with other core management systems.

The basis of the safety-management system is one of continual improvement that uses the risk-assessment process as a starting point and integrates it with the day-to-day management of an organisation. The principles of following this process are evident in Figure 11.5.

Commitment and Policy

The safety-management system is doomed unless there is genuine leadership and commitment from the tourist-diving organisation. Drawing a line in the sand to start the

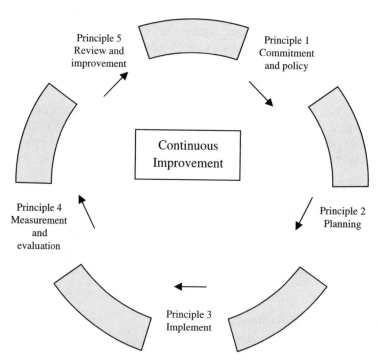

Figure 11.5: Safety-management system principles.
Source: Standards Australia (2001).

process can be underlined by a structured review of the existing safety procedures and developing policies that clearly state the organisation's commitment.

Planning

The primary planning activity is to undertake the detailed risk-assessment process and ensuring as a minimum, compliance with legal and any other requirements. Emergency plans, as well as critical-incident recovery plans, should all be documented. It is appropriate at this stage to set performance and targets as well as to identify performance indicators.

Implementation

Implementing the selected control measures can only be achieved with adequate capability. Budget and other resources should be allocated. Administrative and other support systems may be needed.

Measurement and Evaluation

There should be inspection, testing and monitoring undertaken at fixed intervals or when changes occur in the business. Using a quantifiable self-assessment tool, such as an audit checklist, may be a simple way to measure improvement. Where necessary, corrective or preventative actions such as an incident investigation should be undertaken.

Review and Improvement

The outcomes of the measurement and evaluation stage should act as a guide towards continual improvement. High levels of staff consultation are important to keep the system grounded in the business realities faced by dive instructors and dive masters.

In a tourist-diving organisation, the following are key elements found in a successful safety-management system:

- Appropriate documented work systems are in place with clear allocation of responsibility.
- The staff employed to implement the procedures have necessary skills.
- Appropriate equipment is purchased, inspected, functioning and maintained.
- Correct decisions are made by staff regarding input factors (customers, environment, equipment and workers).
- Emergency plans (complete with appropriate training) are in place.

The documented systems of work should include all selected control measures. Most dive operators collate this into an operations manual. The manual should include routine as well as emergency procedures, combined with position descriptions that clearly describe responsibilities duties. A typical index in a dive operation manual would outline

- Responsibilities and levels of competency of those involved in the diving operation.
- The equipment to be used in the operation with identification of selection, use, inspection, repair and maintenance.

- Diving procedures to be followed (before, during and after each type of dive).
- Diving emergency procedures to be followed (including missing persons, rescue, first aid and evacuation).
- Associated activities and other hazards (such as scuba-cylinder filling).

Any relevant standards that apply to the organisation should be attached or referenced to the manual to help create awareness and build familiarity with legal and other responsibilities. To ensure the implementation of the documented system, diving tourism operators should take an active role in the development, training and assessment programmes of new workers. This should include a structured induction programmes and mentoring of new workers by their more experienced peers. Induction and ongoing training should include assessment. This should assist in developing consistency within the organisation and is valuable when changes have been made to the usual system of work. The emphasis of any assessment should be on practical application of the documented system. For example, the documented system should address the processes to be employed to rescue a diver in distress. However it is only by practical assessment that an operator can be assured that their workers are able to implement the written system. It is advantageous to keep records of any training along with outcomes of any assessments. Many recreational dive training programmes provide examples of training systems designed to assess practical and theoretical competence.

Monitoring and supervision is necessary to provide assurance to the dive operator that the documented system is being followed. Supervisory responsibilities can be allocated to senior staff. Senior and experienced workers can undertake supervisory formal tasks, including inspections, audits, assessments and investigating incidents or near misses. Informal techniques can also be used, including customer and co-worker feedback. Good supervision rewards good work while using difficult or negative outcomes as a prompt for further training and review. Relevant records should be kept of all supervisory activities and outcomes.

The final stage of a functioning safety-management system is its ongoing review. It is critical to identify and adapt to any change in standards. Ongoing consultation with staff can improve and streamline the operational systems. Where control measures are altered, changes should be highlighted in the operations manual, leading to implementation through enhanced staff training and supervision.

Positive Safety Culture

The dive operators who take visitors on underwater tours very often embody the local culture — slick and businesslike or laid back and casual, jocular or sullen (Ecott, 2001). Creating a culture of a positive and proactive approach to safety within a tourist-diving organisation can only occur with meaningful leadership and commitment at the level of owner or manager. This approach shows all those involved that the organisation values safety and is committed to the implementation of the safety-management system. Well-worded policy statements displayed throughout the workplace will help nurture the desired attitude of 'safety is how we do things around here'. Organisational practices can be

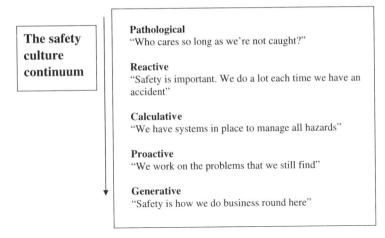

Figure 11.6: Safety culture continuum.
Source: Adapted from Holmes (2004).

changed to demonstrate a management commitment to a positive safety culture. With time this should create an established set of values across the organisation as individuals align their behaviour with proactive practices and processes. The more overtly and enthusiastically that an organisation adopts a safety culture, the more likely it is that individual behaviours will change to 'fit in'. Once a safety culture has begun to evolve in the organisation, increasingly informed and reliable workers will respond to and develop additional safety practices to permeate the tourist-diving organisation. New staff will then seek to improve on the work practices that have become the organisation's culture and attitude towards safety. By following such a process, the organisation can shift the safety attitude from its original position to one that is proactive and even generative. Figure 11.6 above highlights the steps along this process.

The idea of creating a positive safety culture might initially be considered a difficult or unnecessary task for a diving tourism operation that has a well-established culture and has been in business for some years. Also, it is often difficult to identify where and why changes are needed within ones own operation. However, taking an objective view of the situation and asking simple questions can often identify the diving tourism operator's current approach to safety management. Fictional statements such as those listed below, are typical of those sometimes encountered by the authors. They reflect an attitude that does not support or uphold an informed or proactive approach to safety management:

- 'The operations manual? I think it is in the manager's office.'
- 'When I started I was told to follow the documented procedures but I soon saw that no-one else did.'
- 'I showed a newspaper article about a dive incident to the boss but he said it was nothing to do with us.'
- 'Manual, what manual?'

Conclusion

This chapter has sought to provide dive operators with some tools and food for thought regarding the management of risk in their organisation. This has been presented by way of a three-stage approach that involves an assessment of risk, implementing a safety-management system and building a safety culture within the organisation that is proactive or generative. Most dive operators will be familiar with many lists of 'rules' to be followed. Many are also aware of the principles of the risk-assessment process. However, to move beyond this to a well-developed and functioning safety-management system is a challenge that does not have to be viewed with trepidation. There are numerous resources available to assist with hazard identification, standards to guide appropriate selection of control measures and dive-agency training programmes that give examples of working systems. The real decision required is one of making a commitment to developing a positive safety culture in the dive operation. The rewards of which should flow across incident occurrences, customer and worker satisfaction and the bottom line.

References

Cater, C. (2006). Playing with risk? Participant perceptions of risk and management: Implications in adventure tourism. *Tourism Management, 27,* 317–325.

Coxon, C. B. (2006). Safety in the diving tourism industry of Australia. In: J. Wilks, D. Pendergast, & P. Leggat (Eds), *Tourism in turbulent times: Towards safe experiences for visitors* (pp. 199–215). Oxford: Elsevier.

Department of Industrial Relations, Queensland. (2000). *Risk management advisory standard (code of practice).* Brisbane: Department of Industrial Relations.

Department of Industrial Relations, Queensland. (2005a). Recreational diving checklist. www.dir.qld.gov.au/pdf/whs/rec_diving_checklist.pdf (accessed 10 May 2007).

Department of Industrial Relations, Queensland. (2005b) Compressed air recreational diving and recreational snorkelling code of practice 2005. http://www.dir.qld.gov.au/workplace/law/codes/divingcompressed/index.htm (accessed 10 May 2007).

Department of Industrial Relations, Queensland. (2006). Diving Homepage. http://www.dir.qld.gov.au/workplace/subjects/diving/index.htm (accessed 10 May 2007).

Department of Justice, Queensland. (2005a). *In the matter of an inquest into the cause and circumstances surrounding the death of Thomas Creegan.* Brisbane: Department of Justice.

Department of Justice, Queensland. (2005b). *In the matter of the death of Maren Lynsey Dell.* Brisbane: Department of Justice.

Dimmock, K. (2003). Managing recreational scuba experiences: Exploring business challenges for New South Wales diving tourism managers. *Tourism Review International, 7,* 67–80.

Ecott, T. (2001). *Neutral buoyancy — Adventures in a liquid world.* New York: Grove Press.

Edmonds, C. W., & Walker, D.G. (1989). Scuba diving fatalities in Australia and New Zealand. 1. The human factor. *South Pacific Underwater Medicine Society Journal, 19,* 94–104.

Health and Safety Executive. (2006). Diving homepage. http://www.hse.gov.uk/diving/index.htm (accessed 10 May 2007).

Holmes, A. (2004). *Smart risk.* Chichester: Capstone Publishing.

Holyfield, L. (1999). Manufacturing adventure: The buying and selling of emotions. *Journal of Contemporary Ethnography, 28,* 3–32.

Leggat, P. (2006). Travel medicine and tourism health. In: J. Wilks, D. Pendergast, & P. Leggat (Eds), *Tourism in turbulent times*: *Towards safe experiences for visitor* (pp. 22–36). Oxford: Elsevier.

Morgan, D., & Dimmock, K. (2006). Risk management in outdoor adventure tourism. In: J. Wilks, D. Pendergast, & P. Leggat (Eds), *Tourism in turbulent times*: *Towards safe experiences for visitors* (pp. 171–175). Oxford: Elsevier.

Orams, M. (1999). *Marine tourism: Development, impacts and management.* London: Routledge.

Standards Australia. (2000a). *AS/NZS 4005 Training and certification of recreational divers. Part 1: Minimum entry level scuba diving.* Sydney: Standards Australia.

Standards Australia. (2000b). *AS/NZS ISO 9001 Quality management systems — Requirements.* Sydney: Standards Australia.

Standards Australia. (2001). *AS/NZS 4804 Occupational health and safety management systems: General guidelines on principles, systems and supporting techniques.* Sydney: Standards Australia.

Standards Australia. (2003). *AS/NZS 2299 Occupational diving operations. Part 3: Recreational industry diving and snorkelling operations.* Sydney: Standards Australia.

Standards Australia. (2004). *AS/NZS ISO 14001 Environmental management systems – Requirements with guidance for use.* Sydney: Standards Australia.

Tourism Queensland. (2004). Diving tourism. http://www.tq.com.au/fms/tq_corporate/research/fact_sheets/dive_tourism.pdf (accessed 10 May 2007).

Walker, D. (1998). *Report on Australian diving deaths 1972–1993.* Melbourne: J. L. Publications.

Wilks, J. (1992). Introductory scuba diving on the Great Barrier Reef. *Australian Parks and Recreation, 28*, 18–23.

Wilks, J., & Davis, R. (2000). Risk management for scuba diving operators on Australia's Great Barrier Reef. *Tourism Management, 21*, 591–599.

Subject Index